"Describing his own personal experiences, Talbot allows the ⌐ ⌐t spirituality to constructively criticize the Catholic cont⌐ he lives out the Christian life. He encourages hi⌐ should certainly extend beyond Catholici⌐ richer experience of God by the H⌐⌐ the monastic desert spirituality f⌐ fathers and mothers to speak for th⌐ ⌐⌐viding another collection of sayings and qu⌐ ⌐⌐ows in an engaging manner how this transformi⌐ ⌐y has been fruitful in his own life, and has the potential to ⌐ ⌐uce spiritual fruit in the lives of all those who embrace it, making Christ the focus of our life, in the power of the Holy Spirit."

—Father Peter Farrington, priest of the Coptic Orthodox
   Church, UK

"John Michael Talbot knows about the distractions of this world and gives practical suggestions to rediscover the dignity of man and himself in God's ray of light. The book is a testimony to decades of wisdom. Simple and impressive are the examples from everyday life, unsurpassed are the quotations of the desert fathers, which are still so relevant today. The book provides orientation for searching people in a time of disorientation."

—Notker Wolf, OSB
   Abbot Primate Emeritus

"John Michael Talbot is the real deal—a true holy man and spiritual father. This book is a booster shot of grace that will reinvigorate your spiritual life—it is both encouraging and challenging. It's not a how-to, if that means a set formula that is supposed to work for everyone, rather it is a way of empowering the reader to find his or her own way through the desert. From time to time we all need to strip away the barnacles of the distracted life and get back to what is essential. With this book, you can immerse yourself in a world without the annoying distractions of modern technology, then really begin with yourself and go deeper than perhaps you ever have before."

—Jim L. Papandrea
   Professor of Church History and Historical Theology
   Garrett-Evangelical Theological Seminary

"Every generation seems to discover the Desert Fathers as something new, surprising, strange, and radical. Opening heaven's door, we never find what we had expected. This book will be the Desert's doorway for a new generation."

—Mike Aquilina, author of *The Fathers of the Church*

"What a pleasure for me to read John Michael's new book on desert spirituality. It is a beautiful spiritual offering from a great musician who has become a very special author as well. *Desert Dangers and Delights* addresses a hunger for a faith that can be *experienced* in the here and now."

—Tom Booth, composer, retreat leader, and spiritual director

"There has never been a more crucial time to listen to the past. And who better to listen to than the desert fathers, who left everything to embrace a life of simple listening to God in the wilderness. My brother John has done much the same with his life; he has spent a lifetime listening to the fathers and has gifted the church with this remarkable digest of their wisdom."

—Michael Card, faith-based musician and author

"The spiritual life, in Scripture and in church history, is shaped by the garden and the desert. John Michael Talbot, whose fruitful ministry spans fifty years, guides us from that garden to the contemplative life of the Desert Fathers and Mothers. In this new book, he shares the treasures to be found in a place of dangers and delights. Highly recommended."

—Duane W.H. Arnold, PhD, author of *The Early Episcopal Career of Athanasius of Alexandria*

Desert Dangers and Delights

Stories, Teachings, and Sources

John Michael Talbot

LITURGICAL PRESS

Collegeville, Minnesota

www.litpress.org

1	2	3	4	5	6	7	8	9

Library of Congress Cataloging-in-Publication Data

Names: Talbot, John Michael, author.
Title: Desert dangers and delights : stories, teachings, and sources / John Michael Talbot.
Description: Collegeville : Liturgical Press, 2020. | Summary: "A reflection on the author's experience as a spiritual father and a popularizer of Catholic Christian spirituality through his music and teaching. He uses his own stories, Scripture, and the stories and sayings of the desert fathers and mothers to show a radically alternative way of living and thinking in Christ"—Provided by publisher.
Identifiers: LCCN 2019030780 (print) | LCCN 2019030781 (ebook) | ISBN 9780814688038 (paperback) | ISBN 9780814688281 (epub) | ISBN 9780814688281 (mobi) | ISBN 9780814688281 (pdf)
Subjects: LCSH: Spiritual life—Catholic Church. | Christian life—Catholic authors. | Spirituality—Catholic Church. | Desert Fathers.
Classification: LCC BX2350.3 .T347 2020 (print) | LCC BX2350.3 (ebook) | DDC 248.4/82—dc23
LC record available at https://lccn.loc.gov/2019030780
LC ebook record available at https://lccn.loc.gov/2019030781

Contents

Introduction

The desert is delightful. It is also dangerous. It is delightful when used well, but it can kill if entered into wrongly. The difference is in discernment.

As a delight the desert is an awe-inspiring place. The sunrises and sunsets are stunning. The way the light plays off the sands. The mountains and hills in the distance. The clean air refreshes body and soul. The vistas are unobstructed and magnificent. All seems clear and unobstructed in one's soul there as well. It is easy to be inspired by God in such a place. These things are all delightful!

It can also be forbidding! With the delight, there is danger. In the desert everything unessential is stripped away. The hot is very hot, and the cold is very cold. You can die of thirst or exposure to the elements very easily if not properly prepared. And snakes and scorpions lurk under rocks and dwell in the shelter of caves. That's why so few live there, except in properly developed cities or towns with ample services and utilities. Out of cities and towns there is no lush greenery to visually cushion the harsher realities of life. What you see is what you get. This all symbolizes the challenges of our spiritual lives as well. That's why the desert fathers and mothers retreated to deserts.

I have great memories of the desert. Early in the days of Mason Proffit, a country rock band I was with that achieved some success on Warner Brothers Records, we considered buying a ranch outside of Tucson. We loved the saguaro cactus and the activity of the wildlife, flora, and fauna of the desert, often not seen by the casual observer. I spent hours walking that desert in those days.

After my conversion to Catholic monastic life I spent powerful times in the desert of Palestine. I loved the abandoned monastic ruins outside of Bethlehem and enjoyed staying for an extended stay at Shepherd's Field, a hermitage below the pilgrim sites. I especially remember walking down the Wadi Kelt ("Valley of Death") from St. George's Monastery, past the numerous ancient caves that line the cliffs and once served as hermits' cells.

Later in my monastic itinerant ministry, some of my most cherished memories have been of driving back and forth across America, specifically the Southwestern deserts of New Mexico, Arizona, and California. I have enjoyed walking in the desert and finding a shady nook or cranny in the rocks (uninhabited by snakes or scorpions!) in which to pray. I have seriously looked at land where we could make a desert monastic foundation of The Brothers and Sisters of Charity. But the time has not yet come. It is one of my yet unrealized dreams.

These dangers and delights are precisely why the first desert fathers and mothers went to the desert. They went to the desert to live a life stripped of everything but God. The desert fathers and mothers were primarily those who went into the deserts of Upper and Lower Egypt beginning in the third and fourth centuries, influencing monasticism in Palestine, Syria, and throughout the ancient world in later centuries. In the desert all cultural distractions were gone. Only those in the mind remained and demanded that they be brought to Christ. They also went because the people of their culture understood it as the dwelling place of demons, and they sought to do battle with the primary causes of the world's woes. They went to battle demons with the victory only Jesus Christ brings fully. They also had the wisdom to start, not by battling the sins of others, but by battling their own. This takes guts. It takes real courage to endure.

So the desert is a place of danger and delight. It first attracts, then frightens, and then delights in a way untouched by the ups and downs of life. This is the way of the desert fathers and mothers.

I believe the desert fathers and mothers have a special significance in our current cultural and ecclesial climate and crisis.

We live in a world where fewer and fewer folks are staying in a church or faith community. Pew research indicates that the proverbial "nones"—as in "none of the above" on a questionnaire about religious affiliation—are quickly becoming the "dones"—as in those who are simply "done" with it all. Most of these folks still love Jesus or at least still believe in God, perhaps even more strongly than before. It's not so much that they disagree with Catholicism, Christianity, or religion in general. It's simply that they have already given it their level best for decades, gotten very little in return, and are simply "done" with it.

The "dones" are often done with the church, politics, and the Western world in general. Church is a polarized place where liturgies are poorly done and apparent engagement with Jesus is hard to find. Most seem to have a relationship with religion that is *about* Jesus, rather than *with* Jesus who enlivens our religion. As Scripture says of some, "they make a pretense of religion but deny its power" (2 Tim 3:5). The sex scandals have left most feeling gut punched and falling on our faces before God. God knows, politics is even more polarized and helplessly deadlocked along party lines on most issues. Social media has degenerated from a great place for dialogue into a place of unfiltered and hate-filled arguments. This leaves many of us feeling like exiles in our own church and culture.

It was a climate not unlike ours that prompted the rugged souls to "flee the world" for the solitude and silence of the desert. They reach across the ages to resonate with the souls of the "nones" and "dones" today. They provide an ancient model for those in self-imposed exile that is no longer just angry or resentful at the state of the church and the world. Somehow the desert fathers and mothers like Antony, Pachomius, and Mary of Egypt found something deeper in the desert, and their inspiration renewed the religion and even the politics of their over-institutionalized Christian world through the likes of Athanasius and Augustine.

A publisher suggested years ago that I write a book on the desert fathers and mothers. I have always hesitated. Who am I to write such a book? I have written on other monastic subjects, but these radical souls always seemed way above my proverbial pay grade! But I am inspired to give it a try now. Why?

In recent years some health struggles stripped me back to the basics, and the desert fathers and mothers ministered to me in a way that other more active saints such as Francis and Benedict no longer fully did. The notion of simply "being" after years of active ministry speaks deeply to my heart.

As founder and spiritual father of a new integrated monastic community, I have always hearkened to the hermit and community call of the desert fathers and mothers. The collections of their lives and sayings sit close to both my study chair and my bedside. They are my rather constant companions and familiar friends. Even my love for the likes of Western figures like Francis and Benedict, and Romuald of the Camaldolese and Bruno of the Carthusians, was rooted in my love for the first monks of the eastern deserts. They remain the bedrock upon which the entire monastic and consecration of life tradition rises. They have always spoken to a very deep place in my soul as well.

The lives and sayings of the desert fathers and mothers have inspired the likes of St. Augustine, St. Jerome, and St. Benedict in the Christian west. They are the absolute primer for monastic life in the Christian east. They also inspire me. And they still inspire the hermit or monk within all of us today.

There have been increasingly numerous books written on the desert fathers and mothers in recent decades. What was once a scant curriculum in English is now quite bounteous! There is really no great need for the likes of me to write yet another such book of quotes. So I write this book from a more personal perspective. My personal positions are built on quotes, but this book is not a mere omnibus of quotes.

There is also a more personal reason for this treatment. I have recently established a friendship with the only monastics that carry this tradition from the place where it all began: Egypt. It has been a joy to establish a friendship with the monks at St. Mary and Moses Monastery in Texas. Coptic monasticism is thoroughly immersed in the teachings of the desert fathers and mothers in a way that other monastics understand only from a distance. So I have been reimmersed in that tradition out of friendship and love.

As I mentioned, this coincided with some health issues that took me to the point of seeing the other side in Christ. During such times the nonessentials are stripped away. The desert fathers and mothers experienced a similar stripping, not merely through health issues, but as an intentional and alternative way of life in Christ and the church. At this point I find them most inspiring.

It has been suggested that I write about what inspired me from their rich repository of wisdom. So I will try to answer that call. I hope to be at least somewhat successful.

The desert fathers and mothers didn't leave us a monastic rule of life and much less with a mystical theology. Those were for later generations to compile. The desert fathers and mothers left us stories and pithy sayings, or apothegms. They don't explicitly treat the content of what we now call passive contemplation, but they do treat external and internal disciplines, and the battle with thoughts that usher us into contemplation extensively. Passive contemplation is, however, implied throughout.

In this book I will share my own stories, Scripture, and the stories and sayings of the desert fathers and mothers about a radical alternative way of living and thinking in Christ. I try to share from my own experience in hopes that it will assist others in theirs. I hide nothing, for we cannot hide from God.

So I retire into the desert in the twilight of my life, not to run from the world but for its salvation, by first starting with myself. It is an option that can be applied to all of us according to our states of life. If we first leave the world for Christ, then we can bring a salvation that only Jesus can bring.

Questions

1) Do you ever feel alone in the world?

2) Do you ever feel like an exile in the church?

3) Is your primary encounter with religion about Jesus, or with Jesus who enlivens your religion?

4) Do you have a personal love relationship with Jesus Christ?

5) Are you looking for a way to balance this? Would the desert fathers and mothers help inspire you to find a way?

Flee the World

If you want to be saved, flee the world.

—The Lord to Abba Arsenius

thought that I had fled the secular world long ago now. I left a promising secular music career in favor of Jesus. My wife eventually left me. I don't really blame her. In those first throes of being "born again," I was indeed very self-righteous and hard to live with! But I was completely shattered by the divorce. I sought refuge in a Franciscan retreat center in Indianapolis and placed myself under the direction of a friar who would remain my spiritual father until his death. Only after leaving everything for God would God give everything back in a whole new way. But today, after decades of ministry as a spiritual father of a new integrated monastic community, fifty-five successful recordings that have sold millions, thirty-five books that include some best sellers, and concert and teaching live appearances all over the world, I find myself leaving even my religious world in a new way. Like St. Francis at the end of his life, I find myself saying, "Let us (me) now begin, for up until now we (I) have done nothing." The desert fathers are inspiring me again.

Many of the "dones" are fleeing our modern secular and religious world in their own way today. How does that apply to the average Christian in our time?

Let's begin with Scripture for some basics.

Jesus says to "flee to the mountains" during a time of persecution and trouble (Matt 24:16). The Scriptures warn against participating in worldliness. But John 3:16 also says that God so loved the world that he sent his only Son to give his life for the world. And Jesus prays that the Father not take us out of the world, but that he save us from the evil one (John 17:15). The world is not evil. God created the world as good (Gen 1). It is what we do with it that makes it good or evil (Gen 3).

So Scripture differentiates between the *good world* and *bad worldliness*. "Do not love the world or the things of the world. If anyone loves the world, the love of the Father is not in him. For all that is in the world, sensual lust, enticement for the eyes, and a pretentious life, is not from the Father but is from the world. Yet the world and its enticement are passing away. But whoever does the will of God remains forever" (1 John 2:15-17).

The first and most basic sermon of Jesus was, "Repent." Repent comes from the Greek *metanoia*, or "change your mind." Repent means to change your thinking and change radically. If we change our thinking, we change our lives.

So how do we change? Why and how do we flee the world? And from what must we flee?

We flee not so much the world as our *misuse* of it. Sometimes that requires a change of environment. It can even require a change of location. Sometimes that change is for a few hours or days. Sometimes it is for a couple of weeks or months. Sometimes it can be for years or even for a lifetime. Sometimes it means taking on a way of life in Christ that is completely wonderful and new! This is precisely what the desert fathers and mothers did.

Jesus asks us to *renounce three things* when we become his followers: *possessions*, *relationships*, and even our very *selves* (see Luke 14:26). Why? Are possessions, relationships, and the human self bad things? No. It is not that the created world is evil. As we said, God made it! Jesus wants us to have healthy relationships. He blessed marriage at Cana! And he made us in his image and likeness. He made us very, very good!

First, the problem is that our possessions often possess us. We are consumed by what we consume. We must break free of them before we can use them rightly, as good stewards for the world and our loved ones. We must embrace a real gospel simplicity in order to simply live again. As the saying goes, "Live simply so that others may simply live." It also frees us up to live freely again in Christ.

Second, we often fall into bad relationship patterns that enable bad behavior instead of empowering positive things of God. We oppress others and ourselves. We are often controlling and codependent in our relationships. We try to find our happiness by controlling how others behave and live. Furthermore, we allow others to become overly dependent on that control, and we stifle their ability to really mature in Christ for themselves. That is codependency. So, we must disrupt the old patterns in order to let Jesus give us new ones.

Third, we must renounce our old selves. We often settle for a version of ourselves that is far less than the person God originally made us to be. It is not so much that what we have settled for is evil. But it is at the very least incomplete. When we sin, we don't lose God's image. However, we do lose his likeness. We allow our lives to become agitated like the waters of a pond that can no longer fully reflect the beautiful image of God, but only a fractured and broken version of it. We must let the old self die through the cross of Christ in order to be born again, not once, but daily through the resurrection of Christ.

This breaking free must sometimes be intentional and radical. It is like pushing off from the side of a swimming pool in order to swim. We must sometimes push off with great energy and effort in order to establish the momentum we need to swim gracefully. Likewise with possessions, relationships, and our old selves. We must sometimes use great effort in order to really break free of the old, unhealthy patterns. We do this by embracing a discipline in every aspect of how we live. These are three scriptural areas from the example of Jesus Christ.

What are some other things that are perhaps most apparent in modern Western living?

One thing that immediately comes to mind is our use of *media*. The average American spends six hours a day on social media. That doesn't count TV and movies. That's a lot of time! They fill us with expectations of success and pleasure that most of us will never realize. They fill us with angry and unfiltered gossip, slander, and hate-filled and polarizing opinions about everything! If you understand that "we are what we think," then it is easy to grasp why we are often so frustrated and unfulfilled. In order to watch it, read it, or write it, you must first think it. If you think it, it will affect your life (see Prov 23:7, KJV). If you spend a large amount of time thinking it, it will radically affect your soul.

And they are addictive. New studies indicate that habitual use of smartphones and tablets actually rewires the synapses of our brains, creating an addiction every bit as strong as caffeine or nicotine. You may recall the episode of *Star Trek: The Next Generation* called "The Game," which eerily illustrated the consequences of addiction to computer games and such. We are, indeed, in a "brave new world."

So the desert fathers and mothers inspire some wonderful advice! Turn off the TV. Unplug from social media. Put down the phone and tablet for a while. It won't kill us, though we may think that it will! But after the initial pains of withdrawal, we can experience a peace that surpasses all understanding.

We can also make *a retreat* for a day or a week. Typically, this is best done somewhere other than your local parish. It's also not the same as going on vacation to a luxurious hotel or resort. The grace of place of a retreat center or monastery is unlike anything you can find in the secular world.

I also suggest establishing a relationship with a good monastery of monks who are living the desert father and mother life in a developed way. Become an oblate. Our community has an entire "domestic expression" of those who live in the secular world as laity, religious, and clergy. Our community is nothing short of a phenomenon of the Holy Spirit! There is nothing like it anywhere else in the United States. We are an integration of charismatic and contemplative, spontaneous and liturgical, solitary and communal ministry that makes our gatherings much like a Steubenville conference in enthusiasm and gifts of the Spirit, but with a community base of loving, committed relationships that makes it utterly unique in the USA. I invite you to join us!

Our domestics live our monastic life in a way adapted to their own life in a family or parish ministry. We require that our members ordinarily come to the monastery annually to spend some time away from the secular world. This radically helps them to live in Christ in the secular world in a healthy way.

Last, establish a *holy place of prayer* in your home. It could be a prayer corner or room. Place a crucifix, a few holy icons, and candles there. Don't do anything there other than prayer. If it's a corner of your living room or bedroom, have a chair or cushion where you can pray with God alone. This is your modern cell! Even monastics have similar cells within their cells, set apart from the ordinary things of monastic living.

Let me also share some personal insights. For me, there have been *two good kinds of solitude*. The *first* is a respite from the activities of daily life or even active ministry. This kind of solitude and silence is like a filling station. We fill the gas tank of our spiritual lives so that we might continue on the journey of active life and ministry. This is the solitude that most lay people and even monastics experience.

But there is a *second* kind of solitude that is more intense and is more akin to what we find with the desert fathers and mothers. This kind of solitude is more absolute and continual.

I've personally experienced this only during my five-year period of greater reclusion over a decade ago and now in an even
more intense way as I enter into the last decades of my life and
semiretirement. It is this second kind of solitude of which the
desert fathers tend to speak.

In this kind of solitude, any kind of activity that draws you out
of the monastic cell is both painful and counterproductive, even
when there are good reasons for it. In this kind of solitude, all
your focus is on Eternity. In this kind of solitude, the Liturgy of
the Hours becomes a prolonged experience that takes up most
of your day and the words of God in Scripture burn within your
soul. With nothing to do externally beyond maintaining the
meager basics of life, we focus almost entirely on Eternity. All
else pales in contrast to that overwhelming reality. As soon as
we venture out to do ministerial work in a monastic community
or in the greater church and world, the same words become
somehow more secondary to our souls. They burn, but not with
the greater intensity that is found in strict solitude.

The first kind of solitude from the world is with an eye to
going out with greater spiritual fervor to minister to the world.
The second kind of solitude is more focused on the Eternal
realities, the cosmos and the soul. It also ministers to the world,
but in a way that is more mystical, secret, and intensely powerful
in the Spirit of Jesus Christ. The desert teaches us about both
kinds of good solitude.

The world is good, but we have done some bad things with
it. And these patterns are sometimes so deeply ingrained in our
culture and our personal lives that a radical break is needed.
That is what the desert fathers and mothers did in their time.
They fled the negative aspects of their world and felt they could
only achieve this by a radical break that included their location
and environment. We must often do the same.

Questions

1) Do you "flee the world" in the ways about which Jesus taught?

2) How is your Gospel use of possessions, relationships, and even your own self-identity?

3) Do you use available tools to establish and maintain times and places of solitude and silence?

4) Do you have a monastery or retreat center where you can go for these times?

5) Have you considered either joining a monastic community or associating with one that will provide support in using the monastic gifts in your life?

Jesus Christ

"You must be in deep love with our Lord Jesus
Christ. Those who do not possess this will be
like leaves that fall from the tree and die."

—Abba John the Hermit, in Samaan El-Souriany,
The Hermit Fathers

As I get older, I am rather amazed at the phenomenon of
religion in America. I came from the Jesus Movement, a
charismatic movement of ex-hippies who found a completely new way to live through Jesus. We were "Jesus people." It
was a predominately Protestant movement. After the division I
witnessed there and being drawn by patristics and the Franciscan
and monastic traditions, I became a Catholic Christian. What I
saw in the Catholic Church was a stunning and surprising dependence on Jesus. The Mass made no sense without him. At that
time the Franciscans and monastics I met were all about Jesus,
Francis himself to the point of being called an *"alter christus,"*
another Christ. I was also involved in the Catholic charismatic
renewal, a modern extension of that encounter with Jesus with
a special emphasis on the power of the Holy Spirit. Those were
powerful times. Jesus and expectation of renewal was in the air
we breathed. The power of the Holy Spirit was palpable.

I liken it to riding a surfboard. The power of a personal encounter with Jesus Christ was like a huge wave of the Holy Spirit. All we had to do was get up on our surfboards and ride!

In recent years the Catholic Church has lost much of that emphasis and Spirit power, though it is still there theologically. Conservatives often emphasize orthodoxy, apologetics, right ritual, and liturgical correctness. Progressives often emphasize politics and bringing leftist agendas into the church. While both have limited validity, both seem to miss the greater essence of the Catholic faith. Both seem to miss a renewed encounter with the Jesus Christ of the Gospel in the power of the Holy Spirit.

I recently used an analogy with one of our community cell groups to describe this. When a rock is thrown into a pond, there are ripples that flow out in concentric circles. The ripples are beautiful. But we must go back to the rock to find the source of the circles. For us that Rock is Jesus Christ. Jesus is the Rock that sends out the various ripples in the church and in the world of orthodox theology, liturgy and sacraments, or any social or political action. If we miss him, the rest is lifeless.

I also recently did a ministry at a typical Catholic parish. In the narthex was the usual stand with Catholic apologetic material. One of the most prominent and numerous was called "The 2nd Greatest Name under Heaven." I thought it was really nice to have something about Mary there. But I casually looked around for something about "The 1st Greatest Name under Heaven," something about Jesus, and couldn't find anything!

Unfortunately, this often is indicative of the spiritual emphasis of far too many Catholics nowadays. While the Eucharist really makes sense only when focused squarely on Jesus, the actual experience of many Catholics today is far more about the secondary things of devotion to saints, right rubrics and liturgy, or political correctness than Jesus, who is primary to any authentic Catholic Christianity.

Even with my Holy Land pilgrimages, I often find Catholics far more enthusiastic about going to Rome or a Marian shrine than going to walk where Jesus actually walked. Yes, some are concerned about safety in the Holy Land, but this is mostly unfounded in fact. It is a typical excuse for not going. This speaks through the pilgrims' feet what is most important in their heart about their faith. Perhaps Jesus really isn't that important to some Catholics in terms of a real, personal encounter? Their religion remains stuck in the secondary things of Christ. Is it any wonder we struggle to retain members in our increasingly secular and godless world? Folks are hungry for the real thing, for authenticity, and they sense a fraud when they see it.

The desert fathers and mothers stand in stark contrast to any such deviations.

The Christian monk begins and ends his way of life in Jesus Christ. It is through Christ that we are forgiven past sins and empowered to live the Christian and monastic life to some degree of perfection. For the Christian monastic, Jesus Christ is the Monk of monks, the Mystic of mystics, and the Teacher of teachers.

For Christian monasticism, Jesus Christ remains the primary inspiration and focus of all we are about. Scripture was the primary written rule for the early monks. The Holy Spirit was the inner power that inspired the monks. They were often called "Spirit-bearers." For our community, it is only in Christ that monasticism reaches its fullest potential. I would argue that this is also true for all forms of monasticism.

Christian Monks

Jesus is the sole possession of the Christian monastic.

One of the desert fathers used to say that we should possess nothing besides Christ and that we should not esteem anything of value—our possessions or family or even our own selves—except the love of Christ. [1]

---

1. E. A. W. Budge, ed. and trans., *The Paradise or Garden of the Holy Fathers*, 2 vols. (London: Chatto & Windus, 1907), 1:19.

Jesus gave his power to the apostles and their successors. This is called apostolic succession. He also gave it to saints among the clergy, laity, and monastics. I call this the *succession of the saints*. It was through the power of his name that they worked miracles, cast out devils, and healed the sick. This was also seen in countless lives of the desert fathers and mothers. St. Antony and many other fathers and mothers worked many miracles in the name of Jesus Christ. But they never presumed that this was their own power! They performed miracles and healings, not by their own power, but in the name of Jesus Christ, and by his power alone.

It is said that St. Antony did not perform healings by his own power after the manner of a master, but only with prayer and the mention of the Name of Christ, so that it might be clear to everyone that he didn't do these things, but that God did them by his hands.[2]

Spiritual Warfare

St. Antony of the Desert is the first desert father where we see a developed theme of spiritual warfare that includes the inner workings of human psychology and an understanding of the work of demons. The *name* and *cross* of Jesus Christ remained the primary means of combating attacks from within and without, from thoughts and demons. The desert fathers and mothers were no strangers to the devil's tactics, and they knew how to use the name of Jesus Christ to combat the onslaughts of the enemy. They discovered that the demons could not withstand either the name of Jesus or the sign of the cross. These demons appeared to them as thoughts, lusts, or tempting movements of the flesh, and in visible forms as terrifying figures or even as deceiving monks or saints. They learned to use the sign of the cross and the name of Jesus Christ to test the spirits that often came to them as angels of light.

2. Budge, 1:68.

There appeared to Antony an evil spirit that was exceedingly haughty and insolent in appearance. Antony blew a puff of wind at him and rebuked him in the Name of Christ, and the spirit vanished and his words came to an end.[3]

Sometimes the demons were destroyed by the humility of the father or mother. This is similar to the story of St. Francis, in which the devil came and accused Francis of his sins and was ready to take him to hell. Francis humbly admitted his sin, said he was only worthy of hell, but that the devil could do only what Jesus allowed him to do, because Francis had given his life completely to Jesus. At that the devil couldn't withstand either the humility of the saint or the powerful name of Jesus and departed in frustration.

Satan similarly attacked Antony. Antony told him that if he had received power over him from Jesus, then he shouldn't delay, but should do whatever he was supposed to do. But Satan could do only what Jesus let him do. At that Satan was driven away from him "like a sparrow before a hawk, for I am a servant of Jesus the Conqueror."[4]

A similar story recounts that as Satan was departing in haste from the name of Jesus and was running along terrified, he fell down and actually burst asunder.[5] This power over demons wasn't merely the power of the saint's holiness. It was the power of Jesus alone.

Abbess Sarah was fiercely attacked by the demon of lust for thirteen years. She never prayed that the battle should stop, but simply prayed, "Lord, grant me strength." She learned to learn from the struggle. She learned to trust only in Jesus.

The same demon of lust was once attacking her terribly, but she stayed faithful. The spirit in bodily form said she had

---

3. Budge, 1:35.
4. Budge, 1:44.
5. Budge, 1:44.

beaten it. She replied, "It is not I who beat you, but my Lord the Christ."[6]

But a caution is in order here. We shouldn't think that the mere pronunciation of the name of Jesus has power. The name of Jesus isn't a magical incantation. The actual name of Jesus is pronounced differently in different cultures and languages. The name has content. It is the very *person* of Jesus who has the power. It is his life, his death on a cross, and his resurrection from the dead. It is his ascension to prepare our place in Eternity and the gift of the Holy Spirit to empower us on our sojourn on this earth until we also rise to heaven. It isn't about *incantation*, but *incarnation*!

It also has to do with the authenticity of the disciple's life in Christ. We remember the Jewish exorcists who were not really disciples of Jesus but tried to use the name of Jesus to exorcise a demon: "The evil spirit said to them in reply, 'Jesus I recognize, Paul I know, but who are you?' The person with the evil spirit then sprang at them and subdued them all. He so overpowered them that they fled naked and wounded from that house" (Acts 19:15-16).

Philosophy

The use of the name of Jesus didn't apply only to the onslaughts of demons, but also to the attacks of pagan, or secular, philosophers. Again, the content of the name and person of Jesus was what enabled Antony to win arguments even against great philosophers.

Greek philosophers approached Antony and asked questions about his Christian faith to confound him. Specifically, they tried to call into question the Christian teachings about

---

6. Owen Chadwick, ed. and trans., *Western Asceticism* (Philadelphia: Westminster Press, 1958), 62–63.

Jesus and his cross. Antony let them talk for a while. But when they started scoffing at Jesus, he felt pain in his heart and responded.[7] After this St. Athanasius presented St. Antony with a theological understanding of the Trinity and the incarnation that was just as elegant as that of any theologian of his time. His words flowed in the power of the Spirit. He ended his discourse by saying, "If you possess this also, you have no need of much discussion, for the deed itself will convince you that it is not by words, but by powerful works, that our doctrine increases and gives the faith of our Lord Jesus Christ."[8]

We are reminded of the promise of Jesus in such circumstances (Matt 10:19-20): No matter how simple we might be, if we are living a holy and authentic life as disciples of Jesus, the Holy Spirit will give us the words we need to accomplish what God desires for us at the time. We have nothing to worry about.

Dividers

Antony and the other fathers and mothers were also cautious regarding interaction with those who caused division in the community, or heretics. St. Paul told Titus, "After a first and second warning, break off contact with a heretic" (Titus 3:10). The word *heretic* is from the Greek *hairetikos* and simply means one who causes division or schism.

Then, as now, there are those who stubbornly hold to their own views in the face of correction by the church and end up causing division among the people of God. The desert fathers and mothers exhort us to be free from all interaction with those who divide the churches and to follow and understand the true doctrine of our apostolic church fathers and the preaching of the truth of our Lord Jesus Christ, which they received from the Scriptures.[9]

---

7. Budge, 1:60.
8. Budge, 1:65.
9. Budge, 1:72.

Yet regardless of their self-imposed exile and their being "done" with the culture in which they lived, the desert fathers and mothers remained orthodox Catholic Christians. And they felt love in their hearts for everyone, friend or foe.

False Christs

They were aware that, as St. Paul said, "even Satan masquerades as an angel of light" (2 Cor 11:14). In some more extreme desert stories they can even come as Jesus. But they aren't Jesus, and they are lacking in the qualities of the Jesus of the gospels.

The demons, wanting to seduce an old man, asked if he would like to see Christ? The old monk said, "If anyone says to you, 'Lo, here is Christ, or Lo, there, do not believe him.'" And they vanished at the words.[10]

The Cross

It was not only the name of Jesus that vanquished devils, but also the sign of his cross. There are many stories that tell of desert fathers and mothers vanquishing the demons through the sign of the cross. Why? Because it was there that the love of God for all and each of us was manifested fully through pouring out his blood in death so that we might live in him.

Jesus overcame Satan. The devils fear and tremble at the sign of the cross, but also at the existence of the monks in the wilderness and their way of life that they live for Christ's sake.[11]

It is through the cross that our old selves die with Christ, so that we might be born again and rise up daily as a new creation in Christ. The desert fathers interpreted this to mean thinking of him constantly, so that every word and action of our lives can

10. Chadwick, 171.
11. Budge, 2:299.

be conformed to his image and likeness by the way we think, speak, and live. [12]

There is nothing automatic, mechanical, or magical about the use of the name and cross of Jesus Christ. It has substance in the real, incarnate life of Christ and our genuine following of Christ as committed disciples.

Questions

1) Do you see the uniqueness of Jesus in leading people to God in Christian monasticism, or do all monastic expressions seem pretty much different but equal roads up the same mountain for you?

2) Do your external disciplines help you in your personal encounter with Jesus?

3) Do you see the power of the name of Jesus in battling demonic thoughts and temptations?

4) Is the use of his holy Name a magical incantation for you, or does it have power based on the substance of who he is?

5) The previous question can be asked regarding the sign of the cross and holy water as well.

6) Does your devotion to Mary and the saints lead you deeper into a personal encounter with Jesus Christ, or does it stand between you and a direct relationship with him?

12. Budge, 2:327.

Holy Spirit

"Truly, virginity by itself is nothing, nor marriage, nor life as a monk, nor life in the world; for God seeks the love, and gives the Spirit to everyone."

—Macarius, in E. A. W. Budge, *The Paradise or Garden of the Holy Fathers*

The greatest monks of the desert are called "Spirit-bearers." We can be too!

I recently had a security guard at one of my ministry events ask sincerely, "I think I understand a relationship with the Father and the Son, but please explain the Holy Spirit to me." I was touched by his sincerity and tried to respond from my experience.

The Holy Spirit is difficult enough to understand, much less to explain! Jesus said the Spirit is like the wind; we can hear its sound through the trees, but we cannot tell where it comes from or where it is going (John 3:8). But the Spirit is absolutely essential to our relationship with Jesus. In fact, we cannot really have a full relationship with Jesus without the Holy Spirit.

Jesus told his apostles to wait in Jerusalem until they were clothed with the power from on high, the Holy Spirit, before they were to go out and preach his gospel to the world (Luke 24:29; Acts 1:4).

Think of it: They had accompanied him for three years. They had heard him preach, seen him work miracles and stay true to his own teaching to the point of death on a cross. They had even seen him raised up on the third day and ascend into heaven to the right hand of God the Father. You'd think that would be inspiration enough! But it wasn't. They needed the gift of the Holy Spirit to give them the power, the dynamite, to persevere in the struggles and triumphs that still lay ahead of them.

It was not long before the Holy Spirit fell upon the first disciples gathered in the Upper Room as tongues of fire.

The primary sign of the Christians in the Acts of the Apostles is the gift of the Holy Spirit and manifestations of charismatic gifts like tongues and speaking the word of God boldly. It was also living the love of Christ in a community of radical lifestyle change, fellowship, signs and wonders, liturgy, and sharing one's faith with the world (Acts 2; 4).

How do we obtain baptism of the Holy Spirit? You just ask (Luke 11:13)! While it is the Holy Spirit who inspires anyone to call Jesus Christ the Lord (1 Cor 12:3), it is possible to believe in Jesus without the full outpouring of the Spirit. This is evidenced in Paul's address to the first believers baptized by John the Baptist in Ephesus (Acts 19:2-6). We see it in the account of the believers baptized in the name of Jesus in Samaria as well (Acts 8:14-25).

I must admit that these believers remind me of many Catholics today. We want to follow Jesus and be good Catholics. We are conscientious about our faith. We attend Mass regularly and pray various good devotions. We can even be scrupulous to a fault about liturgy, theology, or social justice. But many have no clue about the real power of the Holy Spirit.

History

Catholics are primarily a Eucharistic and liturgical people. The same is true for any liturgical church. It's what we rightly do when we gather on Sunday, the Lord's Day. But let's be honest: real manifestations of the gifts of the Spirit are rarely seen in our parishes or religious communities. How did we get like this?

It goes all the way back to the beginning, after the apostles. It is clear that the early patristic church celebrated the Eucharist every Sunday, and there was a primitive and simple liturgy that accompanied it. But why did they give up the more charismatic aspect of worship so soon?

I suppose it was a combination of, on one hand, individuals like the charismatic Montanus and the Gnostic Valentinus who abused the gifts and placed themselves above the bishops, and, on the other hand, the lack of gifted charismatic individuals who could lead local communities. So the Christian community settled for something that was stable and orthodox, in a more liturgical and sacramental expression. We maintained orthodoxy but lost something of the charismatic fire of the earlier church.

Potentially we can integrate the charismatic and the liturgical in worship. The sacraments symbolize and effect grace, and there are times for spontaneity in the liturgy. But let's be honest. This rarely happens in our liturgical services today. From our ancient past, the desert fathers and mothers help show us how to do it in our own day.

The Desert

The desert fathers and mothers continued that authentic, Spirit-filled tradition. The flowering of the first monastic movement was not unlike the spread of the charismatic renewal in the 1960s. Beginning in more informal small groups of friends and families who wished to live the ascetic life, it soon took deeper root in Egypt, Palestine, and Syria, in local communities that numbered into the hundreds and thousands, and spread throughout Christendom. It was a movement that was unstoppable, because it was a movement of the Holy Spirit.

Except for one story of Pachomius miraculously learning to speak many languages,[1] we won't find any stories of charismatic tongues. But there is ample evidence of holy fathers being rapt in the Spirit and of many miracles of healing, words of knowledge, and prophecies unfolding. There can be no doubt that the desert fathers and mothers were the authentic charismatics of their time.

One account describes a monk rapt in the Spirit and seeming drunk, like at Pentecost.[2] The desert fathers and mothers lifted their hands when they prayed. Humorously, one brother had to lower his hands quickly at the end of his prayer with his brothers, lest he remain in rapture, and began praying the entire 150 psalms again![3]

The Holy Spirit is often described as a fire (Matt 3:11; Acts 2:3). Abba Joseph says to Abba Lot: "If you will it, you can become all flame!"[4] And there's another story of a brother who went to the cell of Abba Arsenius and found him solid flame from head to foot.[5] The desert fathers and mothers were men and women on fire in the Holy Spirit. This fire of the Spirit takes our union with God to such a deep level that it is beyond what we can think with objective thoughts or say with objective words (see Rom 8:26).

---

1. E. A. W. Budge, ed. and trans., *The Paradise or Garden of the Holy Fathers*, 2 vols. (London: Chatto & Windus, 1907), 1:308.

2. Budge, 1:115.

3. Owen Chadwick, ed. and trans., *Western Asceticism* (Philadelphia: Westminster Press, 1958), 143.

4. Chadwick, 142.

5. Chadwick, 187.

The greatest desert fathers and mothers and the monastic saints of the Christian East are not only called "Spirit-bearers" (*pneumatophoroi*) but also "cross-bearers" (*staurophoroi*).[6] The *fruit* of the Spirit is connected to the cross of Jesus (Gal 5:22-15).

Thoughts

The work of the Holy Spirit is related to the thoughts of the desert monks. For them, the words of the Psalter came to life through the Spirit, unlike for the theologians and masters of the theology who knew only the externals of the words.[7] So, they understood the deeper meaning of the words as spiritual thought. This will be developed later in this book.

The Cell

This life in the Spirit usually takes place in a special way *in the cell*, where heaven comes to earth. But simply having a cell isn't a guarantee of the gift of the Holy Spirit. One must live in the cell rightly. Those who live there with bad attitudes are worse than those who live in the world righteously. And those who live there briefly but rightly gain all the benefits of the Spirit. [8]

We all encounter temptations in the cell. But they come and go if we simply come back to worship of God. The fathers call temptations "storms," the passions "waves," and the devils "thieve/s." Our "parents" are the Father, the Son, and the Holy Spirit, One God, in whose image and likeness we are made.[9]

---

6. See Pope John Paul II, Post-Synodal Apostolic Exhortation *Vita Consecrata* (March 25, 1996), n. 6.

7. Budge, 2:306.

8. Budge, 2:284.

9. Budge, 2:293.

Monastic Lifestyle

This personal encounter with the Holy Spirit was lived out in every aspect of the monastic life. They were constantly turning Scriptures on their lips and in their mind. They prayed without ceasing. This radically changes the way a person thinks, speaks, and acts, changing it all for the better! So the desert began to burst forth with the buds of the Spirit and flower with the fruit of the Spirit.

Abba John used to say the fruit of the Spirit manifested various gifts in each of the fathers and mothers as God saw fit and made each individual a special gift from God. There were many rules and ways to live the monastic life. So there is unity in calling but diversity in how that calling is actually lived.[10]

The fathers recognized the Spirit working in one another. Abba Antony said Abba Pambo feared God so greatly that the Spirit of God always dwelled in him.[11] Simple and straightforward, but challenging! I wonder, do we really stand in awe of God as deeply, or in appreciation of the Spirit working in those around us?

Test the Spirit

They also tested the word of the Spirit in one another.

Some of the brothers once came to test Abba John the Short, who always had his mind on God. They tested him by talking about the weather and how it would affect their crops. But Abba John didn't fall for it! He answered by spiritualizing and supernaturalizing rain and crops, offering an analogy to life in the Spirit.[12]

I must admit that I often grow weary of the superficial talk of the monastics of my own community. We are quick to talk about the weather or our work or, God forgive us, politics! But we are not so quick to talk about the things of the Spirit when

10. Budge, 2:148.
11. Budge, 2:183.
12. Chadwick, 132.

we meet outside of prayer, a formal conference, or a spiritual talk. I've talked to monastics in other communities who dread community meals because of political agendas that are foisted on all those gathered to eat. They slowly begin to avoid both formal or informal community meals and social time altogether. They say that they just can't endure it. It is no wonder that monasticism is dying in many monasteries in America!

Holy Spirit Lost?

The full gift of being *filled* with the Holy Spirit and even faith in Christ can be lost, though we are always *indwelt*. This seldom happens in one great rejection of God or Jesus by a monastic, or any serious Christian, but by gradual steps that one by one quench the work of the Holy Spirit in our lives. It is the proverbial "frog in the kettle" syndrome. The frog is cooked so gradually in the water that slowly comes to a boil that it never jumps out of the kettle. By the time it realizes that it is being cooked to death, it is too late.

Orsisius uses the example of mice slowly and almost imperceptibly eating the wick of a lamp to illustrate. The lamp eventually loses its ability to sustain a fire. But all is not lost! God never rejects a sincerely repentant sinner.[13]

Witness

We can also be built up through the witness of others. After we have the fruit of the Spirit in our lives, then our words flow forth with power. We are able to speak that which we really know. Jesus promises that when we are brought before others to give witness about him in our lives, it is the Spirit who will give us the words. That's because they aren't our words. They

---

13. Benedicta Ward, ed., *The Desert Fathers: Sayings of the Early Christian Monks* (New York: Penguin, 2003), 125.

are the word of Jesus within us, and our words flow forth from the Word. This was the case with Abba Ephraim, whose words flowed from the Holy Spirit.[14] We too should often seek out those who are filled with the Holy Spirit to hear their teaching and to grow in the Lord by being close to them.

Actions beyond Words

But this witness is sometimes beyond words. Abba Moses saw the Holy Spirit descending on Zacharias, and he asked Zacharias about his spiritual life in Jesus. Zacharias took his cowl, threw it beneath his feet, and trampled it! Then he said that unless a person tramples his old self underfoot he couldn't really be a monk. The words without the symbol are empty. Yet the symbol without the words still speaks to the one who has the ears to hear.[15]

We must be *more anxious to live the life of the Spirit and not just talk about it.* When we are content with silence in the Spirit, then we can safely speak the words of the Spirit.

Abba Daniel said Abba Arsenius never wanted to discuss any question about the Scripture, though he was wonderful at expounding it when he wanted to. He was also slow to write anyone a letter. He even hid himself at church! In a similar way, we should be slow to speak to ensure that our words are full of the Holy Spirit, rather than just our own excitement, or even worse, our own ego and pride. When we are filled with the Holy Spirit, we become humbler, not hungrier for attention. [16]

Monks and Laity

This gift can be given to anyone. Macarius said God gives his Holy Spirit to everyone, *monk or non-monastic, celibate or mar-*

---

14. Ward, 187.
15. Chadwick, 160–161.
16. Chadwick, 158–159.

ried, according to their earnestness of purpose.[17] As St. John Chrysostom said, all those who live the gospel radically are monks. "The Holy Scriptures do not know any distinctions. They enjoin that all lead the life of monks even if they are married."[18] This might not be true externally, but it is certainly true internally, in one's spirit.

Spirit-bearers

After living faithfully in all the stages of monastic life, some are called to wander completely alone or in small groups in the desert. (In Egypt these are called Spirit-bearers.) The *life of the wandering Spirit-bearer* is often seen as strange and perhaps even mythical to modern believers. Some monks think that such people are purely mythical, offered simply for our inspiration. Others are convinced that they still exist, for they claim to have seen them coming in from the desert to the church late at night, or they glimpse them briefly during a Eucharist. Personally, I believe that they exist. I keep a copy of their lives by my bedside and read it nightly.

Through the power of the Holy Spirit, these Spirit-bearers are even able at times to miraculously travel great distances without the normal mode or time of travel. There are many stories about monks traveling through the desert accompanied by angels or those who later turn out to be one of the apostles. Other monks miraculously cover great distances in just a short time in order to meet a Spirit-bearer just before they die, or to begin the life for themselves under the instruction of an angel, apostle, or Spirit-bearer.[19]

17. Chadwick, 188.
18. John Michael Talbot, *Hermitage: Its Heritage and Challenge for the Future* (New York: Crossroad, 1989), 186.
19. Budge, 1:372.

Asceticism

There is a connection between *disciplining the flesh* through fasting, poverty, vigils, and so on, and the complete outpouring of the Holy Spirit. Abba Poemen used to say that the Spirit of God never enters a house where there are delights and pleasures.[20] This connection even goes so far as *holy begging*,[21] a tradition lived by Jesus and in the West by many great saints, such as St. Francis, but not often seen in the desert.

The Saints

Devotion to the saints is great, but it should never displace one's encounter with Jesus through the power of the Holy Spirit. In one story we encounter Satan trying to get the saints to move their focus from the Trinity and the Holy Spirit to other saints. This is true especially with unhealthy devotion to Mary. When a demon tried to get a "blessed woman" to praise Mary instead of God, she said, "There is dust in thine eyes, Satan. Why should I forsake the Lord and worship a handmaiden?" And Satan disappeared.[22] This circumvents the intention of the saints themselves. Devotion to saints is wonderful and a valued part of apostolic Christianity. But that devotion should always lead us to worship of God and never to worship of saints.

Conclusion

The monastic life of the desert fathers and mothers *was impossible without the empowerment of the Spirit.*

An old man said that when a person follows God with a *sincere* mind, grace abides in him, and his life and deeds are

20. Budge, 2:19.
21. Budge, 2:77.
22. Budge, 2:269–270.

strengthened in the Spirit. He has a holy hatred for the fallen world and a new spiritual life.[23]

A good conclusion is that they say we are only held *worthy* of these through the grace and mercy of our Lord Jesus Christ, the true God and true man, to whom, with his Father and the Holy Spirit, be glory now and always and for ever and ever! Amen.[24]

Questions

1) Are you really open to the power of the Holy Spirit, or does it frighten you?

2) Do you allow the Holy Spirit to set you on fire spiritually?

3) Is your relationship with Jesus really a Spirit-filled personal encounter, or is it simply religious ideology?

4) Do you use the tools of spiritual life in stirring up the power of the Spirit?

5) Can one lose the fullness of being filled with the Holy Spirit? How?

6) Are you willing to ask for the Spirit from a Spirit-filled elder?

7) Do you hear the words of Jesus in Scripture and teaching through the power of the Spirit?

8) Are you demonstrative when you express the Spirit, or do you become humbler and let that proclaim the power of the Spirit?

23. Budge, 2:328.
24. Budge, 2:336.

9) Do you see the connection between your external life and the release of the Spirit in your life?

10) Are you aware of the relationship between the solitude of the cell and the power of the Spirit in monastic life?

11) Can you live monastic life authentically without the Spirit?

The Monk Within

I can remember well when I first heard the monastic call. I had received a vision of community in 1971, but I had no idea how to accomplish it. I was in the public library in Munster, Indiana, browsing through some books on Christian community. I perused some books on the Amish, Mennonites, and Quakers. Next came a book called *The Silent Life*, by Thomas Merton. It was about Catholic monks. This book captivated me! It started me on a journey through monasticism and Franciscanism that continues to this day. Though I was not yet living any form of monastic life, there was a "monk within" that was born or at least called forth that day.

A few years later, after a divorce from a marriage I'd entered rashly as a very young man and a search for things Catholic, I found my spiritual father. Fr. Martin was a Franciscan at the old Alverna Franciscan Center in Indianapolis. Through his gentle and jovial guidance, I moved into a spare room at the Center. He never once pushed me toward the Catholic Church or the Franciscans. But the more I learned, the more I eagerly sought out both. After becoming a Catholic and a Secular Franciscan, I sought permission to build a hermitage in the woods behind a Marian shrine. It was granted, though not without some initial resistance from a couple of the friars. Indeed, it was in that friary that I learned about the ordinary, sometimes humorous, and sometimes tragic life in a monastery. I encountered men with all the same problems as anyone else in modern American life. Yet through all that baggage and sin, Jesus did extraordinary things in them and in that holy place. Many vocations of laity and religious, priests and deacons, and even a provincial minister were found at Alverna. It was there that I first learned that monasteries are places made up of very ordinary people who had the courage and faith to respond to an extraordinary call from God.

Soon people from all states of life, predominantly from the Catholic charismatic renewal movement, began knocking at my hermitage door seeking a more intentional form of community. We established a charismatic expression of the Secular Franciscans that included a house of prayer and hermitage. The community was called the People of Peace Fraternity, and the place where we gathered was the Little Portion House of Prayer on the grounds of Alverna Retreat Center in Indianapolis, Indiana. This community would later become the Brothers and Sisters of Charity in the Diocese of Little Rock, Arkansas, a new, canonical, integrated monastic community that includes an integrated monastery and a domestic expression of those from all states of life who live in their own homes. We are no longer Franciscan, but I will always remain most grateful to the Franciscans and to my spiritual father for the loving and wise support and guidance they afforded me in those formative years.

Kajetan Esser, OFM, said that Francis of Assisi embodied the desert father spirit in the thirteenth century in the West. But Francis expanded on it and saw the world as his cloister, his body as his cell, and his soul as the hermit within. John Wesley developed this when he said that the world was his parish. And for most of us in modern time, we must find a bit of the hermit and monk within in order to make a monastery of our modern and secular world.

Many are mystically, or at least romantically, attracted to the notion of monks and monasteries. But few want to join them!

We might use the words *monk* and *hermit* nowadays, but few understand what these words really mean. Let's look at some words that are common in the monastic vocabulary and see how they apply to us.

History and Patterns

The classic quote of Abba Alonas tells us, "Unless a person says in his heart, 'I alone and God are in the world,' he will not have repose."[1]

The word *monk* comes from the Greek *monos*, which simply means "one" and "alone." The word is found in the Gospels whenever Jesus goes to be "alone" with God (see Matt 14:23). Later, it obviously applied to hermits but it was also used in reference to communities who lived together in solitude from the world. It can be used in regard to one who seeks God and God alone. This is a *monk*.

The word *hermit* comes from the Greek *eremite* and literally means desert or wilderness. It is used in the Gospels when Jesus goes to the wilderness or the desert for solitary prayer to God the Father (see Luke 5:16).

The word *cenobite* or *cenobium* comes from the Greek *koinonia*. It simply means community or communion. Anytime we read those two or similar words in Scripture, the root word is *koinonia* (see Acts 2:42). For instance, the Greek word for *common life* brings together *koine* (for *in common*) and *bios* (for *life*) to form *koinobios*. And *koinobion* is the *place* of common life. So the cenobite lives in the cenobium.

There was a clear pattern to early monastic communities. An individual like St. Antony or St. Paul of the Desert would depart into the wilderness. Others would slowly learn about

---

1. John Wortley, trans., *The Book of the Elders: Sayings of the Desert Fathers: The Systematic Collection* (Collegeville, MN: Cistercian Publications, 2012), 191.

their holiness by eventual contact with the few who traveled or lived nearby. Then others would come from the cities to seek them out for counsel or to ask to share their way of life. A loose colony of hermits living under the direction of the father would form, and then communities would develop. The same happened with spiritual mothers and female monastics.

Today we see four stages and ways to live monastic life in Egypt. Three of these would become normative in the East and also in later reforms in the West. First, one joins a monastic community (a cenobium in the West, a *koinonia* in the East) and is trained there for a decade or so. Second, one can spend greater or lesser amounts of time in solitude in a cluster of hermitages around a spiritual father or mother, called a *souka* or *skete*. After that, a rare few enter the third stage as a pure recluse in the deeper desert or wilderness. The fourth stage is rarer still. It is the pure hermit who wanders the desert or wilderness and eats grass and water from plants, or is taken care of by angels and departed hermits and saints. These are the pure Spirit-bearers, the *El Souah*, or Anchorite, the "Spirit-born."

For Us

These stages might seem alien to most of us. But these patterns can also *apply to our own lives*. When we "flee the world," we must first join with other experienced Christians under spiritual fathers and mothers or elders who show us the way, not to control others, but to simply point out what has or hasn't worked for them in hopes that it will help guide others more effectively. This is manifested in *monasteries*, or small groups of serious Christians within parishes. Most of those who join such communities are content to be there for most of their lives. Some feel called to greater intensity in actual *sketes* or groups for a semi-eremitic life. A few are called to almost complete solitude as *recluses*. This can happen in monastic communities, through a canonical church process directly under a local bishop for individuals who do not live in communities (see Canon 603 in the *Code of Canon Law*), or even informally. A rare breed are those who head out as *pilgrim wanderers*, and even rarer are those who do so in the wilderness (*eremite*).

Sometimes people join more intense communities and ministries and still feel the secular world in which they are located, and to which they minister, too distracting for a truly deeper prayer life. This even applies to those who live in cenobitic or semi-eremitic monastic communities.

Contemplative Heart of the Church

Monks and monasteries have been considered the *beating contemplative and mystic heart of the church* for nearly two thousand years. But in recent centuries, and especially in recent decades, this way of life is disappearing from the church in the West. Communities have often been defined by the active work they did. But ancient monastic life was not about the *work* one did, but about who one *is* in Christ. As the West adopts an increasingly secular and godless ideology, the monastic impetus for monks and those in the world alike is fast disappearing. I am on a mission to help restore the beating mystical and contemplative heart of the church in the secular West again. Much like Peter Damian, I seek to make a monastery of the whole world! We must get the monastic heart of the church beating again!

But this applies to both monastics in monasteries and those who draw inspiration from them alike. Often it has less to do with location and more with *how we live* in a specific location, such as a community or monastery. We can live alone in a hermitage or with a community in a monastery, while our thoughts and hearts can still be constantly in the world with others. We can also live with others in a monastery or in a family, but withdraw into an unhealthy solitude that is merely escapism and isolationism. The location helps set the stage for the deeper reality, but the location alone is never enough. We must fully enter into the spirit of the state of life through the Holy Spirit in order to really understand the meaning of the words and the life they represent.

As the world embraces a more godless secularism, the *need for community* becomes more pronounced. A serious Christian simply cannot make it on his or her own. The sheer peer pressure of the godless, secularized world is too strong. In Europe, more and more serious Christians are entering some form of new or old intentional monastic community. In the United States this is not so evident. We still live under a thin illusion of godliness in our culture, though even that is fast disappearing. Plus, we are a ruggedly individualistic culture. But the shadows of past godliness remain, and we somehow cling to the hope of a godly culture again. But this hope is fast fleeting. Those who are serious about living a godly life as Christians, or in any religion, will soon have to join with others in intentional communities.

The desert fathers and mothers, and monasticism in general, are providing some *paradigms* that can prove helpful. These can be lived in various degrees of external intensity, but folks are now finding that embracing them in some way provides some stability in a highly unstable Western world.

Closing Meditations

Evagrius Ponticus lived in the Egyptian desert in the fourth century and was one of the first monastic writers. While some of his theology was rejected by the church, his writings on monastic life have become staples in the monastic syllabus. We do well to study and meditate on them.

Evagrius says in *On Prayer* that monks should be undistracted and dispassionate. This language gave birth to the later development of descriptive stages from praxis, or the active life of doctine and asceticism, to theoria, or the mystical theology of the life, and apathia, or dispassion in contemplative living. He tells the story of a monk who, while practicing inner prayer as he journeyed in the desert, saw two angels come and walk on either side of him. But "he gave them no attention lest he should detract in some way from 'the better part.'"[2]

Some of his pithy axioms on monastic life, which he presents in a series of numbered statements or "chapters," are:[3]

- "Renounce all things. You then will become heir to all" (36).

- "By true prayer a monk becomes another angel" (113).

His dispassion does not make him insensitive or selfish. He reaches out to others. He says that he can see God in all others. He writes:

- "Happy is the monk who considers all men as god—after God" (123).

- "Happy is the monk who views the welfare and progress of all men with as much joy as if it were his own" (122).

He then goes on to coin some phrases that have become classic.

- "A monk is a man who is separated from all and who is in harmony with all" (124).

- "A monk is a man who considers himself one with all men because he seems constantly to see himself in every man" (125).

2. Evagrius Ponticus, *The Praktikos and Chapters On Prayer*, trans. John Eudes Bamberger (Collegeville, MN: Cistercian Publications, 1972), 74, chap. 112.

3. Each of the following quoted passages is from the same edition of Evagrius Ponticus, *The Praktikos and Chapters On Prayer*, with the "chapter" number identified in parentheses following each.

- "Avoid every lie and all oaths since you desire to pray as a monk. Otherwise you are a vain pretender . . . seeming to be something you are not" (127).

His work *On Prayer* lays the foundation for all future mystical theology in both the Christian East and the West. "If you are a theologian," he writes, "you truly pray. If you truly pray you are a theologian" (60).

From the pithy axioms of Evagrius, we move on to freer and lengthier descriptions of the monasticism of the desert. These describe much of the ideology and daily practice of the ideal monk.

There are several long passages from the earlier desert fathers and mothers describing true monks. I will end with two shorter ones.

> An old man said: "This is the life of a monk: work, obedience, meditation, not to judge others, not to speak evil, not to murmur. For it is written 'You who love God, hate evil.'
>
> "This is the life of the monk: not to go in with the unrighteous, not to see evil, not to be inquisitive, not to be curious, not to hear gossip: not to use the hands for taking, but for giving: not to be proud in heart or wicked in thought: not to fill the belly: in everything to judge wisely. That is where you find a monk."[4]

Monks still fall into temptation, and some give in. Laying a firm foundation with the basics of monastic life can reduce the frequency of both.

> A monk falling into temptation is like a collapsing house. If he is a serious and sober person, he rebuilds the ruined house. He finds the right materials for building, lays foundations, and collects stone and sand, and all the other need-

4. Owen Chadwick, ed. and trans., *Western Asceticism* (Philadelphia: Westminster Press, 1958), 40. (Internal quotation from Ps 97:10.)

ful things, and so his building rapidly grows higher. But the
builder who did not dig or lay foundations, and has none
of the right materials, goes away hoping that some day the
house will be built. So if the monk falls into temptation,
and turns to the Lord, he has the best equipment—meditation on the law of God, psalmody, work with his hands,
prayer, and the others—foundations of his building.[5]

Monks are ordinary people called to an extraordinary vocation. They are tempted, and they sin. They are just like everyone
else, but they dare to answer a unique call from God. And Jesus
is able to forgive and strengthen everyone, even in the face of
the greatest temptation and sin. All it takes is the courage to
respond with true sincerity. The hermit, the monk within you
and me, is the same. Will you answer the call?

Questions

1) What attracts you to monastic and desert spirituality?

2) What is *monos*? Do you live for God and God alone?

3) What is *eremite*? Do you need times for more intense solitude? How do you get it?

4) What is a *cenobitic* way of life? Do you need community?
   How is that manifested in your life?

5) What are the four stages of Coptic, or Egyptian, monasticism?

6) What is a Spirit-bearer? How do you bear the Spirit?

5. Chadwick, 64.

The Cell

"Go sit in your cell, and your cell will teach you everything."

—Abba Moses, in Owen Chadwick,
Western Asceticism

This is a famous saying. It sounds deceptively simple and easy. But it is far from it! It is simple but not simplistic. It is easy to say, but hard to really do.

My first hermit's cell was built at Alverna Franciscan Center. I begged rejected cement blocks from the friary and dug by hand into the hillside behind a Marian shrine. I used the irregular rock wall from the shrine as one wall and started digging the trench for the footing and foundation. Soon I was laying stones on a firm footing and foundation. I found a window frame and a door I could use and roofed it over. I put in a wood floor and brought down a simple desk, chair, and narrow cot to sleep on. I used a lantern as my light and heated it with a simple woodburning stove. It was rugged, and I had to come up to the common house after getting pretty sick during the hard Indiana winter months. But it provided the firm foundation upon which my future life in a semi-eremitic monastic community would develop.

Those first months in hermitage taught me that the lifestyle of the saints, like the desert fathers and mothers, or St. Francis and St. Benedict, is possible for us as well! I would spend long hours in prayer and sacred reading. It was in this hermitage that I first put the Psalter to music; this became the recording called *Come to the Quiet*, which outsold my bestselling *Lord's Supper* three times over. My diet was bread and cheese. I would sit outside my cell in prayer, and birds and squirrels would gather around me. I had to put an end to that when a woodpecker landed on my shoulder as though I was a tree! Seriously, when we are in real communion with God, then all creation is in communion with us. These sacred relationships really are possible for us today in Christ. So be encouraged!

What I dared to believe was that the way of the saints is possible! Most of the ancient saints started out their vocation in hermitages. I decided I'd try to the same thing. I had a great spiritual father who kept me on track and balanced. I discovered that when we pray and are in real communion with God and creation, the creatures gather around without fear. I had all sorts of birds, chipmunks, squirrels, and even a few snakes gather around me when I went out into the woods around my cell. I even had a pet mouse! He'd scamper into my cell. I'd look at him, and he'd look at me. Finally, one day I thought, "Why not?", and I gave him a bit of my cheese and said, "The cheese of Christ!" Seriously, I don't believe it was similar to the Eucharist, but it was kind of cute. He scampered off a bit and munched away!

So dare to believe that you and I can be saints! This stuff isn't for a select few from another era! It really is possible for anyone who dares to give it a serious try. I did. And I discovered much!

Later I would learn that the cell is also a crucible. Away from anything to distract my thoughts, I found out where they went when they wandered. Then I discovered where my heart really was. And that was often painful! I had a naked encounter with myself and with God. I discovered that beneath all my holy words and ideas, I was a sinner and didn't love Jesus nearly as much as I thought I did. Then the real work began.

The early sources reveal that the first desert hermits lived in primitive dwellings. They describe caves, holes in the earth, or huts that could be constructed in a single day with the help of all the monks. Archeology has shown us that the next phase of cells in the Wadi el Natrun were simple, but large enough to spend a great amount of time in them. They often consisted of several small rooms for living, working, and praying. They usually included a small courtyard. They were grouped around a common church where the Divine Liturgy was celebrated on Saturdays and Sundays. The rest of the time was spent in the cell by oneself, or with one or two young cell attendants learning the monastic way of life from an elder monk. Later, monastic communities were like little towns where daily common prayer, work, and meals were shared. Some of the greats ventured into greater solitude in the desert, often inhabiting caves as their cells. A few wandered the desert, eating its meager offerings, charity from Bedouins, or even miraculous food provided by departed saints, apostles, or angels. We must find our own version of this in modern life.

In a previous chapter we addressed turning off the social media and TV for a while, or indefinitely. The cell is the physical place where that can be done. It is a laboratory where we practice the science of solitude and silence. It is where we can become saints. It is really pretty simple. But it's certainly not easy.

What Is the Cell?

What is a monastic cell? The word comes from the Latin *cella*, meaning a small room and *celare*, to hide or conceal. It was applied to monasteries, monastic rooms or hermitages, and later to prison cells, where reforming oneself was at least theoretically possible. I have heard that it also has some indirect connection with words like *celestial*, which comes from the

Latin *caelum*, heaven. The monastic cell is where heaven and earth meet. It is more than just a room or physical monastery. It is the special sanctuary where deeper prayer takes place. It is a place that is sacred and holy, though ordinary things like sleep and work are also done there. The cell is a sacred place.

As Jesus says, "When you pray, go to your inner room, close the door, and pray to your Father in secret. And your Father who sees in secret will repay you" (Matt 6:6).

The Greek for *inner room* here is *tameion* and literally means the storehouse or closet. In modern parlance, it might well mean the pantry! What is a pantry? It's a place where there are no windows and plenty of food! The cell is like that as well. There are no "windows," and the "door" is shut; outer things cannot easily distract us. But there's plenty of spiritual nourishment! There's food of all kinds! Our orthodox Catholic faith is a big pantry! Its walls are solid and stable and lean neither to the right or the left. It is big and balanced. It is *catholicos*—catholic, universal, and full. All we must do is reach out and receive something from the shelf of our rich spiritual tradition as Catholic Christians.

The common pattern was that groups of cells were built around a chapel and eating area, where the monks gathered once a week on Saturday and Sunday for a meal, fellowship, and Eucharist. They would then gather supplies for the week and walk back to their cells, which were a few minutes or hours—never more than a day's journey—away.

St. Pachomius and St. Shenoute pioneered the more intense communal form, called *koinonia*, or cenobitic monasticism. These were monastic villages of many monastic houses where ten to fourteen monks were grouped to a house based on their trade. They prayed and ate in common daily, a few times in the houses and a few times in a large common church and dining hall, or refectory. But even there, monks had their own cell.

Today, Coptic monks often live in large monasteries, but their personal cell is often larger than those of Western monastics, for they spend more time there. The eremitic character of monasticism in general has been better maintained. Even in the cenobitic monasteries of the west, where a dormitory of many monks in one large room was normative for centuries, personal cells are now the rule.

What about Us?

What about average Christians today? How do they practice the cell rule in the more secular environment of the world? The following advice is applicable for them, as well as for monks in monasteries.

I suggest having *a prayer room or corner* in your home, or even in your office if appropriate and workable. It should be a sacred spot used for sacred reading and prayer alone. It should be *monos*, alone for God. I also suggest carving out specific time to retreat there, once or twice a day if possible. Early mornings and evenings are best. I suggest twenty to thirty minutes at a time. A short break around lunchtime is also great. If you can't do it twice in a day, then once is good. If so, I suggest mornings in order to set the tone for the day. If you can't do mornings, then do evenings. But do it! It is the best investment of time you will make in your life. It'll be good for your marriage, your family, your job, and your ministry.

So, we must first go to the cell and let it begin to teach us. This means we must *turn off the outer distractions*.

If we turn off the noise of TV, social media, and the like, we will come face to face with silence, and in the silence we will find God. We will also find ourselves. This is often very appealing at first, when we do so to escape the noise of the family, the workplace, or parish ministry. It is a much-welcomed retreat! It is a great place for recreation, to be created anew.

But when we stay a bit longer, we discover that God reveals to us the *naked truth about ourselves*. And this can be frightening. Thoughts invade our minds. Senses suggest all kinds of things.

Our egos rise up to fill us with fantasies about grand plans for ourselves. Or perhaps we feel left out because someone else gets more notice in ministry or work than we do. But we must face them all down in Christ. Then these temptations often rise up all the stronger, and we often discover that we actually *like* these things. That's why they are so persistent and stubborn when asked to leave. They can be downright terrifying. It is then that we often encounter the fight or flight syndrome. But as Jackson Browne once wrote in his song "Those Bright Baby Blues," "No matter how fast I run, I just can't seem to get away from me."

In the face of this reality, the desert fathers say that the cell is like the "furnace of Babylon" of the book of Daniel. That fire can be very hot! Sometimes it seems like it will kill us if we stay there longer. But God protects us. And in the long run it will purify us and make us stronger.

Stability

Because the cell is sacred, we should not easily leave it. Leaving without good cause, as discerned with our spiritual father or mother, makes us unstable.

We often hear the slogan "Bloom where you're planted." In order to bloom, you have to put down roots and stay put in the soil of your life. If you move the seed or the plant too soon, it will never bring forth life. We must learn how to stay still and bloom where we're planted. One desert father said a tree doesn't bloom if it is transplanted too often.

St. Antony famously said that just as fish die when taken out of water, so do monastics die when they stay too long outside of the cell.[1]

---

1. Owen Chadwick, ed. and trans., *Western Asceticism* (Philadelphia: Westminster Press, 1958), 40.

St. Syncletica, a great desert mother, used a similar analogy when she said that if a chicken stops sitting on the eggs they won't hatch, and the monk or nun who moves from place to place often grows cold in monastic life and loses his or her faith.[2]

But life in the cell without worldly or even religious projects to distract us, can be very difficult. An old man said that the monk's cell is the furnace of Babylon in which the three young people found the Son of God. It is the pillar of cloud out of which God spoke to Moses.[3] It can be painful at first, but if we stay put, we will discover graces that are unavailable in almost any other place.

The desert fathers tell numerous stories of how *the devil tries*, with ferocious insistence and in ingenious ways, *to get monks to leave their cells*. Some of these ways are simply sinful, such as to commit fornication or to lust for more property. But most are seemingly valid reasons, such as boredom, to visit another monk, or to find a more secluded cell. Few people follow the devil outright. He uses seemingly good reasons to get us off course in our vocation with God. Some might decide they don't get along with their community or elder, so they go looking for another. Others consider a change to the pure eremitic life in order to avoid others and the occasion for sin. A common one is the desire to go out and minister in order to save the world. The list goes on. But they are all deceptions to get us out of our original calling and cell. That cell, that vocation, that community is our wall of defense. Once it falls, the devil can wage open war on us, and we are utterly alone.

This idea gave rise to the great Benedictine commitment to *stability*. This means a commitment to living in a particular community and avoiding frivolous trips outside the monastery.

2. Chadwick, 85.
3. Chadwick, 93.

But it can also apply to one's family, work, or church. For any good monastic, it means stability in cell.

One of the great temptations in life in general is to constantly be on the move in order to entertain ourselves with *newness and novelty*. New and successful projects are exciting! But they can also distract us from the deeper work of God in our souls. While successful work, ministry, or projects can be a gift of God, they can also distract us from the deeper work of God in our lives.

We become like rocks skipping across the surface of the waters of our souls. We never allow ourselves to sink deep beyond the shallows and to find the deeper things of God within us. We only know the surface of our selves, others, or God. Spiritual life remains superficial, and ministry is never effective in the true spiritual sense.

Even in religious and monastic life, it is easy to get all caught up in going from one project to another, one person to another, and one ministry to another. We can even ramble from one spirituality to another and never really plumb the depths of any of them. The problem is that we never really let God into the deeper work on ourselves, and we never really develop our spirituality, work, or relationships in ways that last throughout life. Stability is needed.

So once we enter into our sacred cell, we are often tempted to leave it for a variety of seemingly good reasons. There are always good reasons to leave! We have ministry to do, or we left a work undone somewhere. Or maybe we just get up for a drink of water or a snack. Such things offer an endless stream of reasons to leave our solitude and silence. But they are distractions. They are not from God, who is calling us deeper into the desert through the cell of solitude and silence.

Unhealthy Attachment

We must also be careful *not to become attached to our cell*. We can make a god of our cell. It is only a tool from God to lead us back to God, but it is not God. It is temporal and passing. We have a heavenly mansion waiting for us, as promised by Christ. John of Lycus had several cells, one for the needs of the body, another for a workshop, and the third for greater solitude.[4] Macarius the Alexandrian dug a half-mile-long trench or tunnel from his primary cell to a cave farther out in the desert as a means to find solitude and silence away from the crowds that gathered around him to seek his guidance.[5]

So while stability in one's cell is fundamental, attachment to it isn't. There has to be a poverty of spirit regarding the physical cell.

I am reminded of St. Francis, who would leave a cell if anyone called it "his." He wanted to be totally poor. He didn't want to own the cells he stayed in, or clothing, books, or anything whatsoever. There are similar desert stories.

The legendary hermits of Coptic monasticism reportedly wandered the desert in complete solitude after having been trained in monastic community life. They had a lonely cave as a cell, or they simply wandered. They lived on what others—both humans and angels—brought to them for sustenance. The apostles and the angels were their primary friends. They attended liturgy nearly invisibly or late at night when the church was almost empty. They revealed their lives to anyone only as their deaths approached, so that their life stories might be told and their bodies buried. Most chose to die completely unknown. Some say these hermits are only myths. Others believe that they are real. I personally believe they existed. But, hey, I'm a believer! They stand as a reminder never to get attached to one place on earth and always to press on toward heaven.

---

4. E. A. W. Budge, ed. and trans., *The Paradise or Garden of the Holy Fathers*, 2 vols. (London: Chatto & Windus, 1907), 1:169.

5. Budge, 1:116.

Questions

1) Are you afraid of the solitude and the naked encounter with yourself and God that a cell or special place of prayer allows to happen?

2) Do you have a cell or prayer place where heaven comes to earth, so that secular pursuits do not pollute your prayer?

3) Where is your cell or prayer place?

4) Are you stable in your cell and prayer place, or do you allow yourself to be taken away from it too easily?

5) Do you believe that the relationships with God and creation attained by the great saints are still possible for you today, or do you rationalize and end up compromising your own holiness?

6

Work

The cell is where heaven comes to earth. This is experienced mainly in prayer. But work is also done in the cell. The cell is a place where the mundane things of the earth take on heavenly significance. The normal things of daily life are done there. There are a bed, desk, and chairs, as well as study and prayer spaces, and an area for some handiwork or hobby. There's even a small bathroom in the hermit's cell. These are ordinary things. But the calling is extraordinary. So in the cell there is a balance between the mundane and the miraculous.

I've lived in the same cell at Little Portion Hermitage and Monastery in Arkansas since 1983. I have loved watching saplings outside of my cell grow almost imperceptibly into tall trees. Hopefully I too have been growing, in the Spirit, throughout those years.

My cell was very simple at first. There was little there but a bed, a desk, and a couple of chairs. I had my guitar and a few books. Then with the advent of digital recording, I set up one side for recording equipment, and I had to get a TV when I went into television ministry. I also brought in books for writing and preparing talks. No doubt, it isn't the same as when I began. But a spirit of simplicity still prevails. Two rooms and small lofts for storage have proven to be sufficient for Viola (our Spiritual Mother) and myself through the years. But I do regret the TV! Every day I divide my time between *prayer and work*. When I'm at the monastery, I join the community for Common Prayer and Mass several days a week, and I pray the Divine Office on my own the remaining days. I often augment the Roman Office with the Coptic (Egyptian) *Agpeya* (Hours) simply to pray more psalms and the truly beautiful litanies and prayers. Saturdays are unscheduled, and a rather busy Sunday includes community Mass, a council meeting, and monastic chapter, or spiritual talk and business meeting. Daily, I'm up around five o'clock in the morning, and I spend most of my time in study and prayer. It's difficult to determine where study leaves off and prayer begins. I write music and work on records. I still write some books, like this one. I also go up the hill to the monastery for the various meetings and conferences throughout the week. It is a full day and week. Indeed, it's a full and wonderful life! And most of it occurs in my cell.

We do a *regular inspection* of the monks' cells at Little Portion Hermitage, not always preannounced. I want to see the ordinary upkeep of the cell. I sometimes find a real mess. This often indicates a messy monk. If you cannot keep your cell organized and straight, your mind and soul is often unorganized and unfocused as well. The other extreme is also harmful. A cell that is so neat that it looks like no one lives there often indicates a spiritual life that is so regimented that no real spiritual growth is happening there. What I look for is something in between the extremes. I want a reasonably neat and clean cell, but one that is really lived in. This indicates a focused, but lively spiritual life.

Work in the Desert
What did the first monks do in the cell?

We know the story of St. Antony, who was taught by an angel to balance his time between prayer and work.[1]

All of us must work. Adam worked in the Garden of Eden. Jesus presumably worked in the home in Nazareth. The saints were all great workers for God. We must also continue with daily work if our prayer is to be balanced and lifegiving.

The monks of the desert were men and women of *work*. This work was usually manual labor. Some, like Evagrius, copied and wrote books as his work. The main work of the hermits was cutting reeds for plaiting ropes and weaving baskets, which they sold in order to support their frugal and simple lifestyle. The Pachomian and koinonia monks of Upper Egypt had extensive occupations, ranging from baking and farming to woodworking and ironworking. They even arranged their living quarters according to the work skills of the monks and sent the fruit of their labor up the Nile on barges they themselves owned to sell in big towns and cities such as Alexandria.

Today, Coptic monasteries in Egypt are actively involved in large farms, bakeries, and retreat work, reaching thousands weekly. It is said that for every monk in the monastery, there are about ten lay employees who help him in what have become rather large and industrious spiritual enterprises! Western monasteries are also very busy places. They operate farms, bakeries, breweries, and schools of higher education. Most people are surprised to learn how busy and industrious good monastics are. Good monastics often do the work of two or three people (and more!) in half the time. Only halfhearted monastics are lazy or inefficient in their work. It's said that if you want to get something done right, give it to a busy person! So the image of a monk idly praying his days away is false. Work was, and remains, a most important part of monastic life in the East and the West.

---

1. E. A. W. Budge, ed. and trans., *The Paradise or Garden of the Holy Fathers*, 2 vols. (London: Chatto & Windus, 1907), 2:30.

For the desert fathers and mothers, stability in cell is linked to staying busy in cell. If we try to pray constantly, then we can neither support ourselves nor stay mentally agile. Work in cell is a big part of desert monasticism. Some stated flatly that the life of the desert monk is work, obedience, and silence.

An old man said, "This is the life of a monk: work, obedience, meditation, not to judge others, not to speak evil, not to complain."[2] Stark, simple, and most demanding.

Against Idleness

There are humorous stories about young monks who wanted to be so spiritual that they would pray without ceasing, lived the angelic life, and therefore did not believe they needed to work. These dreamers were met with the older monks' lesson that since they were now living the angelic life, they also no longer needed to eat. Needless to say, the young monastics changed their tune and readily began working just like the other monks!

There are other stories in which the quickness and quality of an aspiring monk's work served as a confirmation of his vocation to that lifestyle. This was true in the case of the older aspirant Macarius, who St. Antony doubted could keep up with the tougher regimen of the younger monks and at first encouraged him to go back to the world. It was Macarius's willingness to work that convinced Antony that he could cut the mustard of a more austere monastic life. Macarius went on to become a great saint.[3]

This dedication to work is also seen in stories of older monks who worked so quickly that the younger monks couldn't keep up. One older monastic plaited ropes so quickly that the younger brothers were amazed.

---

2. Owen Chadwick, ed. and trans., *Western Asceticism* (Philadelphia: Westminster Press, 1958), 40.
3. Chadwick, 84.

I have witnessed this in our monastery. The Sisters of the Incarnate Word and Blessed Sacrament trained our Spiritual Mother, Viola. She was trained "old school." She was taught to work, not for her own pleasure, but for the will of Jesus, and to find great joy in even the lowliest of tasks. She was rarely given an obedience—an instruction that a monastic is obligated to obey—very nicely, but she says it trained her to do things cheerfully for God alone, and she is now the first to be cheerful in giving obediences today. Though she rebelled many times during formation, the formation took hold and molded her into a selfless servant. Our younger members are always amazed at how much she gets done with such ease and joy. They are either inspired or put off. Those who are put off cannot get past their more "me oriented" ego formation. Those who let go of such things are deeply inspired and learn a new way of living in Christ than what the fallen world has taught them.

Work is an antidote to idleness. Idleness is the enemy to the soul (see 2 Thess 3:6-13). Idle hands are the devil's workshop. A monk should be working at some good task every day in solitude. The Rule of Benedict says clearly, "Idleness is the enemy of the soul. Therefore, the brothers should have specified periods for manual labor as well as for prayerful reading."[4]

Abba Poemen said that as people use smoke to clear bees from their hive to steal the honey, so does idleness drive the fear of God from the soul and steals away good works.[5]

As he was dying, Abba Pambo said that from the time he came to the desert he did not remember having eaten anything that his hands had not worked for.[6]

And Isidore, the priest for Scete said, "My brothers, is not work the reason why we are here?" When he saw that the monks

---

4. *Rule of Saint Benedict 1980* (hereafter *RB*), Timothy Fry, ed. (Collegeville, MN: Liturgical Press, 1981), 48.1.
    5. Chadwick, 54.
    6. Chadwick, 39.

at a particular monastery didn't work, he took his cloak and went away. He said, "I am going where there is work, and there I shall find rest."[7]

Against Workaholism

But *work is not an end unto itself*. Nor is work a substitute for real prayer, either communal or private. We hear it said all too often, "My work is my prayer." But this is just workaholism for Christ! St. Francis did say, "I seek, not so much to pray, as to become a prayer." But this did not keep him from insisting on set times for the Divine Office and private prayer or from founding over twenty hermitages in his short lifetime! Francis was no "workaholic for Christ"! He was a contemplative hermit whose prayer overflowed into ministry that was filled with the power of the Spirit. Without that foundation, his ministry would have been religious, but spiritually weak.

Do we see work as an aid to prayer or as an obstacle to prayer? Does our work provide a healthy break from intensity or boredom of prayer? Conversely, do we try to hide from prayer through work?

Questions

1) Do you see the value on hard work?

2) Are you stable in your work?

3) Do you understand work to be in conflict with prayer?

7. Chadwick, 85.

4) Do you see the balance between work and prayer in a good life of stability?

5) Do you sometimes want to pray but not work? How realistic is this?

6) Do you do high quality work?

7) Do you overcharge for your labor?

8) Do you value the variety of kinds of work, or do you see only manual labor as valuable?

Private Prayer

"There is no need of much speaking in our prayers."

—St. Macarius, in James O. Hannay,
The Wisdom of the Desert

Prayer is communication with God. It is simple, but not simplistic. St. John Vianney described contemplative prayer saying, "I look at him, and he looks at me."

I remember well my childhood experiences of God. It usually amounted to sitting outside in the yard and pondering God in nature. I never much liked the ritual prayers at our church. But I always had a natural propensity to the simple prayer of just being with God.

After my adult conversion back to Jesus, I also loved to study Scripture. I studied voraciously. But I also prayed. I would leisurely read a passage of Scripture and let it slowly sink into my being, beyond mere thought to deep intuition. Later, it would often become a song that helped the words sink into the soul of the listener. Through the years of experience, I learned about the stages and levels of prayer.

The desert fathers and mothers had not yet developed a systematic treatment of prayer. We would look in vain to find it in their lives and sayings. But *prayer permeates all that they did*. And we can discern much from their almost casual comments about prayer.

They treat both *private prayer* in their cells and *public prayer*. They treat both *spontaneous* prayer and the extensive use of the Psalms as *liturgy*. Contrary to what some have claimed in times past, they also engaged in liturgical prayer in the Divine Office and a weekly Eucharist. They address true devotion to Mary and the saints. It was up to the likes of Evagrius, the great desert writer and mystic, to directly address what today we call contemplative prayer.

Physicality

We know that the *cell* was the normal place for private prayer. They also prayed in a common *church*, around which private hermit cells were arranged. Prayer was in *a place*. It had *physicality as well as spirituality*. Jesus is the Word Incarnate. He went to the desert to pray, and ministered in specific public places. Our spirituality is both spiritual and physical.

The Body

They also used their *bodies* in prayer. They stood, knelt, fell prostrate, and raised their hands.

One Saturday evening, Arsenius turned his back to the setting sun, stretched out his hands toward heaven, and then he prayed until the sun shone on his face once more at dawn on Sunday.[1]

Macarius *prayed always*, and he prayed *with his arms and hands extended in the form of a cross*.[2] Following St. Paul, prayer

1. Benedicta Ward, ed., *The Desert Fathers: Sayings of the Early Christian Monks* (New York: Penguin, 2003), 130.
2. E. A. W. Budge, ed. and trans., *The Paradise or Garden of the Holy Fathers*, 2 vols. (London: Chatto & Windus, 1907), 1:110.

is to be *unceasing* (1 Thess 5:17). It involves actions of the body, thoughts of the spiritual mind of the soul, and contemplative intuitions beyond thought, image, or idea.

Why this use of raised hands in prayer? Certainly it is scriptural. Moses raised his hands in order for the battle to go well and had them propped up when they began to droop from exhaustion (see Exod 17:11-13). The Psalms are filled with admonitions to pray with uplifted hands (see Pss 63:4; 134:2; 141:2; among others). And St. Paul instructed Christians to pray everywhere with uplifted holy hands (1 Tim 2:8). Why?

I believe it is because *God doesn't just want our spirit and soul. He wants our body as well!* He doesn't just want our faith. He also wants our morality! He wants all that we are—spirit, soul, and body. God is a God of incarnation. Jesus is the Word Incarnate! *Incarnate* comes from *carne*, which means *flesh* or *red meat!* The body must be involved in prayer. At Mass we fold hands, open hands, and raise hands. This is an ancient prayer posture.

Raising hands is a great way to get beyond our false humility and self-obsession. Often we don't want to do such things because "that's not my way." It's true that we are all different, but often we hang on to our false selves under religious clothes to keep Jesus from breaking us free to be born again and become a completely new creation in him. Often it can just be introverted pride.

For me, raising hands in prayer gets past my personal preferences and hang-ups, and it lets me pour out my heart to God with no obstructions. It expresses and stirs up my soul. It raises my poor self to God, who alone cares for me fully, and can raise me up in him. This is most powerful in private. It is expressive and liberating as long as it is done in the Spirit of God.

Even in public prayer it is powerful for an entire community. But when the community where I am praying is simply not into such things, I can do so discreetly without calling attention to myself. I also do not confuse the role of the presiding priest with the role of the laity. In Eastern liturgy, the laity is free to make spontaneous signs of the cross or prostrations as the Spirit inspires them. But again, we don't do this to draw attention to ourselves through a fake show of piety or humility. So I recommend raising hands in liturgy when done in the right spirit. It is very liberating in the Spirit of God.

In the practice of the desert mothers and fathers, we see some humor in their raising of hands at prayer. One father couldn't stop praying if his hands were raised. He would come to the end of his lengthy prayers, start to lower his hands, get inspired again, raise his hands, and start all over again! If they couldn't get this father to lower his hands, they would be there for days on end! It was said that Abba Sisois lowered his hands quickly when he stood up to pray, because if he didn't he went into rapture and his mind was simply with God for a while. So if he was praying with another brother, he quickly lowered his hands and ended the prayer, so that his mind should not be rapt or remain in prayer too long for his brother.[3]

Abba Dulas, the disciple of Abba Bessarion, found his spiritual father standing in prayer in his cell, with his hands stretched toward heaven. He stayed like that for fourteen days![4] We too should get the body involved in prayer. It helps stir up the Spirit.

Today we also *sit, stand, kneel, or prostrate ourselves in private and public prayer.*

The Mind

One hermit used to say that ceaseless prayer *heals the mind.*[5]

Prayer is the *antidote against temptation.* Time and time again we see the fathers incorporating prayer in the battle against

---

3. Owen Chadwick, ed. and trans., *Western Asceticism* (Philadelphia: Westminster Press, 1958), 142–143.

4. Chadwick, 141.

5. Ward, 132.

tempting feelings or thoughts. Syncletica said that strong antidotes are needed to cure some animals' poison; in the same way, fasting and prayer drive temptation from the soul.[6]

Thoughts and Feelings

There is also a relationship between *thoughts and feelings*. Sometimes we use too many words in prayer. All that is needed is a repentant heart. Abba Dulas also said that when a bad thought enters the heart, or the emotions, we should not cast around here and there in our prayer, but simply be penitent. This will sharpen our swords against the thought that assails us.[7]

Ceaseless Prayer and Daily Life

The prayer of the desert was to be *without ceasing*. But that didn't mean the other normal things of life didn't have to be done. This is humorously demonstrated by several stories. The following one is indicative of the attitude of the desert fathers and mothers.

A group who sought to pray constantly sought out the desert fathers. Abba Lucius asked them what they did as a way of life. They responded that they prayed but did no work. Lucius asked whether they ate, and they said they did. Lucius asked who prayed while they ate, and they had no answer. He then asked whether they slept, and they said they did. He then asked who prayed for them while they slept. They were again silent. Then Lucius said, "Forgive me, brothers, but you do not practice what you preach. I will show you how I pray without ceasing, though I work with my hands. With God's help, I sit and collect a few palm leaves and weave them. While I work I say: 'Have mercy

6. Chadwick, 55.
7. Chadwick, 142.

upon me, O God, after thy great mercy: and according to the multitude of thy mercies do away with mine iniquity' [Ps 51:1]. And he said to them: 'Is that prayer, or is it not?' They said: 'It is prayer.'"[8]

Young Abba John wanted to live like an angel, so he wouldn't work and went naked into the wilderness. But he got hungry! He came back to an abba's cell and begged forgiveness.[9]

We've had similar situations in our hermitage. Some would-be monastics are hyper-spiritual and want to pray all the time. They are often very critical of the ordinary things we do in the monastery. They never last long. They go back to secular life. It always strikes me as funny that those who seek unattainable and extraordinary monastic goals end up with very ordinary secular Christian lives, while we merely "ordinary" monastics are still here!

The fathers did come up with some ingenious and sometimes humorous ways of trying to fulfill the command to pray without ceasing! Pachomian monks didn't sleep in beds, but in primitive wooden recliner chairs.[10] Some sat up without leaning against a wall, held a book, or suspended themselves by straps so they wouldn't lie down and nod off to sleep![11] I wouldn't recommend this to the average monastic or Christian today, though some Coptic monks still sleep in a simple reclining chair.

They also came up with ingenious ways to keep the cycle of prayer going constantly. Some of this is just common sense. Lucius worked and prayed throughout the day. He left some of the money he earned from selling his baskets outside his door for the poor. Those who received the money prayed in his place,

8. Chadwick, 142–143.
9. Chadwick, 110–111.
10. Budge, 1:145.
11. Budge, 2:234.

"filling in the gaps," while he was eating and sleeping.[12] They fulfilled the command: Pray without ceasing.

When we at our monastery help others, we make lifelong friends. These are people that come to our door, or even some whom we meet doing the normal business of the monastery. We promise to pray for them. We see many conversions, healings, and miracles in Christ. These friends support our humble way of life through prayer when we have to work, and we pray for them in their secular life as Christians in the world. There is a healthy balance and a natural alternation of giving and receiving. It is beautiful when it unfolds.

Asceticism

But some *real asceticism is also required* for pure prayer. While holy water displaces ungodliness, it is also true that you need to cleanse a dirty vessel before you pour water into it. Otherwise, the water will become muddy.

The desert mothers and fathers use the analogy of water (a favorite in mystical religion) to describe the purity of thought needed for real contemplation. One father said that just as one can't see his face reflected in muddy water, so the soul cannot pray in contemplation of God unless first cleansed of harmful thoughts.[13]

Obedience

There is also a connection between prayer and *obedience*. If you are disobedient to God or God's valid ministers on earth, you will not have a good life of prayer. Obedience means listening

---

12. James O. Hannay, *The Wisdom of the Desert* (1904; repr. n.p.: Glass Darkly, 2012), 65. Citations refer to the Glass Darkly edition, available at https://archive.org/details/WisdomOfTheDesert.

13. Chadwick, 143.

without resistance or grumbling and responding promptly to what you hear.

Abba Hyperichius said the monk's life is obedience. He who possesses obedience will have his prayers answered and will stand by the Crucified with confident faith. For that was how the Lord went to his cross. He was obedient even unto death.[14]

Devotion to Saints and Mary

It would be an understatement to say that the fathers and mothers were very devoted in their prayers! They also had a great love for *the saints* and patriarchs that came before them. *The Hermit Fathers* describes men and women who went into radical solitude as wanderers in the desert and were visited supernaturally by apostles, saints, and angels who assisted them in a variety of ways. At various times, these visitors supplied food, led them to a special cave or spring to live in, or helped them journey long distances in short periods of time.[15] These are miraculous indications of the great devotion of these desert dwellers to the intercessory role of the angels and the saints in helping lead them to Jesus Christ, the final Intercessor.

But they were also aware that *demons can take the form of angels and saints*. They can even appear as Jesus! Therefore, great discernment is needed. They often appeal to St. Paul who said, "Even Satan masquerades as an angel of light" (2 Cor 11:14).

One story says that Satan told a monk that he should pray saying, "Glory be to you, Mary, mother of Christ." But the monk answered and said to him, "There is dust in your eyes, Satan. Why should I forsake the Lord and worship a handmaiden?" And Satan immediately disappeared.[16]

14. Chadwick, 152.

15. Samaan El-Souriany, *The Hermit Fathers* (Putty, Australia: St. Shenouda Press, 2010).

16. Budge, 2:270.

Proper Marian devotion is one thing, but ceasing to pray to God directly in favor of primarily or only praying to Mary or saints is not real devotion. Real devotion to Mary always flows from and leads back to Jesus. The prayer that the devil suggested to the monk in the story above substituted the Mother of God for Jesus and the Trinity, but it wasn't from God. It was a deception. Real discernment is always needed.

But this doesn't mean that the desert fathers and mothers didn't nurture a real devotion to Mary. They did!

Abba Isaac once said that Abba Poemen was in a state of great ecstasy and rapture, and he asked him what was in his mind at that moment. He eventually said, "My mind was in the place of the Crucifixion, where the holy woman Mary, the God-bearer, was standing and weeping by the Cross of our Redeemer, and I was wishing that I might at all times feel thus."[17]

This illustrates the right place of Mary in orthodox prayer. The Eastern tradition extols Mary to an even higher degree than the Catholic West, but with a different emphasis of doctrine.

Pure Prayer

Later generations would categorize prayer as active and contemplative, knowing and unknowing, cataphatic and apophatic stages. The first involves the things we can know and practice about God. This is the world of apostolic teaching, sacraments and liturgy, and positive prayer disciplines and practices. The second is beyond our full comprehension. "We see indistinctly, as in a mirror" (1 Cor 13:12), and can only grasp such things even incompletely through contemplative intuition. We must practice and substantially master the first before God allows us, at first only in glimpses and snatches, the second. Then, after

17. Budge, 2:235.

years of faithfulness, we begin to pass over into contemplation as a gift from God.

It is Evagrius who first gives us *the most sophisticated approach to prayer from the desert.* These words span from knowing to unknowing, from cataphatic to apophatic, from positive to negative. He paves the way for all future systems and theologies of mystical prayer.

Evagrius speaks of this pure prayer in the brief but rich and insightful aphorisms that he offers in his work, *On Prayer.* His insights are reflected in what we have said above. I will offer but a few lines of his teaching, indicating the "chapter" numbers following each.

- "The state of prayer is one of dispassion" (53).

- "Blessed is the intellect that is completely free from forms during prayer" (117).

- "Blessed is the intellect undistracted in its prayer" (118).

- "Blessed is the intellect that during prayer is free from materiality and stripped of all possessions" (119).

- "Blessed is the intellect that has acquired complete freedom from sensations during prayer" (120).

- "The man who always dedicates his first thoughts to God has perfect prayer" (126).

Questions

1) What is prayer for you?

2) Do you involve your body in prayer, through practices like raising your hands?

3) Is your prayer unceasing? What does that mean for you?

4) Does prayer help you in temptation?

5) Is your prayer simple or complicated?

6) How does prayer affect your thoughts?

7) Is your prayer positively affected by obedience and negatively affected by disobedience?

8) Do we adapt our prayer to meet the needs of charity?

9) Is Mary a part of your prayer life? How does that work for you?

10) Do we move beyond images, forms, and ideas in contemplative prayer?

8

Liturgical Prayer

Now we move on to public prayer. We begin with the Psalms that developed into the Liturgy of the Hours, or the Divine Office, and move on to the Divine Liturgy, or what we in the West call the Mass.

Psalmody

Jesus teaches about private prayer. He says, "When you pray, go to your inner room, close the door, and pray to your Father in secret. And your Father who sees in secret will repay you" (Matt 6:6). But he also goes to the temple, institutes the Eucharist at the Last Supper (Matt 26:26-30), and confirms it on the road to Emmaus (Luke 24:13-35).

When we started Little Portion Hermitage, we wanted to emulate the desert fathers and mothers and spend most of our time in solitude and silence. But we had to actually *do* something in that solitude! Otherwise we would just aimlessly waste our time away, drift from a real life with God, and end up in delusion. Plus, we weren't just individuals but a community of hermits who gathered daily. So we had to *do* something when we got together. The same was true of the first desert fathers and mothers and of all communities of hermits ever since.

That's where the use of the Psalter came in. At first, the desert fathers and mothers left things up to the individual and the Holy Spirit. But some folks weren't that good at discerning the Spirit yet, so the more experienced fathers set down that the monks should all pray at the same hour, the ninth hour (three o'clock in the afternoon), the time of Jesus' death on the cross. They also recommended that the monks pray the entire Psalter every day, as well as much of the New Testament. Soon a pattern of praying at certain hours developed, with each hour having significance in the life of Jesus Christ. This took on special significance when an elder had one or two younger monks living either with him in cell or right next to him in their own cells. There was a communal dimension to their solitude.

They also gathered from their hermitages that were within walking distance from a common chapel and common building on Saturday and Sunday every week. On Saturday they would share an agape meal together and a Eucharist, and on Sunday they would celebrate the Lord's Day Eucharist, presided over by one or more of the monks who had been ordained as priests by the local bishop.

So pretty early in the desert tradition, a daily pattern of praying the Psalter at set hours and celebrating the Eucharist on Saturday and Sunday developed. Today we pray it in the Liturgy of the Hours in most Roman and Eastern traditions. The Coptic tradition prays most of the Psalter daily. The Roman tradition first mitigated it to praying the 150 psalms weekly with St. Benedict, and we now pray the Psalter in a monthly cycle. This is to emphasize quality over quantity. But the Copts all say that to pray the sheer volume of psalms and extra prayers, they actually get under the words to hear what the Spirit is saying. That is the point.

Abba Isidore, a priest at Scete, said that when he was young he stayed in his cell and made no limit to the number of psalms he prayed to God as part of his daily service. Both night and day were spent in psalmody.[1]

But temptations still come while praying Scripture. Abba Evagrius said it is a great thing to pray without temptations and distractions. It is even greater to sing psalms without them.[2] Abba Hyperichius said to keep praising God with hymnody, meditate continually, and you will lift the burden of the temptations that come upon you.[3]

Praying the entire Psalter was work. And it took time, a large part of every day. Some who visited saw this as excessive and complained. One story says that one father tried to be charitable to visitors by feeding them amply and letting up on their heavy prayer schedule. The guests complained about their laxity. So he taught them a little lesson by requiring that they pray the normal monastic cycle of psalms. Then they complained about the length of the prayers! So the hosting monks sent word to the monks whom these guests planned to visit next with the message, "Don't water the vegetables." This became a code meaning not to be too charitable, for whatever they did would be criticized.

So the next hermit welcomed the visiting brothers. But he immediately put them to regular monastic work. Afterward he served a normal, meager monastic meal. Then he kept them up all night praying the usual number of prayers. In the morning the hermit served them extra breakfast, but it still was almost nothing and disgusted the guests. This was to teach the upstarts a very real lesson in monastic life. Well, the brothers couldn't wait to get out of there. The holy hermit begged them

1. Owen Chadwick, ed. and trans., *Western Asceticism* (Philadelphia: Westminster Press, 1958), 134.

2. Chadwick, 132.

3. Chadwick, 87.

to stay at least three days in order to experience real eremitic life, and the guests snuck away in shame![4]

Despite the length of the daily routine, prayer is *not to be the rote repetition* of psalms or other prayers. Jesus warned clearly about vain repetitions (Matt 6:7). Liturgical and private prayer is to be filled with the fire of the Holy Spirit. It was not passive. It was active and fiery!

We should not simply sing or recite the psalms or any other liturgical prayer. We must be on fire in the Spirit when we pray them. Abba Joseph rose, spread out his hands to heaven, and his fingers shone like ten candles. He said, "If you will, you could become a living flame."[5]

The Divine Office

From spontaneous prayer, the Liturgy of the Hours emerged. It consists mainly of the Psalter. It also includes biblical canticles and readings. It developed slowly from monastic and cathedral traditions that eventually intertwined. The first monks prayed all 150 psalms daily. In the West, St. Benedict reduced it to a weekly cycle, which later happened in the East as well. The current Roman Liturgy of the Hours uses a monthly cycle. It provides a structure that guides and supports our more continual prayers throughout each day.

The Coptic (Egyptian) *Agpeya* (Hours), *canonical hours* in the East, and the Divine Office in the West developed from both the cathedral tradition of praying the psalms grouped according to themes and the numerical monastic tradition of praying all 150 psalms daily. John Cassian reports that an angel demonstrated by beautiful example that twelve psalms were to be prayed at each liturgical hour. Some scholars say that standardized prayer

4. Chadwick, 127–128.
5. Chadwick, 142.

first appeared in the desert with the fathers praying at the hour of Jesus death, the ninth hour. Others say that the desert fathers used some more complete form of the canonical hours inherited from the Jews or used in an early form in the diocesan cathedrals. Evidence from the compilations suggests that the use of the canonical hours was adopted pretty quickly.

My Experience

I first was introduced to the Liturgy of Hours at a Franciscan community where I lived during my conversion. I prayed this prayer daily with the friars. I also prayed it in a hermitage. I loved praying the Hours sitting at a primitive desk with a lone kerosene lantern in the solitude of my cell. Much of one of my early recordings called *Come to the Quiet* is the result of that initial prayer. Later, I learned about the history of Liturgy of the Hours in the East and the West. I have prayed the Roman Liturgy of the Hours for four decades, and it has given me the foundation for much of my personal prayer.

My experience of the Divine Office has varied and hopefully matured through the decades. Originally I used the Roman Office, or Breviary, for that's what the Franciscans who birthed me into the church used. Later I learned about the Benedictine Office that uses all 150 psalms weekly, though some use a two-week cycle nowadays. Later I learned the Coptic Office that uses nearly all the psalms daily. I find all enriching to my prayer life.

For myself, I have always tried to sing and recite the psalms with attention and enthusiasm both in private and in public prayer in monastic choir. Unfortunately, this often stands in some contrast to the rather passive or even apparently bored way that many monastics tend to pray the Office, even in the community I founded! If the psalm says to raise your hands, I discreetly do so in my choir stall. If it says to shout to the Lord, I add a bit of an emphasis in my singing. If it says to rejoice, I really try to rejoice. As one nun once told me, "If Jesus is in your heart, please inform your face!" And I must admit that it can be really disheartening to look across the church to the other side of the choir stalls and see only downcast, disengaged, and even miserable-looking faces. I don't try to draw attention to myself, but at this point in my life I figure I don't have that much time left, so I really try to pray the liturgies for God and God alone. Others can do so or not. That is up to them.

This has been more intense with me personally since the onset of the health issues and crises that often come with age. When you are more intensely aware that your death is more imminent, you no longer have time to fool around with mediocre religion. It is literally life or death to get completely real in your prayer expressions. So I no longer really much care whether or not folks like the way I pray. I am deeply aware that our monastic church is filled with angels and saints while we pray. It is a crowded church! How can I stay stuck in mundane mediocrity in the midst of such a spiritual reality? So I pray freely, yet discreetly, regardless of the quality of the liturgical prayer in which I find myself.

But lately I have found an even greater new power when I pray the Coptic Office in my hermit's cell alone. When I am no longer thinking about what I have to do in community or ministry, I can pray meditating only on the Eternal. I can take my time. In that context the words of the psalms and prayers literally jump from the page or from my memory and burn like a fire into my soul. Rejoicing or weeping is completely free because I don't have to worry about others in choir. I don't have to worry about the time, for I am alone in my cell. I find my hands rising spontaneously and my heart stirring as I linger over a word or phrase before moving on. I can rejoice, pray in tongues, or weep. Everything takes on a sole orientation to God alone in whom we and, in a powerfully personal way, I will spend our Eternity. It is in this context that the words of the desert fathers and mothers really hit home. No longer am I praying as a restful break in an otherwise busy day of service and ministry in community, the church, or the world. I simply exist to pray. All else fades.

I must add that while I still venture out of my hermitage to fulfill my necessary ministry responsibilities, I am now really discovering that venturing out takes me to a level of prayer that is far less intense. You cannot go out and maintain the same level of intensity that requires a more absolute solitude.

The Desert Fathers

The use of the Office should never replace ceaseless prayer of the heart. It is not enough to just recite or sing the Office.

An abbot of a monastery in Palestine told Bishop Epiphanius of Cyprus that they kept their rule, observing the offices of Terce, Sext, None, and Vespers. But Epiphanius rebuked him and said, "Then you are surely failing to pray at other times. The true monk ought to pray without ceasing, ought always to be singing psalms in his heart."[6] So the Hours were already being prayed.

Wandering Mind

Even with the beauty in our liturgies we can still find our minds wandering during prayer. I certainly experienced this in my younger days. I still do on occasion. And I see it with young and old monastics today if they don't stay on fire for God and use the available means to stay on focus and on fire during liturgical prayer. It is far too easy to blame it on the mediocrity of the execution or the monotony of the liturgy. Usually the problem is not "them" or "out there." The problem is us! Wandering minds during the Divine Office is not a new problem!

Once the brethren asked one of the fathers what he did to prevent his mind from wandering when singing the psalms. The old man said that first he tried to understand the meaning of the words of the psalms. The fathers didn't do did this as

6. Chadwick, 142.

an exercise in Scripture study or interpretation like Basil and John Chrysostom. Rather, they did this spiritually, according to the way of the desert fathers. They applied all the psalms to their own lives and works, to their passions, spiritual life, and to the spiritual warfare.[7]

Today we often find folks reverting to rote ritual prayers in an attempt to please God. This is often a reaction to the failed Catholic experiments of more liberal use of spontaneous prayer. But a simple reversion to a pre-Vatican II approach to liturgy is not the answer either. If it had worked well then, liturgical reform wouldn't have been called for, and it doesn't work now.

We see this especially among our youth. These are good, conscientious young people. They love God and they love the church. They just want to do the right thing. But because they have rarely seen the beauty of real charismatic and contemplative liturgy in a monastic setting, they settle for whatever they can find. All they can find among many of today's orthodox priests is getting the rubrics right. Anything spontaneous is viewed as suspect or even sacrilegious. So they often degenerate into modern scribes and Pharisees. Sadly, they rob themselves of really entering into the spiritual beauty of the liturgy, and they judge everyone else who does (see Matt 23:13)! The result is a technically correct but lifeless liturgical prayer where few really find the wealth that the liturgy was intended for in the first place. All real enthusiasm is gone. This is not the way of the desert fathers.

So our typical parish liturgies are often passive experiences where folks mumble responses and songs as they wait for the Real Presence of Jesus in the Eucharist. Rather than preparing us for the Eucharist, they are something to be endured to get the Eucharist! While it may be correct to focus on Jesus in the Eucharist and we cannot judge the inner faith of any

7. E. A. W. Budge, ed. and trans., *The Paradise or Garden of the Holy Fathers*, 2 vols. (London: Chatto & Windus, 1907), 2:306.

congregants, we can judge the quality of the liturgies. And the external aspect of most liturgies in America and Europe today is pretty awful. The fire of the desert fathers and mothers has much to teach us!

Our Little Portion Chant is based on ancient chant and modern tones. It isn't too fast or too slow. Chant should be *sung speech*. Too fast and it feels like a freight train that runs over anyone in the way! Too slow and it feels like wading through molasses and brings an oppressive spirit to the community. Chant should *lilt* and lift the soul to God. It should be loud enough to be heard and express some spirit, but not so loud as to jar folks like a rude intruder into prayer. There should be a healthy balance.

And deeper prayer comes *after* the psalm or canticle. Some space for silence is important to let the Scripture soak into the soul. We also allow for monks to repeat the line or phrase that the Spirit spoke to them to allow us to get a sense of what God is saying to the community. But like the prophets in Corinth, we allow two or three at most (1 Cor 14:29); otherwise it can drag on too long.

I encourage you to pray the psalms in any form. Today the Roman Liturgy of the Hours is best for laypeople and more active communities. Some laity in the West use popular publications organized similarly to the Office, but these can seem too brief for most who are seriously interested in this liturgical way of prayer. If the Liturgy of the Hours seems too complicated, find a local community that prays it together regularly to learn. It's actually pretty easy once you get the hang of it. Others might want to use one of the many online versions or liturgical apps. Today there is really no excuse not to pray the Office if you really want to.

The Eucharist

In previous decades, some tried to represent the desert fathers and mothers as sort of "proto-Protestants," rejecting the liturgies and sacraments of the church. But this has been proven to be untrue.

It is clear that the fathers gathered from their individual hermitages on Saturday for the "Synaxis," or gathering prayers, a common meal, Eucharist, and vigils, and on Sunday for Eucharist. After that they would gather their weekly supplies and walk back to their respective hermitages.

They definitely believed in the Real Presence of Jesus in the Eucharist.

When one father didn't believe that the Eucharist was the Body and Blood of Jesus Christ, but only a symbol, the other monks begged him to desist from such a belief, for it is not what was passed on from the apostles and their successors.[8]

Abba Poemen used to say the monks who are in the desert are often burned up by the envy of evil devils. They wait for Saturday and Sunday that they may come to the fountain of water, the Body of Christ, to sweeten and purify themselves from the gall of the Evil One.[9]

Another monk said to a brother in his cell that they did no good just sitting in solitude in their cells. He said they couldn't receive the Body and Blood of Jesus there, while three miles away was a monastery with a presbyter. He implored the brother to go on Sunday, or every other Sunday, to receive the Body and Blood of Christ.[10]

From this we can see that, contrary to what some teach, the Divine Office and the Eucharist on Saturday and Sunday were most important aspects of the life of the first desert fathers and mothers. You can find examples of those who stayed in solitude for decades without seeing another human. But these are exceptions. The clear rule is that they came together for

8. Budge, 2:159–160.
9. Budge, 2:165.
10. Chadwick, 89.

common prayer and Eucharist weekly. Even hermits needed some fellowship in prayer. We do, too!

The Eucharist and the Spirit

Participation in the common table and Eucharist are connected to the Holy Spirit. There was a great old man who saw in the Spirit some of the brethren eating honey, others eating bread, and others dung during the Eucharist. Those eating honey are the best, those eating bread are the average faithful, and those eating dung are the worst and always complain.[11]

The fathers relate that one of the qualities that was especially honored among monks was spiritual gladness in participating in the Holy Mysteries and the table of the brethren.[12]

The desert fathers and mothers saw the Eucharist as a source of healing. Abba Moses was healed through the Eucharist.[13] Abba Apollo's legs were healed by adopting the life of a hermit wanderer and receiving the Eucharist every Sunday.[14]

Questions

1) Do you pray the psalms?

2) Does your mind wander when you pray? If so, how do you remedy that?

3) Do you pray the Liturgy of the Hours? Do you find it too complicated or dry?

11. Budge, 2:79–80.
12. Budge, 2:79–80.
13. Budge, 2:290.
14. Budge, 1:357.

4) Do you find rote prayer helpful?

5) Is it enough to just recite the words of liturgy, or should we experience the fire of the Spirit?

6) Is frequent, weekly Eucharist important to your prayer?

9

Sacred Reading and the Writings of the Fathers and Scripture

> "Whatever you do, do it after the example of Holy Scripture."
>
> —Abba Antony, in James O. Hannay,
> *The Wisdom of the Desert*

I was raised a good Methodist boy. I went to church. I loved the music and good preaching. But I wasn't really experiencing a personal encounter with Christ in the power of the Holy Spirit. That came later after falling away from the faith of my childhood and ambling through the dangerous paths of the secular music world. After seeing an endless stream of people passed out on floors strewn with drug paraphernalia and alcohol bottles after concerts, I decided that I wanted to find something deeper. I started my search for God. I started reading everything I could about every major religion of the world. But I didn't have a personal encounter with the God I was reading about. That came after a year and a half of praying daily and asking God, "Who are you—a he, a she, or an it?" I didn't have, as we say in Arkansas, "a dog in the hunt"! I just wanted to know. The answer finally came in a personal encounter with Jesus Christ.

Suddenly the Bible I had been reading alongside of the other religious books and texts came to life through a personal encounter with Jesus Christ! So I started my rediscovered Christian life with a great love for Scripture. I used to sit for endless hours reading a pocket-sized King James Version. I read in hotel rooms across America while touring with our country rock band, Mason Proffit, and then with The Talbot Brothers. I used to find spots of nature around hotels or parks to just sit and read the Bible. After getting out of the music business for a more serious Christian lifestyle and study, I graduated to the Scofield Study Bible where I learned the ins and outs of premillennial dispensationalism. I also read the typical litany of Scripture study aids like *The Interpreter's Bible Commentary*, *Unger's Bible Dictionary*, and *Barclay's Bible Commentary*, just to name three that are well known. Then I mellowed out a bit with the notes from the *Thompson Chain-Reference Bible* and then the lovely New International Version of the Bible. After growing frustrated with the division in Christendom, I immersed myself in the church fathers like Clement of Rome, Ignatius of Antioch, the *Didache*, and Irenaeus of Lyons. At the same time, I was discovering the saints of the Franciscan and monastic traditions. And these were only what got me started into a life of sacred study. Through those first decades of my Christian experience, sacred reading was a most important part of my spiritual life.

Previously, we saw that work provides a healthy balance to prayer. We also saw that St. Benedict of Nursia addresses spiritual reading, not in a chapter of its own in the Rule, but in the context of addressing work. This brings out the natural balance between the two.

Lectio Divina, Sacred Reading

This also gave rise to what would be called *lectio divina*, or sacred reading. While Origen considered all study of Scripture to be *lectio divina*, in the later monastic tradition it developed as a practice unto itself, distinct from simple Scripture study. It amounted to a slow and prayerful reading of Scripture that led to prayer, meditation, and contemplation.

Benedict also expanded the content of such common or private reading to include the early monastic fathers. He says, "Someone should read from the *Conferences* or the *Lives* of the Fathers or at any rate something else that will benefit the hearers" (RB 42.3).

Lectio divina should also be *orderly*. Benedict says, "Then after their meal they will devote themselves to their reading or to the psalms" (RB 48.13). He continues, "Each one is to receive a book from the library, and is to read the whole of it straight through. . . . Above all, one or two seniors must surely be deputed to make the rounds of the monastery while the brothers are reading. Their duty is to see that no brother is so apathetic as to waste time or engage in idle talk to the neglect of his reading, and so not only harm himself but also distract others" (RB 48.15, 17-18).

We live in a time when information is bombarding us. We often experience information overload. "Googling" takes the place of study, and information is usually mistaken as knowledge. Wisdom is rarely found. While more and more books are being published, they are often popularized to the point of dumbing down the meaty wisdom of the ages into infant's milk at best. While bringing ancient wisdom from the top to the bottom shelf in order to be available to more people is a good thing, this has brought the experience of good book reading to an all-time low. Very few really read anymore. I mean really, really read. You know what I mean—sitting down with a book and slowly letting its wisdom sink in on the deepest level of mind and soul.

The desert fathers and mothers were people of *knowledge and wisdom*, not just of information. Because of that, many went on to become true saints and mystics.

The Word

The desert fathers and mothers were men and women of *the Word*. Particularly they were men and women who committed the *Scriptures to memory*. They meditated on the Psalter as part of their daily prayer, and the New Testament, especially the gospels, had a most important place in their life. Eventually, they prayed all 150 psalms daily.

Interestingly, for the ancients, meditation was not just something done mentally in silence; it included saying the words aloud with the lips. "For one believes with the heart and so is justified, and one confesses with the mouth and so is saved" (Rom 10:10). Saying a word with the lips forces us to slow down a bit. It also solidifies what we read in the mind. It incarnates ideas. So meditating with the mind and the lips together is a powerful tool for those who use it.

I am reminded of one of my mentors who used to quietly form the words of Scripture as he was meditating on it. I asked him why he did that. He answered that he has been trained to do it that way, and it helped to slow his reading down and to concretize the words deep in his soul. Most moderns are trained to speedread. We read entire sentences, paragraphs, and pages at once. But we run the risk of reading the information but not receiving the knowledge and wisdom of the words when we read sacred texts in such a way. We skip like a rock across the pond of God's wisdom, rather than sinking slowly to the depths of the deep water of the Spirit.

Church Fathers, Patristics

The desert monastics were also men and women who read the great fathers and mothers of the *church* and *monastic communities* who preceded them. In fact, they quickly learned that Scriptures could be quoted wrongly, so right interpretation by the church and the monastic fathers and mothers played a uniquely important role in how they read the Scriptures. Some even said the fathers and mothers should be read first, and then the Scriptures, in order to avoid falling into the trap of heresy.

The *Scriptures took a while to be written and compiled in the early church*. Scholars tell us that the Jewish Scriptures were themselves still in some flux at the time of Christ. The New Testament took time to be birthed from the church. But by the time of the desert fathers and mothers, the gospels and most of the epistles were in place. The Jewish Scriptures were also more stable. So these became the primary rule of life for monastics. The various founders of monastic settlements simply put them together in ways that best fit their particular community or group of communities.

The early church depended on apostolic teaching to ensure the true teaching of Jesus (see Acts 2:42). This originated in Jesus himself. On the road to Emmaus, Jesus himself explained which of the Jewish Scriptures referred to him (Luke 24:27). It continues in the apostles. Paul tells Timothy to be faithful to both the Scriptures and the teaching he received from him and to pass it on to others (2 Tim 2:2; 3:15).

Slowly the New Testament was written and compiled. It was seen first in letters from apostles and their successors to churches, then in gospels, and finally in the Apocalypse. But there were many writings that bore the apostles' names that didn't teach the same thing they had received and passed on to their successors. It was the authority of the church that discerned which books matched apostolic teaching or were simply more useful than others, though they could be read for edification.

We would like to think that this happened neatly and quickly, but it didn't. It unfolded over many centuries and sometimes in messy ways. God doesn't paint his masterpiece quickly or with all right angles and straight lines. So we see different lists in various church fathers. Generally, the books of the current New Testament were being accepted and used by the third century. The East was less defined than the West, first including some of the apostolic fathers, the *Shepherd of Hermas*, and the *Didache*, though both agreed on most of the basic books we now call the New Testament. By the fourth century, St. Augustine (354–430) considered the canon closed. But the debate was far from over. It went on for centuries, and as late as the Reformation Martin Luther excluded Hebrews, James, and the Apocalypse; removed the deuterocanonical books (the Apocrypha) from the main body of the Jewish Scriptures; and kept them only as a separate section. Later Protestants would exclude the Apocrypha altogether. The Council of Trent (1546) defined it once and for all for Catholics. Orthodox Christianity now agrees with this list, and Protestants are discovering the value of the Apocrypha once again.

Scripture

By means of this process of development, the *authority of Scripture is even surer than if the books it contains had simply dropped down from heaven*. It is incarnational and develops within the greater authority of the church, a community of people established by the Word Incarnate. Jesus didn't write a book. He established a people and empowered them with the Spirit and an apostolic leadership. It was from this that the Scriptures developed.

The Scriptures were *the earliest, and surest written form of apostolic teaching*. They both carried on the apostolic tradition and provided the guide by which to discern all further inspiration. They are the "canon," or measuring rule by which all later teaching was measured.

But they were always *read in the context of the church* from which they were birthed. There was no conflict between the church and the Scriptures, for they were one and the same river of inspiration from Jesus via the apostles and their successors and the power of the Holy Spirit.

The reading of the Scriptures and the church fathers is a very important part of the life of the desert fathers. The hermits used to say that God demands of Christians that they obey the inspired Scriptures, which contain the pattern of what they must say and do, and agree with the teaching of the orthodox bishops and teachers. So both simplicity and apostolic development is seen in the way that Scripture and apostolic teaching was understood and lived.[1]

The religion of the Jewish people stands in contrast to the other religions of their region. It retains an often stark monotheism that is absent in other religions of the Middle Eastern world. But that doesn't mean that there was no development or no integration of some ideas that were not in conflict with that monotheism. Concepts such as blood sacrifice and priesthood were common concepts in the religion of the region and indeed of the primitive religions of the world.

It is true that Scripture also contains some Hellenized or Greek concepts the Jewish people integrated into their religious thinking. The early church did the same. Notions such as the immortality of the soul only slowly found their way into the belief system of the Jewish people. Paul himself used Greek concepts to evangelize the Greeks in Athens (see Acts 17:22). This continued to develop in the theology of the early church. This is proper, so long as it didn't conflict with the primary teaching of the early church.

But it can be taken too far, going beyond integration and into syncretism, a noncritical universalism where "all religions are just separate but equal roads up the same mountain."

---

1. Owen Chadwick, ed. and trans., *Western Asceticism* (Philadelphia: Westminster Press, 1958), 152.

Antony of the Desert was most aware of the shortcomings of Greek and pagan philosophy without the revelation of Jesus Christ. One of the greatest desert treatments of the incarnation of the Word in Jesus Christ is found in his dialogue with pagan philosophers.

He says, "Behold, we are not learned in books, yet we believe in God, and we possess understanding concerning His creation, and concerning the mercy of the Providence of His grace, and we have confidence through the faith of Jesus Christ that our faith is sure, [whilst] ye have only words which are full of contentions; in your case the phantom of the adornment of your idols gradually cometh to an end, but in ours our faith increases and becomes more abundant day by day everywhere."[2]

The Scriptures are seen as *containing the power of the Spirit*, and *the devil could not withstand them* when they were quoted and lived rightly. Jesus quoted Scripture to combat the devil, and so did the desert monastics.

An old man said that whenever someone reads the sacred Scripture, the devils are afraid.[3]

Taking Scripture for Granted

But it was easy to *neglect this precious gift or to take the Scriptures for granted*. We often think that if we simply mouth the Scriptures in the liturgies, this is enough. But it isn't. They must be studied with *humility*. And they must be studied with *prayer*. Only then can the *power of the Spirit* be stirred up in our lives. Then it is the Spirit within us that leaps at the presence of Jesus and the Spirit in the written words of Scriptures and the teachings of the fathers and mothers.

---

2. E. A. W. Budge, ed. and trans., *The Paradise or Garden of the Holy Fathers*, 2 vols. (London: Chatto & Windus, 1907), 1:63.

3. Budge, 2:24.

An old man said that the prophets wrote books. The fathers came after them and studied them closely. Then their successors memorized them. But this generation has come, and it copies them on papyrus and parchment and leaves them unused on the window ledge.[4] This reminds me of the story of St. Francis, who used to clean up church buildings. Whenever he found the Scriptures laying around on windowsills, he would reverently remove them and enthrone them in a proper place in the church.

This deep study must be *daily and repetitive*. Only then can real wisdom be written deeply on the heart. Ordinarily, it *cannot be obtained quickly*. It must happen daily, steadily, and repeatedly. It is like water that can wear down the hard rocks of stubbornness and sin in our lives when prayerfully and humbly read every day.

One day John, who had been exiled by Marcion, went into Syria to see Poemen to ask him about hardness of heart. He used the *example of water cutting through rock to describe the power of the daily and repetitive reading and meditating on the word of God* to illustrate his point. He said the nature of water is soft, while the nature of stone is hard. But if a bottle is hung above a stone letting water drip down, it wears away the stone. It is like that with the word of God; it is soft and our hearts are hard, but if a person hears the word of God often, it will break open his heart to the fear of God.[5] This analogy of water is often used in the mystical traditions of various religions to describe humility conquering pride. It holds true for those of any faith.

Put into Practice

It is not enough to simply read the stories of the saints, fathers, and mothers without putting them into practice. That is a com-

4. Chadwick, 131.
5. Budge, 2:145.

mon mistake, and it constitutes an illusion. Reading must *give birth to a radically changed life in Christ.*

In one account, we read that Abba Theodore of Parmê possessed some beautiful books, and he went to Abba Macarius and said unto him, "Father, I have three books, and I gain profit from them, and the brethren borrow them from me, and they also have profited from them; tell me, now, what shall I do with them?" And the old man answered and said, "Ascetic labors are beautiful, but the greatest of them all is voluntary poverty." And when Abba Theodore heard these words he went and sold the books and gave the price of them to the poor.[6]

Indeed, sometimes divesting oneself from the possession of books is far better than reading them. The mere possession of books can create possessiveness and pride. So the practice of poverty by divesting ourselves of owning the gospels is often a better way to actually live the gospels. This is again similar to St. Francis who said that Jesus is more glorified by selling an expensive gospel book and giving the proceeds to the poor than by keeping the gospel book and depriving the poor. He said the same thing regarding altar decorations. But he also honored the word of God and loved to ornately decorate altars out of love of God, so this cannot be legalistically interpreted.

While the fathers and mothers disdained reading without action and manual labor was valued as particularly helpful to desert dwellers, *study* was also seen as a proper work for some. This teaches us that work is according to the gifts and talents that God has granted to each individual. One of those talents can be intellectual life. But it is always done after having our pride humbled through asceticism and manual labor, and in a way that doesn't allow pride to gain its way back into our lives.

Evagrius lived by the labor of his hands. His work was to write books. It took him fifteen years of ascetic life before wisdom

6. Budge, 2:35.

and understanding about the spirits were given to him. He then composed three volumes, teaching us the cunning of devils and the snares of the thoughts.[7]

Prayer

This caused Evagrius to coin the great phrase, "If you are a theologian, you will pray truly. And if you pray truly, you are a theologian."[8] Prayer is always seen as necessary to properly study the word of God in Scripture or the apostolic and monastic tradition in the desert fathers and mothers. In the East this equation of prayer and theology is jealously maintained, and in the West it is maintained at least in theory, but both admittedly fall short in practice. In the West study is often disjointed from real training under a monastic elder and becomes the main prerequisite for theology degrees. This is always unfortunate and creates a religion that finds it difficult to drop theology from the head to the heart.

The writings of *Scripture, patristics, and the lives of the fathers and mothers* are a true gift from God. It is how most of us come into contact with the venerable tradition that came before us and makes imitation of the best of that tradition possible in the present. We should cherish them and use them rightly on a daily basis. If we do, we will discover over time that this is one of the delights of the desert.

For myself, I first discovered Scripture. Then I discovered silence and solitude in order to go deeper into Scripture. Let's look at them next.

---

7. Budge, 1:225.

8. Quoted in Allyne Smith, ed., *Philokalia: The Eastern Christian Spiritual Texts: Selections Annotated and Explained*, trans. G. E. H. Palmer, Philip Sherrard, and Kallistos Ware (Woodstock, VT: SkyLight Paths Publishing, 2012), xi.

Questions

1) Do you spend more time in spiritual reading or in Googling?

2) Do you read slowly or skip across the surface of Scripture? Have you tried forming the words with your lips as you meditate?

3) Do you appreciate the development of Scripture, and read it in full communion with the church, or do you try to separate Scripture from the church?

4) Do you take advantage of spiritual reading?

5) Do you use modern or ancient sources in your reading?

6) Do you live what we read?

7) Do you overly compartmentalize dogmatic and mystical theology, or do you use a more integrated approach?

8) If you write, do you ask for the power of the Spirit in humility?

Sacred Silence

"Flee from the crowd, keep silence, and you
will live."

> —Anonymous Old Man, in E. A. W. Budge,
> *The Paradise or Garden of the Holy Fathers*

"To live without speaking is better than to
speak without living."

> —Abba Isidore, in Christine Valters Paintner,
> *Desert Fathers and Mothers: Early Christian
> Wisdom Sayings, Annotated and Explained*

It is said of Abba Pambo (or Agatho[1]) that in order to learn silence he carried a pebble in his mouth for three years. Many times I wish I had put one in mine! Silence is hard to learn, but it is a priceless treasure to those who learn it.

I remember all too well one of the most embarrassing things I ever did in community (and there are many!). We were young, and I was a young leader, so we didn't always handle guests very well. Plus, we took ourselves way too seriously! People

---

1. Owen Chadwick, ed. and trans., *Western Asceticism* (Philadelphia: Westminster Press, 1958), 49.

who come to monasteries often love the idea of silence but have virtually no experience of actually practicing it. Once we had a particularly talkative guest. I don't mean that she talked a bit too much. I mean that she talked constantly, everywhere, and very, very loudly! This guest was truly delightful, but the constant, boisterous talking started getting on some people's nerves. So in my inexperience, I tried to apply the discipline of Abbot Pambo on her. I actually asked this guest to put a pebble in her mouth for a while. And she actually obeyed . . . at least for a while! This was only one of the most arrogant things I did in my inexperience. Believe it or not, she is still a dear friend. She was most forgiving of my youthful arrogance and inexperience. I am still working on not being such a jerk!

Putting pebbles in our mouths is for us, not others! It is a symbol of using established disciplines to help us learn the wonderful monastic gift of silence. After this I occasionally put a pebble in my own mouth to remind myself to keep quiet unless it was really helpful to say something. I should have done this before I imposed it on someone else!

In our community we have times and places for silence and times and places for speech and even recreation. At all times and places, we teach to beware of speaking if you cannot be silent and conversely to beware of silence if you cannot speak when the occasion calls for it. This is a beautiful balance, but few of even our monastic community members really find it. I'm still working on it too!

Silence is a most appealing concept in the context of our noisy modern world. The constant sound of people in crowded places or just in a family home can sometimes feel quite imprisoning. The same goes for the sounds of cars or traveling on a train or airplane. But even beyond the obvious, just getting away from the constant hum of the electricity we have grown so accustomed to seems like being immersed in a warm bath of natural life again. Such silence can be most renewing of the human spirit.

But it can also be terrifying! Real silence is usually difficult. It reminds me of the old commercial for Rice Krispies cereal, where the monks were trying to keep silence. But the natural sound of the "snap, crackle, and pop" of the cereal in milk disrupted their silence. It started with looks, then giggles, and ends with the monks laughing out loud. It was a very cute commercial. But it captures the real experience of any group or community who tries to live with times or places of silence. It takes some work and some forgiveness of those who naturally break the silence.

I also remember our community exalting silence at a new hermitage and then constantly breaking it! It's hard to eat in silence when we come from families where meals are noisy affairs. Soon every clink and clank of silverware and plates, not to mention noisy eaters and drinkers, became almost humorous. So we would sometimes laugh or just forget and talk. It came up at almost every Friday chapter of faults. After weeks and months of this, it got to the point of seriously considering whether we should drop the discipline of silence altogether. I mean, why exalt silence and then constantly break it? But we still loved silence so much that we decided to keep it as a community discipline regardless of how many times we broke silence. After decades I'm glad we made the right decision. Times and places of silence create a sacred environment throughout the monastery. But we still struggle with breaking silence. And I don't know a monastery that doesn't still struggle with it at times.

Silence is an appealing concept for many modern seekers.

Silence and solitude are among the more immediately appealing aspects of the desert fathers and mothers. But it was as hard for them to practice as it often is for us. Otherwise they would not have spent so much time talking about silence!

Then there's silence from the technology of the millennial generation. This is almost absurdly apparent. Nowadays folks are constantly messing about with their smartphones, tablets, or computers, not to mention smart TVs! Silence is indeed "golden" for anyone who wants to have some time to think without being brainwashed or to create without being manipulated.

But silence isn't easy. As soon as we get away from our gadgets that constantly tether us to the gods of the digital world, we get anxious and nervous. We begin to fidget. Soon, almost unconsciously, our hands are reaching once more to the smartphone or tablet to keep us connected to the digital beast. Studies show the average modern person lasts about thirty seconds in inactivity before reaching to his or her smartphone! They say it is as addictive as heroin, caffeine, or nicotine. I believe it!

It's even true when we're around other people. As soon as we get with others, we are talking constantly on our gadgets to others with whom we aren't sitting face-to-face. Worse yet, the new generation even prefers to text those who are sitting just a few feet away in the same room with them! And let's be honest, the older generation does it too. And we dare to call it Facebook! There is no substitute for face-to-face communication.

But even when we disconnect from the gods of the digital universe, we often cannot really be silent. We begin to chitchat with others about anything at all. We might maintain serious and godly conversation for a while, but all too soon our talk degenerates into either meaningless chatter or godless, negative judgments about things we really don't know much about to begin with. As Proverbs 10:19 says, "Where words are many, sin is not wanting."

And then there are our thoughts. They play like a constant movie of memories and fantasies. They talk all the time, and we struggle to turn them off. The Eastern religions call this, "monkey mind," because our thoughts jump from bar to bar within the cage. Truth be known, we think all the time. Even at night our minds process what we experience in daily life through dreams—or nightmares! We can never stop thoughts. But we can slow them down, direct them, and focus them on the things of God, the superficial and deep, active and contemplative.

Scripture

Scripture teaches much about silence and speech. Without quoting all the references in Sirach, Wisdom, and Proverbs, I have come to believe that the most distinguishing sign of wisdom is knowing when to be silent and when to speak. And we learn this wisdom only when we learn to silence our rather constant need to speak. Wisdom usually knows when to be silent, when to speak, and who to speak to if we really need to do so.

Jesus is silent in the desert of temptation. It is only when he is fighting the thoughts and temptations the devil put into his mind through images of worldly power and false worship, and through wrongly quoting Scripture, that Jesus responds by quoting Scripture rightly to silence the devil (see Matt 4:1-11). We are told that he often retired to deserted places to pray (see Luke 5:16). We are also told that the devil tempted Jesus repeatedly (see Luke 4:13). Silence and solitude were important to the interior life of Jesus.

We also know that while heaven is filled with the joyful and awe-filled praises of God being sung by the angels and saints, there is also silence there when something dramatic occurs on earth (Rev 8:1). Sometimes it's better to be quiet and wait than to comment right away. Silence is important.

The Desert

The fathers and mothers understood these Scriptures, and they experienced problems similar to ours in their own culture. They were mystics, but they were also rugged realists.

There is a relationship between thoughts and words. You cannot talk until you at least superficially think. Conversely, you cannot control your thoughts until you learn to control your tongue.

Abba Sisois said that if we cannot guard our words, we cannot guard our hearts.[2] We have seen that Abbot Pambo placed a pebble in his mouth for three years in order to learn silence.

---

2. Chadwick, 136.

We often seek a place of solitude in order to find silence. But even the most remote spot has distractions. If we find ourselves distracted by inanimate objects in solitude, we haven't yet found real interior silence. The problem is usually not the place, but our hearts. Abba Arsenius reminds us that even in solitude and silence, if we are distracted by something as simple as the sounds of the wind through the reeds, then we are not really silent. [3]

To conclude, I explain silence in the more meditational music of my repertoire. You have to hear not only the notes but also the space between the notes to hear God's music. And you have to hear not only the words but also the silence between the words to hear God's word. And sometimes that word is sacred silence itself. This lesson in music has much to teach us about silence in the spiritual life in Christ, the word in silence.

Questions

1) Do you see a need for silence in your life?

2) Do you put a pebble in your mouth? What other tools can you use to help with silence?

3) Is silence hard for you?

4) Is exterior silence the same as interior silence?

5) Do you sometimes practice exterior silence and still find that you are internally noisy?

6) Do you see the connection between silence and defeating demonic temptation?

7) Can you hear the space between the notes in the music of your life? Can you hear the word of God in silence?

3. Chadwick, 41.

Sacred Solitude

11

> "The man who abides in solitude and is quiet,
> is delivered from fighting three battles—those
> of hearing, speech and sight. Then he will have
> but one battle to fight—the battle of the heart."
>
> —St. Antony, in Owen Chadwick,
> *Western Asceticism*

Sacred stillness is best found in solitude. The body must be situated in an environment. For the desert fathers, that was the desert and a cell. The cell could be in a monastery, a hermit's cave, or the total isolation one finds by wandering around an area.

It is often said that if we are afraid of solitude, then we should be afraid of community. And if we are afraid of relationships in community, we should be afraid of solitude. Both solitude and community are naked encounters with God and self. We come face-to-face with God who gradually reveals the ego attachments of the old self and the call of Jesus to let them die in order to be born again and rise up a new creation in him. It is a lifetime process.

Those who think that solitude is some beautiful and blissful experience with God have never lived in solitude for any length of time. Solitude can be a welcome respite after intense times of activity in community, ministry, or work. But the longer period of solitude in the hermit's cell is a rugged encounter with the demons that come to us through senses or thoughts. It is a naked encounter with one's self. It is a naked encounter with God. It is a place to choose between God and evil.

Imagine living in a place where contact with the world is almost completely cut off. No internet, no smartphones, and no social media to constantly draw us back into the endless rise and fall of the currents of the passing world. This is frightening. Indeed, it is often terrifying. But it also forces us into communion with God, who does not rise or fall with the world. It forces us to look honestly, with no distractions or illusions, at ourselves. This is the beginning of the lifelong journey of self-discovery and repentance in Christ before the eternal God.

The hermit fathers are filled with stories of those who hadn't talked to anyone in decades (though they did normally participate in weekly Eucharist, sometimes without being seen by others) and only being found at the end of their lives. The ones who discover them often want to join them but are told that they couldn't bear the satanic wars they have faced through the decades of dire poverty and isolation.

Solitude is a naked embrace of one's *self* with no distractions in public prayer, common meals, work, or ministry that are part of life together in community. That naked embrace can be frightening! In solitude we simply pray and work. There we often discover that worship of God and menial tasks are not enough to satisfy us. This stems from our ego attachments to doing something "big" for God, often in order to be appreciated or noticed by others. At that point we have a choice: we can either run back to community, or we can stay in solitude and face down the devils that we have allowed ourselves to become attached to.

Community is also a naked embrace of ourselves before God. In community we learn obedience by serving God and others under a rule and an abbot or abbess. This means we rub shoulders with people who, in the positive, have heard a similar call from God as ours, but who, in the negative, we wouldn't choose to "hang out" with in the world. We may like or dislike them to varying degrees, but they wouldn't necessarily be our friends. As I say, our community members aren't necessarily the folks we'd choose to share pizza and a beer with! I also say that we all choose Jesus in monastic life, but in the monastery we sometimes look around and think, "Who are all these other people?!"

And it isn't as simple as a secular job or even a parish ministry where we are able to go home and get away from the troublesome coworker or boss in one's private life. In monastic community we share prayers, meals, and work with them! And there is little escape. We are around them all the time, except for the few hours in cell before we sleep and at night when we sleep. The rest of the time we are in close quarters with our brother and sister monastics.

In the training ground of community, we learn how to love everyone by letting go of our ego attachments to likes and dislikes of people, things, or activities. We learn how to live for God and others. We learn how to do so under a particular monastic family, a rule, and a spiritual father or mother. This brings the lofty ideals down into real life. It is like the incarnation of the Word in flesh. It is incarnational. When we learn this, we discover a whole new way of living for ourselves that is free and happy in any situation with anyone.

Monastic Tradition

Because of the very real challenges of community life and the even greater ones in solitude, monastic tradition has encouraged that we enter into solitude gradually. We begin by living in community for ten years or so. Then we can try some time in the solitude of hermit days once or a few times a week. Eventually, we might move into the hermitage throughout the week and come out into community only for weekly Eucharist and important meetings. This is done by beginning the process as cenobites in community, then becoming semi-eremites or hermits in colonies, and then perhaps by entering into strict eremitic life in reclusion. These steps are discerned with the help of a spiritual director and an abbot or abbess. But most monastics are not called to this stricter solitude. Community is the way for most.

The Rule of St. Benedict classifies hermits as the second of the four kinds of monks. "Second, there are the anchorites or hermits, who have come through the test of living in a monastery for a long time, and have passed beyond the first fervor of monastic life. Thanks to the help and guidance of many, they are now trained to fight against the devil. They have built up their strength and go from the battle line in the ranks of their brothers to the single combat of the desert. Self-reliant now, without the support of another, they are ready with God's help to grapple single-handed with the vices of body and mind" (RB 1.3-5). This came to Benedict as a rather established tradition going back to Cassian, who himself got it from others. The word *anchorite* comes from the Greek *anachōréō*, "to withdraw, to retire." An anchorite, then, is one who has withdrawn or retired from the world.

The Desert

An early account tells us, "When Abba Arsenius was still at the palace, he prayed the Lord asking: 'Lord, show me the way to salvation.' And a voice came to him: 'Arsenius, run from men and you shall be saved.' He went to become a monk, and again prayed in the same words. And he heard a voice saying: 'Arsenius, be solitary: be silent: be at rest. These are the roots of a life without sin.'"[1]

---

1. Owen Chadwick, ed. and trans., *Western Asceticism* (Philadelphia: Westminster Press, 1958), 40.

Abba Poemen added some discipline to solitude, saying that if a monk controls his stomach and his tongue and stays in solitude, he can trust that he is not dying.[2]

We are told that the solitude of the desert is the place where the muddy waters of the soul settle and become clear so that one can see one's reflection like in a mirror.[3]

The first desert fathers and mothers didn't have a tradition to build on, so they entered into solitude in various ways. Some went directly into greater solitude, like St. Antony of the Desert or St. Paul the Hermit. Some established colonies of hermits in *lauras* and *sketes* (in Coptic, *Shiheet*, meaning "the weight"), like St. Makarios and Ammon. These were cells within walking distance from a common chapel and common center for weekly prayer and meals. Later, but still in the lifetime of St. Antony, some, such as St. Pachomius or Shenouda the Great, built strict communities based on *koinonia,* or communion. These were monastic towns around a church that also included houses and places for work. Most of the popular desert father and mother material comes from either the semi-eremitical or the strict eremitical tradition.

Solitude, like *hesychia* (stillness), helps us to see the naked truth of who we really are. When we live in the midst of the agitation of the secular or religious world, things often move so quickly that we lose ourselves in the process. One of the repeated stories of the desert says that striving for solitude is like trying to see your face in the reflection of water that is agitated in a large jug. We have to allow the waters to settle. Then we can see a reflection of our faces in the water. So it is with sacred solitude and stillness. We must allow the waters to settle before we can see our own faces reflected in the water.

2. Chadwick, 62.
3. Chadwick, 43.

Otherwise we not only do not know God, we cannot even know our own selves.[4]

Questions

1) Do you see a need for more solitude in your life?

2) Do you see the connection between solitude and silence?

3) Are you afraid of relationships in community?

4) Are you afraid of the naked truth about yourself in solitude?

5) How do you practice solitude in your life?

6) Are you easing into solitude, or do you try to do it all at once?

---

4. Chadwick, 143.

Sacred Stillness and *Hesychia*

12

The external prepares for the internal. External silence and solitude are only a means to interior silence. This is often called *hesychia*, or sacred stillness. It includes the external means to provide the environment and means for inner stillness and the inner stillness itself. *Hesychia* is a special gift of Eastern Christian monasticism. In the fourteenth century the Hesychast movement became a major contributor to the East and is now being appreciated and practiced in the West. Both consider it a cherished gift today.

Sometimes the greatest action is found by being still. And sometimes the greatest action is sacred stillness itself.

To explain meditational music in concerts I say that we must listen, not only to the notes, but to the spaces between the notes. That's where God's music is often best found. Likewise, we must hear not only the words, but the silence between the words. That's where God's word is often found. And sometimes the word *is* silence. We must learn sacred stillness before we can safely act. Otherwise we are addicted only to action.

I learned this during one of my first extended times in the hermitage. Though I learned the mechanics of it long before, in the actual experience of the Jesus Prayer in this extended solitude and silence, I learned to simply breathe in order to find the presence of Jesus in my life. I breathed in Jesus and breathed out anything whatsoever that was standing between Jesus and me and the church he gives us. I didn't necessarily need to study, actively pray, or work all the time. I didn't need distractions of any kind. I could simply sit and breathe Jesus. That was enough. So I ended up for hours every day simply being and breathing in Jesus. It brought me peace beyond description. This is a result of sacred stillness, or *hesychia*.

But like silence and solitude, sometimes just sitting in *hesychia* is agonizing, at least at first. And I mean for the first few minutes, days, weeks, months, and even years! It takes time to settle down, and this is cyclical as we go deeper and deeper. I often want to scratch, twitch, shift, get up and walk around, or do a project. Anything that will give me something to do! Natural as this might sound, and may even be recommended at times, it can often short-circuit the prayer time. These are often just carnal or mental distractions. Once you give in to them, you have to start over to get to the point where the distraction stole your attention. You have to fight the urge and just sit still and breathe. *Be* in *hesychia*. Pray. Nothing else. Once you do, these distractions dissipate. Then you can go on to the deeper things God has in store.

But you don't "do nothing" in *hesychia* either. You have to give your body, emotions, and mind something to do. But you bring that activity to a bare minimum. You still the body, calm the emotions, and focus the mind. You sit still, and with each breath you own and calm the body, emotions, and mind through the cross of Jesus Christ. Don't worry, *hesychia* won't leave you without a body, emotions, or thoughts. Such nihilism isn't part of authentic Christian meditation. There's always resurrection at the end of and *in* every cross!

Christian tradition unites each breath with the name of Jesus. This isn't a New Age or Eastern religion method. It is part of ancient Christianity. You breathe in Jesus and breathe out anything that isn't of Jesus. This is best done through the Jesus Prayer, as taught by an experienced spiritual father or mother. Books can help, but they cannot replace the guidance of a spiritual father or mother. That's how I learned it. That's how I pass it on. Only at the very beginning (in order to get started) or much later after you learn the discipline of the verbatim prayer can you amend the words.

The word *hesychia* is used in Scripture. Paul urges us to pray for those in civil authority "that we may lead a quiet [*hesychia*] and tranquil life in all devotion and dignity" (1 Tim 2:2). Paul uses it elsewhere when he writes, "If anyone was unwilling to work, neither should that one eat. . . . Such people we instruct and urge in the Lord Jesus Christ to work quietly [*hesychia*] and to eat their own food" (2 Thess 3:10, 12). So *hesychia* is not an excuse for getting out of work in a monastery, at a job, or at home. Surprisingly, it is not the word used by Jesus to quiet and still the waters (Mark 4:39) or to quiet the demons he cast out (Mark 1:25). But, perhaps because of its more ordinary and positive connotation, *hesychia* is the word that ended up being used by monastic tradition.

Hesychia is both *a beginning* for training and *an end* in contemplation in mystical theology. St. John of the Ladder (Climacus) treats it at the very end of *The Ladder of Divine Ascent* as the goal of monastic life.[1] That chapter is a veritable gold mine for anyone interested in contemplative life. Yet we also see it in the desert fathers as a condition for spiritual progress.

As we have seen, one desert father said that just as no one can see one's face reflected in muddy water, so the soul can-

---

1. John Climacus, *The Ladder of Divine Ascent*, trans. Colm Luibheid (Mahwah, NJ: Paulist Press, 1982).

not pray to God with contemplation unless first cleansed of harmful thoughts.[2]

Stillness can be likened to a pond. Most of the time the pond of one's soul is agitated. The water is muddied and fractured so that you cannot really see what is within the pond, nor can the pond rightly reflect an image while fractured and choppy. It is only when the pond settles in stillness and the sediment settles once more to the bottom that the water becomes clear and we can see into the deeper waters of the soul. Likewise, we can begin to reflect the image and likeness of God more perfectly without that image being fractured and broken.

But that is just the beginning. Once we see clearly into the pond of the soul, we see the garbage that we have let fall into it. Then we must reach down and pull it out! That stirs up mud and creates agitation so that once more we can no longer see clearly. So we have to let things settle. Once the pond clears, the process begins again. This goes on over and over for most of our lives, until we have cleared the pond of our soul, and we settle into a more continual stillness that clearly and calmly reflects the image of God again. This is cyclical going deeper each time and culminating in a more continual state of stillness.

Matthew 4 says Jesus is led by the Spirit into the *eremos*, the rugged Judean desert or wilderness, to face the temptations of the devil to prepare for his public ministry. He was still. Then the temptations came. Then he could defeat them by rightly quoting the Scriptures. Only then was he ready for public ministry. St. Paul also goes into solitude and stillness of Arabia, southeast of Damascus, before he is ready for his public ministry, though he offers few details about what happened there (see Gal 1:17). But the pattern is clear: stillness and solitude often precede the battle with heart and mind. And only when we

---

2. Owen Chadwick, ed. and trans., *Western Asceticism* (Philadelphia: Westminster Press, 1958), 143.

are at least substantially (if not completely) cleansed of negative thoughts and emotions does ministry of any real worth happen. The rest is just hyperactivity in the name of God.

The Desert

The desert fathers had not yet developed the more sophisticated mystical theology of the Hesychasts of the Eastern church in the fourteenth century, but they were certainly most aware of the value of stillness and *hesychia*. They express it in typical rugged simplicity. But it is the foundation upon which all further reflection could build.

St. Antony said that in *hesychia* we are delivered from three battles—hearing, speech, and sight. But then he says that we must still fight the battle of the heart.[3] I would add that this is the hardest battle of all!

One often encounters this when staying put in sacred stillness in the cell. A brother asked Abba Poemen, "What am I to do, for I become a weakling just by sitting in my cell?" The old man said, "Despise no one: condemn no one: abuse no one: and God will give you quietness, and you will sit tranquil in your cell."[4] In some translations, the word *hesychia* is used.

The activity in cell included praying the Psalter but went beyond it. What we in the West call the Work of God, or the Divine Office, is just a pointer to lead us into prayer and *hesychia*. Monastic scholars tell us that the real prayer happened after each psalm in silence. The desert monks prayed the Rite of the Twelve Psalms at each of the hours and at least all 150 psalms daily. For the monks in the desert, the Psalter took up a lot of each day and was important. But even the great prayer

3. Chadwick, 40.
4. Chadwick, 104.

of the Psalter is just a pathway to the deeper prayer of quiet, or *hesychia*.

Here we expand to a rule of life in the cell that includes *fasting and prayer* that help to cleanse thoughts. We silence the cravings of the body and the activity of the spiritual mind of the soul to open the way for the emergence of the pure intuition of God in the spirit. Abba Lot said, "As far as I can, I keep a moderate rule, with a little fasting, and prayer, and meditation, and quiet: and as far as I can I try to cleanse my heart of evil thoughts."[5]

External stillness is not enough. Abba Arsenius teaches us that if we still the rustling of the reeds in the wind or the sound of a bird as a distraction, then we do not yet have true *hesychia*.[6] I would add that once such distractions are cleansed, every sound becomes a praise of God.

So, *hesychia* quiets the senses, emotions, and thoughts of the body. It quiets the soul. And it opens the way for the pure intuition of the spirit. The first are part of the active life, the things that we actually *do* to create and nurture *hesychia*. The last is pure *hesychia* itself.

Questions

1) What is *hesychia*?

2) Do you have trouble sitting still?

3) Do you "do nothing" in stillness, or are there tools that can help you? If so, what are they?

4) How is your soul like a pond?

5. Chadwick, 142.
6. Chadwick, 41.

5) Does stillness always bring peace, or does it sometimes reveal your sin?

6) Do you use appropriate means like fasting, asceticism, and prayer to remove the sin from your life?

7) Have you ever broken through in *hesychia* to the pure intuition of the Spirit of God in your spirit?

13

Thoughts and Demons

"The beginning of evil is to spread the mind."

—Abba Poemen, in Owen Chadwick,
Western Asceticism

cripture says we are what we think (see Prov 23:7, King James Version). It is said that the battle for the soul is in the mind. I agree.

An old father said, "No one can see his face reflected in muddy water: and the soul cannot pray to God with contemplation unless first cleansed of harmful thoughts."[1]

Abba Evagrius said, "While you sit in your cell, draw in your mind, and remember the day of your death." He elaborates that meditation like this could include meditating on the goodness of God on Jesus, and on heaven and hell. Evagrius continued, "Keep these memories in your mind and so cast out of it the sordid thoughts which harm you."[2]

Scripture is filled with admonitions to have the mind of Christ (see 1 Cor 2:16) and to focus our minds through the

1. Owen Chadwick, ed. and trans., *Western Asceticism* (Philadelphia: Westminster Press, 1958), 143.
2. Chadwick, 44.

Holy Spirit (see Rom 12:2, Eph 4:23-24, and Phil 4:8). Jesus warns that sins begin in the thoughts of the heart (Matt 15:19).

I went into the hermitage to find peace. But soon I discovered an inner war in my thoughts and emotions and an outer war in my senses. The war was with myself. The war was with the temptations from the devil. No sooner had I been clothed with the habit and completed my hermitage in the woods than my peace was disturbed by the rude appearance of thoughts and sins I thought I had moved beyond long before. My thoughts were disturbed. My flesh was aroused. Hunger and thirst, hot and cold, the need for cozy comforts, and even sexual arousal came out of nowhere! I was in the hermitage to get beyond all that stuff I thought I had left behind. But there it was, stronger than ever, like a spoiled brat refusing to take no for an answer. I had to learn the deeper art of spiritual warfare. Fortunately, the fathers and mothers and my own spiritual father were there to help me out. It has been a lifelong struggle, but it does get a bit easier with experience and age.

How often I have retired to pray, when out of the blue my mind is besieged by a seemingly endless litany of ideas, agendas, and ministry projects. These aren't always bad thoughts, and some of my best musical and book projects have been born from times of prayer. But sometimes they come in an undisciplined and scattered way at the wrong time, lead nowhere, and completely disrupt real prayer. Sometimes I simply can't turn them off! Some meditation teachers call this all-too-familiar experience "monkey mind," for thoughts jump around our minds like monkeys in a cage. Before I could make progress in prayer, my spiritual father had to teach me how to silence, and sometimes even use, these thoughts to overcome thoughts that aren't from God.

The desert fathers and mothers were experts in spiritual battle. This battle was primarily, though not exclusively, fought in the thoughts.

There is a clear reason for this. In order to do or say something, we must first think it. Likewise, if we sense something, we immediately process it through a thought. It is the control tower for the flight of the soul. It has the power to help us take off and land in Christ. It can also keep us on course through the flight of our spiritual lives. But if neglected, it can dysfunction and cause tragic crashes and horrific devastation. It can end in spiritual and physical death!

In the West we are often taught Descartes's principle, "I think, therefore I am." But the perspective of the East is more typically, "I am, therefore I think." Both are true and can complement one another. We are not merely conceptual thought, but if we are alive we ordinarily have thought. Conversely, we are not our thoughts, but we have thoughts. There is a difference.

The Greek word used by the Eastern fathers for thoughts is *logismos*, and the biblical word is *logizomai*. We also read in Scripture of *dialozomai*, which literally means "with the words of the mind." A similar word is *dianoia*, in which the *dia* means "with, through, or by," and the *noia*, from *nous*, means "mind." So basically *dianoia* means "with the mind." But it refers more to an intuition or image than an objective thought. And if we really "think" about it, we realize that the mind thinks in images. Concepts are first visualized before they become speculative ideas or words alone.

Regarding the classical Eastern Christian concept of *nous*, one's deepest self goes beyond objective thought to pure intuition. Various traditions have used various ways to try to describe this, but the basic point is similar in all: one's deepest self goes beyond objective thought to something far deeper and spiritually intuitive. It is pure being.

Using Pauline language, we are spirit, soul, and body (see 1 Thess 5:23). Spirit is that place of pure, spiritual intuition. The soul is the spiritual mind. And the body includes thought (neurology), the chemistry of emotions (psychiatry), and senses. The body is the vehicle where the spirit and soul live in creation. Together, they make up the complete, well-ordered, and integrated human person created in the image and likeness of God.

We lost the likeness to God in sin, but the image of God remains and creates the inner longing for God and all things good. Jesus restores that likeness to complete the longings of the image.

In our sinful state we have gotten this order and priority reversed. We usually lead with our body of carnal senses, emotions that are chemical, and thought that is electrical and chemical. Then the spiritual soul of the *nous* and the intuitions of the spirit get lost, covered up, and forgotten. Then we wonder why we are frustrated and angry! Our deepest self, the image of God, still longs to be reborn and set free. We must bring this incomplete and disordered self to the cross and let it die so that we can be reborn in Christ, and the spirit and soul can take the lead once again.

The desert fathers and mothers describe in some detail the inner battles with thoughts and emotions of anger, judgment, and, of course, with lust for sex and all sorts of carnal delights. These are often graphically laced throughout various stories and sayings. These stories are sometimes humorous, sometimes painful, and almost always helpful. They are not yet a methodical teaching. But they are primary. Later these will be more fully developed into the eight thoughts in the Christian East and the seven capital or cardinal sins in the West. The desert fathers and mothers really pave the way and become the first Christian spiritual directors and psychologists.

They also connect these thoughts with *demons*. The words for devil (*diabolos*) and demon (*daimonion*) in Scripture mean a god or spirit higher than humanity who *accuses, slanders, and lies*. Jesus calls the devil a liar (John 8:44). The more personal word, *Satan*, comes from *Satanas*, which has Aramaic origins and primarily means *adversary*, the prince of demons. Demons can place temptations and thoughts into our minds, but they can't make us choose to follow the temptation. That is in our power alone.

The eastern monastic tradition is clear that *thoughts come from three sources*: 1) the *divine* from God, 2) the *demonic* from the devil, and 3) the *human* from one's own mind. The ancient writings offer the classic example of gold. The thought of using gold to ornament something for God is positive and from God. The thought of using it greedily is negative and demonic. Or the thought of simply seeing it as a pretty rock is neutral and human. The thought of gold itself is neutral. It is neither good nor bad. It is what we do with that thought that makes it divine or demonic.

The desert fathers and mothers first lived in Egypt. Egyptian cosmology taught that the *desert was the dwelling place of demons*. So they went to the desert, not so much to run away from the world, but to do full-on battle with the core problem of the world, evil. And instead of beginning with *other* people's demons and problems, they began with their *own*. While demons are mentioned in Scripture, the desert fathers and mothers were the first Christians to become experts in a more developed demonology.

We too must be willing to do battle with demons. Lucifer was the first one to fall by trying to be *like God* without God (see Isa 14:12-15). Adam and Eve fell for this same temptation (Gen 4:4). And humanity has done the same ever since. When we try to live apart from God and his revelation of truth and love, we are left to our own devices. They lead to *temptation, sin, and death*. The letter of James says, "Each person is tempted when he is lured and enticed by his own desire. Then desire conceives and brings forth sin, and when sin reaches maturity it gives birth to death" (Jas 1:14-16). St. Paul says flatly, "The wages of sin is death" (Rom 6:23).

We must know the *seriousness of the battle* and be unafraid to wage war in Christ against the spiritual darkness that blinds so much of humanity to God and enslaves the earth and creation to its deception.

But this *does not mean that we should see a devil "under every rock"*! Paranoia about demons can have a terrible effect on the Christian. It can cause us to live in fear. We know that "perfect love drives out fear" (1 John 4:18). There is a good fear, or awe, that is the beginning of wisdom and knowledge (Sir 1:20; Prov 1:7) and inspires us to greater efforts in love of God. There is also a negative fear that can cripple us from journeying forward in Christ. This principle is seen with sorrow as well. "For godly sorrow produces a salutary repentance without regret, but worldly sorrow produces death"(2 Cor 7:10). One inspires us forward, the other cripples us in the past. We know that the love of God through the shed blood of Jesus and the powerful name of Jesus can defeat the demons that assail us through our thoughts.

So the *spiritual battle is in the mind*, but we do well to remember the *serious consequences* of the battle. This is not optional. Nor is it to be trifled with. It is serious. But it is the common lot of every human being. It is nothing more, and nothing less, than what comes to every person who ever lived, including Jesus, who was tempted in every way we are yet was without sin (see Heb 4:15). Our mental patterns can create optimism and beauty in our lives, or they can cause discouragement, depression, and devastation. Life is both positive and negative. To deny either is unrealistic. But our focus must remain positive and balanced for health. We can focus on the negative and die, or we can focus on the positive and live. The choice is up to us.

The desert fathers and mothers teach us this orientation and balance. Their understanding of it was still primitive in its development. But it was real and taken very seriously. It was one of the main activities and achievements of the way of the desert.

Eight Thoughts

Evagrius and John Cassian developed a system of eight principal thoughts or sins, which led the way to a great body of thinking on sin. It is from this list that we get the more well-known seven cardinal, or capital, sins.

The eight thoughts in Cassian are:

1) gluttony

2) sexual sin, or *porneia*, and fornication

3) avarice or the need to control and possess

4) anger

5) bitterness or dejection

6) boredom, or acedia

7) self-glory

8) pride

Out of these eight, three—gluttony, avarice, and self-glory—lead the way.

There is *logic to the list*. *Gluttony* is small sense gratification that leads the way to sexual sin, which is serious sense gratification. *Avarice*, or the need to control possessions, people, or situations, leads to *anger*. When anger is left unhealed, it takes up residence in the inner recesses of the heart and soul as *bitterness* and poisons everything in one's life. Then one gets *bored* as soon as the novelty of even the best life for God wears off. *Self-glorification* is the need to be noticed and appreciated for the things we do, and this leads to *pride*, which is the mother of all vices. So basically, smaller tempting thoughts lead to bigger tempting thoughts, and temptation leads to sin if left unchecked.

The first desert fathers and mothers didn't teach this developed list, but it developed by the time of Evagrius. John Cassian brought it to the West in his *Lives* and *Conferences*. With St. Gregory the Great in the West and St. John Climacus at St. Catherine's in the Sinai, the list was adapted to seven, which has become the better-known version in the West. The

Western list begins with pride, and the East sees pride as the culmination of all other sins. Both approaches have great wisdom. Personally, I still prefer the earlier list of eight due to its more rugged logic and pastoral application.

There is also a *progression from tempting thoughts to actual sin*. In the East they break it down into anywhere from five to nine stages. These are very insightful for the serious inquirer. In the West St. Augustine simplifies it to *three steps*: 1) the *thought* of temptation; 2) playing with and *entertaining thoughts* of temptation; and 3) *acting* on temptation through words or actions. The first is not sinful. The second and third are. I like this simple list. It is easy to remember and covers most of the bases.

Jesus

Jesus was tempted just like everyone else, but he didn't sin (see Heb 4:15). He understands what it is to be sorely tempted. He also knows how to overcome it and empowers us to do the same.

In Matthew 4, his own initial temptation gives us a great *pattern* to help us when we are tempted. First, the Spirit sometimes leads us to a *place* of temptation in order to test us and prepare us for greater spiritual battle and ministry. But God doesn't actually tempt us. He allows it only for our testing and victory in Christ (see Jas 1:13). Second, we must fast and purify our flesh and desires through appropriate *discipline*. Third, we overcome the temptations of the flesh with the right use of the *Word of God*. Fourth, we must *not put God to the test* by demanding miracles to prove his sovereignty. Fifth, we must *not worship the false god* of the power of this world, but worship only God. And sixth, such temptations *do not happen only once*, but throughout the life of Christ (see Luke 4:13). They will happen throughout our lives, too, no matter how advanced we think we are.

The Desert

The desert tradition places great importance on effectively fighting tempting thoughts and on getting direction from more experienced monks on how to overcome them in Christ on a daily basis.

As one of many stories reports, "The brothers surrounded Abba John the Short when he was sitting in front of the church, and each of them asked him about their thoughts."[3]

In another, an old man said to a brother: "When a proud or vain thought tempts you, examine your conscience to see if you are keeping God's commandments; but don't think you have corrected all your faults yet. This one thought alone can undo all the other good you have done."[4]

For the desert fathers and mothers, thoughts were the doorway to the soul. The battle for the soul was in the mind. It is for us too!

Questions

1) Do you see the connection between your thoughts and your spirituality in Christ?

2) What are the eight thoughts? How do they function? Are they interconnected, and if so, how?

3) How are the eight thoughts combated, and by what tools?

4) What are the three stages of temptation, and how do they work in your personal life?

3. Chadwick, 176.
4. Chadwick, 168.

Angels

As we look at demons and thoughts, it would be easy to get overwhelmed by focusing too much on the negative. It's more important to focus on the positive spirits, or angels, who constantly protect us on our journey.

I have friends who at one time or another became so obsessed with evil that they forgot the good and that good ultimately triumphs in Jesus! They saw the proverbial "devil under every rock." They became paranoid, judgmental, and miserable. Jesus gave the apostles and their successors authority over demons in a special way, and he gives it to us as well. It is best to focus on the positive in Christ and let Jesus take care of most devils.

Angels have become especially popular in the past decade or two in the West. It was recently said that if you wanted a best-selling book, write about angels! Writing about God or Jesus too directly was off-putting to many people. But angels are no replacement for God. Angels serve God. Angels announced the birth of Jesus, but they worshipped Jesus. They never want to be worshipped instead of Jesus.

Angels are spirit messengers of God. There is an entire spiritual world and beings all around us all the time. We cannot ordinarily see them with bodily eyes, but they are real and we can see them with the eyes of the Spirit.

All through Scripture they are announcing God's plans and defending God's people. For our purposes, let's just look at the birth of Jesus. They announced the birth of Jesus to Mary and Joseph (see Luke 1:26-28 and Matt 1:18-21). They are spiritual beings distinct from humans. They do not have bodies, though they can assume them when we need a bodily manifestation. Humans are temporality lower than angels (see Heb 2:6-7). We have "guardian angels" assigned to us from the very beginning of our lives (see Matt 18:10). The Apocalypse is filled with references to angels who help carry out God's plans on earth.

The Greek word for angel in Scripture is *aggelos* and simply means "messenger." The Greek word for prophets, *prophetes*, has a similar meaning. What is the difference? Angels are pure spirits. Human beings are embodied spirits. Angels haven't sinned. Demons have. And fallen angels, demons, are trying to get us to join them in their sin!

The Desert

Contrary to common thought, *angels are even more active in the lives of the desert fathers and mothers than the demons.* They direct Antony about finding balance in his life as a hermit in the desert. They miraculously help the hermit fathers and mothers by leading them to find their caves, providing food, and guiding other monks to them before they pass to the Lord.

When discouraged about hard work, the fathers and mothers are reminded that the angels count every step they take in service and sacrifice for God.[1] When discouraged or frightened about the activity of demons around them, elders remind them that the angels are even more active than they are able to see![2]

---

1. E. A. W. Budge, ed. and trans., *The Paradise or Garden of the Holy Fathers*, 2 vols. (London: Chatto & Windus, 1907), 2:46.

2. Budge, 2:126–127.

There is a classic story of an angel teaching St. Antony about finding *balance*. When Antony cannot keep his mind focused while trying to pray for long periods of time, an angel shows him a monk who prays for a while, then works for a while. He says, "Do this and you will be saved." With the typical brevity of a desert father, the text says, "He did this, and was saved."[3]

Humility

An angel also taught Antony *humility* by pointing out that there was a man who resembled him and who was holier than he was. This man was a physician and prayed throughout the day, giving his profits to the poor.[4] So holiness is the point, not slavishly imitating the monastic way of life. Holiness is for everyone, and there are non-monastics who surpass a great number of monastics in really following Jesus.

There are several stories that tell of younger monks who rather self-righteously criticized older monks who spent their time in work. They often pointed out that he didn't need to work since he had opted for an "angelic life." Yet these younger monks were always ready to eat with the older monks when mealtime came around! So the older monks finally denied them food, telling them that since they were now living as angels, they should not eat, for angels do not require physical food. The young monks quickly repented and learned their lesson, at least for a time![5]

Encouragement

Angels give great *encouragement* to monks who are tired or discouraged. One monk lived ten miles from the monastery

3. Budge, 2:30.

4. Budge, 2:150.

5. James O. Hannay, *The Wisdom of the Desert* (1904; repr. n.p.: Glass Darkly, 2012), 64. Citations refer to the Glass Darkly edition.

and had to draw water from the monastery well. He would have to carry the water ten miles back to his hermitage. He finally decided to move his cell closer to the stream. He then turned around and saw a man walking behind him. The man told the monk he was an angel sent by God to count his footsteps so he could be rewarded for his sacrifice. The old hermit was consoled and then decided to move his hermitage five miles farther out into the desert! So angels encourage us in our sacrifices for God.

Angels live in glory, but they come to earth to *minister* to us and carry out God's plans. Which is better—to see the glory of angels or to see our sins so that we might repent? The desert tradition says that it is preferable to see our sins so that we might repent, then to see the glory of angels. One story says that an old man was asked why some people see the glory of angels. The old man said, "Blessed is he who sees his sins continually."[6]

Outnumbered

Angels *outnumber demons*! When discouraged about the number of demons, we are encouraged to meditate on the fact that they are far outnumbered by the angels who did not fall.

Once Abba Moses of Patara was waging war against the demon of fornication, and he went to Abba Isadore and said, "I can't bear it any longer." Abba Isidore had him look to the west to see the demons waging war of humanity and doing the work of the devil. Then he had him look to the east to see the angels ministering to God's saints and doing the work of God. He asked which were more numerous? Abba Moses said that the demons were numerous but countable, and the angels were beyond number. Abba Isidore said they were always victorious

6. Budge, 2:112.

in the end. Abba Moses went home encouraged. [7] Sometimes
we also feel like we cannot bear the evil attacks of demons. But
the angels far outnumber the demons, God is infinite, and Jesus
has won the victory for us. So we also must be encouraged.

Holiness in Speech

The angels are also close to us when we maintain holiness in
our speech.

On one occasion the fathers were sitting and talking together
about ascetic excellence. An old man who was a seer of visions
saw angels flying about over them. But when they talked about
worldly things, the angels departed, and he saw pigs rolling
about among them and wallowing in the mire.[8] Holy conversation delights the angels and draws them close, while unholy talk
repels them and leaves us to wallow in our own filth.

The Eucharist

The angels are *especially active during the celebration of the
Eucharist.* One monk doubted the Real Presence of Jesus in the
Eucharist while in solitude. Perhaps it was only a symbol? So
two older monks took him to the weekly monastic celebration
of the Eucharist with the other brothers. God revealed a Child
Jesus on the altar and an angel of the Lord coming from heaven
to open the side of the Child with a heavenly knife. Real blood
flowed from the Child into the Eucharistic cup, and when the
priest broke the bread, the monk saw real flesh. When he was
given the flesh, he professed: "I believe, O Lord, that the bread
is Thy Body, and that the cup is Thy Blood," and he immediately
saw the Eucharistic Bread instead of the flesh in his hand. He

7. Budge, 2:126–127.
8. Budge, 2:152.

believed. The old man explained: "God knows the nature of men, and that it is unable to eat living flesh, and for this reason he turns his Body into bread, and his Blood into wine, for those who receive him in faith." The role of the angel on the altar is real. When we celebrate, the Eucharist Jesus is personally present, as are the angels and saints of God.[9]

We see another connection between angels and the Eucharist, this time with regard to healing, in the story of a monk who had an open wound that oozed puss and infection. The angel told him not to fear, for the gift of the Holy Spirit that enabled him to partake of the Eucharist would be sufficient. And after healing him, the angel advised him, "Leave this place and go into the inner wilderness." So at once the saint went forth and fed on the shrubs of the wilderness, but every Sunday he would return to his old cave to partake of the Holy Communion.[10]

Angels Lead to Jesus

However wonderful the angels are, we should not give too much attention to them, for they always serve and glorify God and lead us to Jesus.

One father said that once when he was journeying along the road, two angels walked along with him. But he added, "I did not look at them." Why? Because it is written, "Neither . . . angels, nor principalities . . . will be able to separate us from the love of God in Christ Jesus our Lord" (Rom 8:39).[11] And Abba Arsenius and Abba Moses the Ethiopian comment that the monastic way of life is superior in the same way that the Spirit of God is more exalted than the holy angels.[12] So angels are good, but they are only messengers of the Good.

9. Budge, 2:160.
10. Budge, 1:357.
11. Budge, 2:247.
12. Budge, 2:284.

Angels *help us fight against demons who assail us in thoughts.* We are told that when we engage in holy discipline and healthy asceticism, angels assist us. They fight against the demons who are trying to get us to give up our struggle and drive them away. We can tell that this has happened because we feel ourselves filled with the light of God, renewed fervor, and spiritual joy at such times.[13]

At Death

The end of the lives of Sisois and Isezoros teaches us that *angels are sent to us at the time of our death.*[14] They prepare us for death and escort us to God in Christ when we pass away. Angels were sent time after time to the hermit fathers who lived in isolation beyond the monasteries, or semi-eremitic *sketes.*

I have seen the other side only on rare occasions when very ill. I was too ill and too awestruck to make that journey alone. Angels were there to help me in that small and distant glimpse of Paradise.

And then there are the hermits, the Spirit-bearers of Coptic monasticism, who live alone in the desert for decades, come to the Eucharist almost unseen by others, and either live in secluded caves or wander the desert virtually unknown during their lifetime. The angels and even the glorified apostles make frequent appearances in their stories. It is often the angels who lead them to the place prepared for them by God. They minister to them during spiritual battle. They often bring them food. They prepare them for death. It is almost impossible to separate the lives of the Coptic hermits from the angels who minister to them for God.

13. Budge, 2:296.
14. Hannay, 133.

Questions

1) Do you believe in angels?

2) Are you aware of your personal angel and greater angels protecting major areas, nations, or situations?

3) Are you aware of the presence of angels when you worship or live a holy life?

4) Do you use discernment when you feel or see angels?

5) Are you aware of angels in sickness and death?

15

Watchfulness

We hear and read a lot today about "mindfulness." The word comes from popular Buddhism. It has now worked its way into the lexicon of psychologists, health professionals, and self-help gurus. It is now a standard part of Christian lingo as well. It is similar to the desert tradition of *watchfulness*. In Eastern Christianity there is a rich traditional teaching on watchfulness. But our Christian tradition of watchfulness is unique from mindfulness, and a special gift. That is what we will emphasize here.

I am a student of religion. More specifically, I am a student of the monastic and mystical traditions of the religions of the world. I do this from a specifically Catholic Christian perspective. I am a firm believer in the fullness of God in Jesus Christ, but I recognize the truth found in other traditions and am glad to share common ground with believers of other faiths.

But I am also aware of the dangers of a universalism and syncretism that reduces all religions to seemingly separate but equal paths up the same mountain. All paths are not equal, and all roads are not as safe or direct as others. And all paths go both up and down. I am also aware of the dangers of fundamentalism in any faith that is militantly exclusive and reduces any path other than its own to being demonic and evil. This leads to a world of religious war and violence.

In our monastery, I have found that very few can integrate the mindfulness authentically taught in eastern religion together in a way that doesn't confuse their own Christianity. Other religious traditions can be most sophisticated, elegant, and persuasive. They can rival the greatest of Christian theology, mysticism, and metaphysics. Unless one is firmly grounded in one's Christian faith, dabbling in meditation techniques from other faith traditions can lead to becoming confused regarding faith and eventually even morality. Some lose their Christianity altogether. I am understandably cautious about integrating it too soon into a young monastic's spirituality. So I teach watchfulness from a solid and rich Christian tradition.

I have taught Christian meditation for decades. We have many areas of experiential common ground on the psychological and spiritual levels with other religions. But after much experience, I now teach clear Christian meditation unto itself, without trying to intermingle one tradition with the other too freely.

Watchfulness is related to both sacred stillness and thoughts. It is also related to stability in the cell. Watchfulness grows from stilling the body and emotions so that thoughts can be observed.

We modern people are often mentally obsessive, but not mindful or watchful in our thoughts. Externally, we suffer from a constant barrage of unedited news images and ideas via the onslaught of social media, TV, and such. Our thoughts are constantly active. Consequently, we cannot really process them with good discernment. The average news cycle is a day or two at best before a new "alert" demands our attention. This leaves us agitated and upset, and the obsession gets even worse.

Watchfulness means calmly watching over our lives, our passions, and our thoughts so as to discern whether or not they are from God, from demons, or from ourselves. It is the first step in discernment.

Scripture

Jesus says to watch out for evil coming to us under the form of religion, "Watch out, guard against the leaven of the Pharisees and the leaven of Herod" (Mark 8:15). He tells us to watch for coming persecutions (Mark 13:23), to watch daily for his second coming, and not to be surprised by it (Mark 13:35-36). So Jesus speaks of watching for the good and the bad that enters our lives and of being ready for his return. As St. Bernard says, there are three comings of Christ: the first in his Incarnation, the second at the end of our lives or the end of time, and the third in an intermediate coming through the Spirit in word and sacrament. We must be watchful for all three.[1]

St. Paul speaks of watchfulness of one's life of prayer in the Spirit of Christ. "With all prayer and supplication, pray at every opportunity in the Spirit. To that end, be watchful with all perseverance and supplication for all the holy ones" (Eph 6:18). And again, "Persevere in prayer, being watchful in it with thanksgiving" (Col 4:2).

The Desert

The desert fathers and mothers gave birth to a more specialized watchfulness, called in Greek *nepsis*. Interestingly, this is not the word used in Scripture. There we read of being watchful and of keeping watch in the night. *Nepsis* is more specialized. It is the intense, but not scrupulous, watching of thoughts and passions that enter the house of one's soul.

Watchfulness is conditioned by *hesychia*, or sacred stillness. As we have already seen, this can be likened to an agitated and muddy pond that has been stilled. Only when the sediment that has been stirred up through agitation has settled back to

1. Sermo 5, In Adventu Domini, 1–3: Opera Omnia, Edit. Cisterc. 4 (1966), 188–190.

the bottom does the water become clear enough to see what is really in the pond of one's soul. This is when we can become calmly but intensely watchful according to *nepsis*.

It's also said by St. Hesychios the Priest in the later *Philokalia*, a collection of beautiful eastern monastic wisdom, that watchfulness is like a spider that does the work of spinning the web but afterward is very still so as to perceive anything stirring the web. It is the same with watchfulness.[2] We do the work of asceticism but then enter into sacred stillness so we can perceive what disturbs the web of our life. If it is good, it is nourishing. If bad, it can be rejected.

So we must be very still in *hesychia* in order to see what is going on in the depths of our soul, whether that be from God, the devil, or just ourselves. Then we must make the choice for Jesus.

John of Damascus in the *Philokalia* also says that just as it is easier to cut off the head of a snake when it tries to enter your home than to wait until its entire body has gotten through the door, so it is with watchfulness of thoughts.[3] If we see them as soon as they enter the doorway of the soul, it is easier to cut off the head of the snake of bad thoughts, rather than waiting until they have fully entered the house. Then it is much more difficult.

The earlier desert fathers don't yet have a developed method or theology of watchfulness. But it is certainly present and an essential part of their way of life. For example, Serapion said that if you want to make progress, stay in your cell, *keep a watch upon yourself,* and attend to the work of your hands.[4] And when Abba Poemen was asked how one should to sit in his cell, he said

2. G. E. H. Palmer, Philip Sherrard, and Kallistos Ware, trans. and ed., *The Philokalia*, vol. 1 (London: Faber & Faber, 1983), 26.166.

3. Palmer, Sherrard, and Ware, *The Philokalia*, vol. 1, 76.

4. Owen Chadwick, ed. and trans., *Western Asceticism* (Philadelphia: Westminster Press, 1958), 99.

that to "sit" in the cell is, externally, to work with the hands, eat once a day, keep silence, and meditate. Internally it is to make progress by bearing injury and fault through self-accusation and asking forgiveness of God, keeping the hours of prayer, and keeping a watch on the secret thoughts of the heart.[5] So watchfulness has both an external and an internal dimension.

To be effective in watchfulness we must still the body and the emotions. Only then will thoughts become clear. To still the body we must also *stay still in one place*. We are so tempted to get up and move around constantly. We must learn to simply sit alone with God. Recall the image offered by the fathers of a spider on a web.

We cannot still the body if we cannot still *the breath*. The Jesus Prayer unites prayer with breathing. This allows our thoughts to drop from the conceptual mind to the intuitive mind, the *nous*, the heart, the center of our being. Settling the breath settles the body. Then the emotions and thoughts settle down. When done rightly it can even reduce blood pressure. Done wrongly, and it will actually increase it!

But there is a necessary caution in order. It is easy to become *scrupulous* with our thoughts in a way that makes us nervous and uptight. That isn't authentic watchfulness. Desert watchfulness is peaceful and calm.

The Cloud of Unknowing (chap. 32) says to gently look around thoughts that tempt or bother us. I expand on this and say to see thoughts as objects coming slowly toward us. If they aren't from God, we calmly move our head to one side and let them pass. I like this analogy. We don't get upset when our watchfulness reveals something bad in our thoughts. We simply move aside and let them pass. It is peaceful. It is calm. It is lifegiving.

If we find actions in our lives that are sinful or simply unfruitful, we just repent. We change our minds. We let them go. No

5. Chadwick, 118.

need to get worried or overly upset. But we must actually do it. Jesus forgives everyone who turns back to him with a humble and contrite heart.

So I recommend taking time daily for simply sitting in watch-fulness. You cannot stop thoughts and emotions. But you can settle them in order to see them more clearly. Once seen clearly, they can be brought to the cross of Jesus and transformed through the resurrection.

Questions

1) Are you watchful of thoughts?

2) Do you still the muddy waters of your life through times of prayer?

3) Do you incorporate your breathing in prayer?

4) Do you recognize the uniquely Christian aspect of this practice?

16

Spiritual Direction and Revelation of Thoughts

"If he is able to, a monk ought to tell his elders confidently how many steps he takes and how many drops of water he drinks in his cell, in case he is in error about it."

—St. Antony, in Christine Valters Paintner, *Desert Fathers and Mothers: Early Christian Wisdom Sayings, Annotated and Explained*

The lives and stories of the desert fathers and mothers simply assume the revelation of thoughts to a trusted elder. It was essential to the way of life.

We live in a culture where respect for elders is quickly disappearing. For the first time in recorded human history, youth and novelty is regarded as more important than eldership and time-tested wisdom. In the past the older something was, the more we venerated it. The oldest was the most precious. Now we worship the god of youth and novelty. Consequently, what was once wrong is often considered right, and what was once right is now wrong. This is often the work of the father of lies (John 8:44).

But we must be careful of extreme reactions against novelty. Both St. Benedict and St. Francis were open to the opinions of novices. So a certain balance must be maintained between veneration of the old and openness to the new. Then the body of Christ in the church and various expressions of community can really grow.

Why should we venerate our elders? Obviously, they have lived much longer, and they know the successes and mistakes of various spiritual paths, not just in theory but also in actual experience. The desert fathers and mothers give us similar guidance.

It is often very hard to make sense of the flurry of thoughts that arise in our minds. Some are positive and some are negative. We often get confused. When we allow negative or confused thoughts, they can become unhealthy mental patterns. These can become deeply ingrained and negatively impact our entire lives. We need discernment. We need help.

Some of that help comes directly though the Holy Spirit, our comforter and advocate, who teaches us everything that Jesus said (see John 14:26). Some of it comes from Scripture and apostolic tradition that is inspired and useful for instruction (see 2 Tim 3:16). Some can come from the teaching authority of the church. For the average Christian, this is often enough. But for the more serious follower of Jesus, these are often too general, and we can interpret them too subjectively. We can get off the path. We can sin.

This is why we need spiritual direction. We need someone to share our thoughts with so that we can receive some feedback. This person must be more experienced than we are. He or she must be a proven man or woman of the Spirit. And this person must know the way of life we are trying to live in Christ. Ordinarily, it is hard for those in the married or secular state to advise one living the monastic or consecrated life, though monastics all come from families and can often offer advice for families. Experience on the part of the director is needed.

In the desert these were called abbas and ammas, spiritual fathers and mothers. They are also called elders, or even "old man." Jesus cautioned against calling anyone father (Matt 23:9). But St. Paul was called father (1 Cor 4:15). In ancient Judaism, Christendom, and monasticism, consulting an elder was a sign of wisdom (Sir 6:34-37). It guaranteed a good training in the way of the Lord.

We Westerners are suspicious of this. We are rugged individualists. We are extremely vocal socially, yet extremely private regarding our innermost selves. We talk a lot but communicate little. We Americans have a suspicion of authority that is deeply rooted in our founding history. This suspicion of authority has been reinforced by the religious scandals of our more recent history and by our distrust of politics. Caution is good. Suspicion is not.

We have also come to realize the imperfections of our own mothers and fathers in a way that can be positive when used for healing, but negative when it perpetrates the "blame game." We love to blame others for our problems. We all have some "mommy and daddy issues," but we simply cannot continually blame others for our problems and expect any maturity or happiness in this life. We must take responsibility, forgive, and move forward.

This all affects how we approach spiritual fathers and mothers and elders. We are often inherently distrustful. Yet we inwardly long for someone to trust and help guide us through the minefields of spiritual battle. We want someone we can trust to accompany us on our spiritual journeys in Christ.

So we tend to fight spiritual and relational battles on our own. We read books on self-help and spirituality. We watch talks on social media and the internet, go to conferences, or perhaps make an occasional retreat. But we are left largely on our own as to how to apply what we read and hear.

We need spiritual fathers and mothers or elders to accompany us on our spiritual journeys in Christ. We have the Spirit, but we need a trusted elder to help discern the spirits in and around our lives. It is one thing to say that we defeat the onslaughts of demons and thoughts in the solitude and silence of a changed life of prayer or monastic life. It is quite another to actually do so! How do we do it? How do we learn how to do it?

The Fathers

The desert fathers were clear that we learn from one who has experienced it and is able to pass it on to others through example and words. They can say from personal experience, "Don't step there, it is loose ground next to a sheer cliff." Or, "Walk this way, for it is more level and smooth." This is nothing terribly mystical. It's just common sense. It's not about controlling others. It's about helping.

In one sense that is what the various collections of the desert fathers and mothers are for. It is a blessing to have collections of their lives and sayings to guide us so many generations later. But those same sayings and lives are clear that you cannot get the essence of the teaching from books alone. You must have a teacher, a spiritual father or mother, an elder to pass on the teaching face to face, from one real life to another.

There is an old saying: Better to have a spiritual director than not, but better no spiritual director than a bad one! So I recommend a good spiritual father or mother in Christ.

But you must be ready and willing to submit to their direction or it all fails anyway. There's a saying: When the disciple is ready, the master appears. Often we only *think* we want a good spiritual director and complain that we can't find one, when in fact we are not ready. Sometimes they are there all along. We just couldn't or wouldn't see them.

If you really cannot find a good spiritual director, the fathers say to steep yourself in the writings of the ancient fathers, mothers, and saints.[1] But this is always more dangerous than having

---

1. "Appendix B: The Spiritual Instructions of St. Seraphim," in Harry M. Boosalis, *The Joy of the Holy: Saint Seraphim of Sarov and Orthodox Spiritual Life*, trans. S. D. Arhipov (South Canaan, PA: St. Tikhon's Seminary Press, 1993), 160.

a good spiritual director. It is never an excuse for avoiding the revelation of thoughts to a trusted elder. That individualistic way can lead to delusion.

My Experience

I was most fortunate to have a spiritual father to guide me on my early path in the Catholic Church and in monastic and Franciscan life. He was a master of "balance." He drilled it into me every time I tended to go to one extreme or the other. So balance is part of my spiritual DNA, and I owe that to being fathered and birthed into the church and monastic life by my spiritual father.

On another level, he was quite human. He could also be quite aggravating! He talked too much, but the word of God flowed through him. He ate too much, but was not a glutton, and he shared the joy of life. He forgave too much, but he found a happiness that he could pass on to others. I could tell many stories about his lovable and sometimes infuriating imperfections! He was not perfect by any means. But he was my spiritual father, and God used him mightily in my life. Despite his human shortcomings, I learned to trust that God spoke to me through him. And I was not disappointed. I will never be able to repay the debt of gratitude I owe him for his spiritual fatherhood.

So having a spiritual father or mother isn't always about finding someone who is perfect. It's about finding someone who is anointed by the Spirit and someone with more experience than we have. That's what I learned, and hopefully I can pass on a bit to others who are interested.

Revelation of Thoughts

The desert fathers are really the early Christian originators of what today we call spiritual direction. They specifically describe something called the "revelation of thoughts."

Abba Cassian said that Abba Moses told us not to hide the thoughts, but to reveal them to old men; "but not to men who are old merely in years, for many have found final despair instead of comfort by confessing to men" who were aged in years, but not in experience.[2]

Monastic and Sacramental Confession

Monastic revelation of thoughts is different than modern spiritual direction or sacramental confession.

The sacramental confession that we know today developed from the monastic confession of thoughts and sins. Monastic confession wasn't the sacrament of penance. It was with a spiritual father or mother for men and women respectively. But lay folks around the monasteries saw that it worked to mentally, emotionally, and spiritually liberate the monks, so they asked for something like it as well. The bishops responded by using the sacramental means from earlier centuries in the church's history.

Prior to the tenth century, sacramental confession was only done once or twice in a lifetime, and only for major sins that were more public knowledge. This was concerning public scandals such as murder, adultery, theft, and so on. The bishop or priest would impose public penances to determine whether the penitent was serious. These could last for a period of years. If the penitent persevered in the public penance, the bishop would publicly forgive him or her. It was then over and done with. This might sound tough to modern ears, but it was lenient compared to the rigorists who said serious Christians couldn't sin after baptism because they had the Holy Spirit. This was in response to those who had lapsed in the face of persecution, while others had remained faithful and given up life and limb

---

2. Owen Chadwick, ed. and trans., *Western Asceticism* (Philadelphia: Westminster Press, 1958), 60.

for the faith. The church thought this rigorism too extreme and allowed for forgiveness after baptism. But it wasn't the frequent confession that came to be practiced later.

So sacramental confession is for actual sins in thought, word, and deed, for things we have done and failed to do. Monastic confession reveals not only sins but also temptations in order for the older monastic to help with the struggle. Sacramental confession is for sins. Monastic confession is for temptations *and* sins. One forgives sin. The other helps avoid them!

Monastic confession is also different from modern spiritual direction in the West, though the latter came from it. Modern spiritual direction is more of a counseling session, though not full therapy in the clinical sense. It can take an hour or so. Monastic confession is a simple, rather short revelation of thoughts. It allows little or no opportunity to make excuses. It's not about what other people did to tempt us. It's about our response. It forces us to take full responsibility for our response to thoughts.

This revelation of thoughts really just makes sense. How can spiritual fathers or mothers offer advice and direction, if they do not know the inner workings of the person they are directing? How can they know how to help someone if they are not willing to open up their thoughts and temptations to their discernment? A spiritual son, daughter, or younger brother or sister must be willing to open up his or her soul in order to receive any real help from another.

Trust

This requires trust. And trust has so often been broken in modern life. Broken marriages and families have eroded our trust in spouses, fathers and mothers, and brothers and sisters. Abusive bosses have eroded our trust in business leaders. And clerical abuses have eroded our trust in spiritual leaders. So we are now left almost completely on our own to figure out the often complicated thoughts that assail us almost constantly from an increasingly godless secular world. We are left between the proverbial "devil and the deep blue sea."

Companion

Perhaps this is one of the reasons Pope Francis has suggested the language of *companionship* in spiritual direction. Companions walk with us. They do not walk separately from, push, pull, prod, or cajole us. They share rather than argue and dialogue rather debate. Over time this builds the trust that we have so often lost.

They help carry our burdens in Christ. One account tells of a brother who gave in to great temptation during the week, sleeping with one of the village women. He confessed to his spiritual father. The old man said, "Do you repent?" The brother said, "Yes." The old man said, "I will carry half the burden of the sin with you." Then the brother said, "Now I know that we can stay together." And they remained together as spiritual companions until death separated them.[3]

Gradual Progress

Progress with a spiritual director is usually gradual, not sudden or fast. The progress is little by little, by God's grace. We can advance in the ascetic life until we reach the first level. Then we receive the power to resist thoughts and to vanquish them.[4]

One spiritual father said not to fight all thoughts at once, but one by one. "Do not strive against them all, but against one, for all devilish thoughts have only one head, and it is necessary for

---

3. Chadwick, 184.
4. E. A. W. Budge, ed. and trans., *The Paradise or Garden of the Holy Fathers*, 2 vols. (London: Chatto & Windus, 1907), 2:5.

a man to understand and to make war upon this head only, for afterwards all the rest will perforce be brought low"[5]

In my role as spiritual father in my community, I have frequent personal conferences with the brothers. In those conferences I ask them to share with me one or two of the eight thoughts they have struggled with in their personal spiritual life or in community relationships. This provides ample material from which to get more specific about how that is actually working out.

In these conferences I listen a lot, encourage, and sometimes challenge. I try not to force my will on the monks in an obtrusive way. But I'm not afraid to direct with my authority when needed, though it rarely is. I jokingly say that my role as spiritual father is often more like a referee trying to get others to get along with one another. I have even joked that I should start wearing a striped shirt, hat, and whistle instead of my monastic habit! Seriously, after listening I offer some advice and pray with them. This is most important! And I try to carry their burden in my personal prayer after the conference.

These conferences are usually not longer than thirty minutes. I let the brothers speak freely but remember that in the multitude of words sin is seldom lacking. I try to keep them on point. That way they are not a drain on their energy or mine. These conversations are simple, short and sweet, and hopefully uplifting in the Spirit. Also, as each brother matures, we don't always need to meet every week. But dropping out of touch completely effectively destroys the father/son relationship.

And I must admit that while we use the term "spiritual father" for my role, it mainly applies to the community in general. I have rarely felt that someone has entered into the role with me fully. It is not my place to force it on others. It must be *caught* rather than *taught*. As the Buddhists say, if you man-

5. Budge, 2:67.

age to pass on the spirit of the teaching to one other person in your whole life, you can count yourself fortunate. We can teach many, but if only one really gets the spirit and essence of your teaching, you're blessed indeed. I pray that at the end of my life I have managed to really pass on my monastic life in Christ to at least one other soul. That would make my entire life worthwhile.

Questions

1) Do you have a spiritual director?

2) How would you go about finding one?

3) Is spiritual direction more about talking in order to justify your problems, or are you really ready to change through simple confession of thoughts?

4) If you live in monastic community, do you consider your abbot or abbess a spiritual father or mother, or just a functional leader?

5) Are you willing to submit yourself to a relationship with a spiritual father or mother as an obedient child of God?

Obedience

Related to finding a spiritual father or mother and the revelation of thoughts is the topic of obedience. You cannot have a good relationship with a spiritual father or mother without being obedient to his or her direction. But what is obedience?

Monastic obedience is often misunderstood. It is not a military obedience, nor is it oppressive or restrictive. When rightly understood and practiced, it is most liberating.

The root of obedience is to *listen*. Most of the time we do not really listen to what people are saying. We often are formulating our opinions and arguments to justify our position before they even finish speaking. To be obedient means to really be silent, listen, and hear what others are saying. This is especially true in our relationship with the leaders God has brought into our lives.

It also means to *promptly respond* to those God has put into positions of leadership in our lives. It is not enough to simply listen, politely agree, and say "amen." Often, we go about our business unchanged by the input of those God has put into a position to really help us live better lives in Christ. No. We must actually do what they are asking us to do. It is not for their benefit. It is for ours.

Most of the time this is just the ordinary stuff of running a monastery or the church. Sometimes it requires us to trust the leaders and carry out a command we might not yet understand or agree with. There might not always be time for them to explain. Or God might be asking us to simply grow in faith.

But obedience is *not blind*. We *choose* to live in monastic obedience. Once we have discerned the right community or spiritual father or mother, we freely choose to place ourselves under obedience to a leader and a community. In modern times there are mechanisms in place to address situations where a leader is habitually leading in ways that defy the teaching of the church or are in major conflict with a rule and way of life. But under ordinary circumstances, even when leaders are wrong in minor ways, we do not spurn their authority but give them the benefit of the doubt, understanding that no leader is perfect. They can even make major mistakes, but unless they become habitual and truly harmful, we do not spurn their authority. Today there are appropriate checks and balances in place for the extraordinary times when we have truly bad leaders.

I have positive and negative memories of childhood leaders. I had teachers whom I deeply loved and respected. They were smart and loving and listened well. They imparted wisdom and understanding to me, and I could share my problems with trust that they wouldn't just condemn or dismiss me out of hand. My mom and dad were just the best, and I could trust them with any problem I might bring to them. They would listen, understand, and really try to help.

I also had some negative experiences with leadership. I loved to swim as a kid, and I was like a fish in water. But I knew how to swim only underwater. I needed to learn the correct way to swim above water. So I enrolled in some YMCA swimming classes in Oklahoma City. I really respected my instructor. But I remember all too well how embarrassed I was when he corrected me in front of the pool full of students. I was left with no enthusiasm or motivation to continue. In hindsight, he really had no other place in which to do it. I was using a flawed technique, and he was on the side of the pool. I was just very sensitive. And that swimming flaw haunts me to this day! But it is a negative memory of how I didn't take the correction of a skilled instructor and suffered for it in the long run.

Scripture

Scripture is filled with teachings about being obedient. The main Hebrew word is *shamaʿ*, which means to hearken or listen, among other things. It means to listen attentively. This is the word Samuel uses in 1 Samuel 15:22, when he tells Saul, "Obedience is better than sacrifice, / to listen, better than the fat of rams."

In the New Testament, Jesus teaches obedience even to bad leaders: "The scribes and the Pharisees have taken their seat on the chair of Moses. Therefore, do and observe all things whatsoever they tell you, but do not follow their example. For they preach but they do not practice" (Matt 23: 2-3). And Jesus was obedient to God—even "obedient to death" (Phil 2:8)—working through bad religious and civil leaders.

On a more positive note, Jesus commissions the apostles to "Go, therefore, and make disciples of all nations, baptizing them in the name of the Father, and of the Son, and of the holy Spirit, teaching them to observe all that I have commanded you. And behold, I am with you always, until the end of the age" (Matt 28:19-20). The apostles also establish successors (see Acts 14:23). This was the guarantee for authentic teaching of the gospel of Jesus in the early church, and it was through this that the Scriptures were both written and compiled.

St. Paul says to Timothy, "Remain faithful to what you have learned and believed, because you know from whom you learned it" (2 Tim 3:14).

Hebrews 13:17 says, "Obey your leaders and defer to them, for they keep watch over you and will have to give an account, that they may fulfill their task with joy and not with sorrow, for that would be of no advantage to you."

Benedict

The Rule of Benedict says very clearly that obedience makes
sense only if we can see the work of God in the obediences given
us by our fathers and mothers. The abbot "is believed to hold the
place of Christ in the monastery, since he is addressed by a title
of Christ" (RB 2.2). And monks are exhorted to "carry out the
superior's order as promptly as if the command came from God
himself" (RB 5.4). We must spiritualize obedience, or it fails.
We have to look beyond the human leader to the leadership of
Christ, or we won't ever be fully satisfied with any earthly leader.

The Desert

The desert fathers and mothers present us with the first monastic applications of these scriptural teachings regarding obedience. There are some radical and miraculous stories, as well
as direct teachings.

There is the classic story of Abba John the Short who had his
disciple plant a dead branch in the ground and water it faithfully. And it took root and sprouted! Abba John told him, "Pour
a jug of water over its base every day until it bears fruit."[1] I'm
sure the disciple didn't understand the command and thought
it unreasonable. But because he obeyed in humility, without
voicing his reasonable and logical objections, the dead branch
sprouted, and grew into a tree.

We might say that clearly the superior didn't understand. We
might even tell ourselves and others that we have the superior's
best interest at heart and are objecting to protect the superior.
But these can all be guises under which ego and pride can hide.
No, this story encourages being obedient even when we don't
fully understand all the reasons for it.

---

1. Owen Chadwick, ed. and trans., *Western Asceticism* (Philadelphia:
Westminster Press, 1958), 150.

Obedience is to be *prompt and humble,* making no excuses for tardiness or negligence.

There's a common desert story about a disciple of Sylvanus who was a copyist. On one occasion when he heard a command from his teacher, he stopped work immediately and fulfilled Sylvanus's obedience. Now what is remarkable about this story is not merely that the disciple dropped his work immediately, but that he did not even finish the letter *O* that he was copying![2]

This is pretty remarkable. Most of us would consider it acceptable to fulfill the obedience when we are finished with our current work. And most superiors would ordinarily consider it reasonable. But the response of this disciple was prompt. He didn't make excuses that could have easily hidden ego and pride beneath putting the superior's command off until it was comfortable to respond.

Benedict concurs: "Almost at the same moment, then, as the master gives the instruction the disciple quickly puts it into practice in the fear of God; and both actions together are swiftly completed as one. It is love that impels them" (RB 5.9-10).

Love is the key! This is why St. Benedict teaches us that obedience is to be joyful and without grumbling. And that is precisely the difference between military and monastic obedience! Military personnel often obey externally but grumble internally. Monks cannot allow that in themselves:

> This very obedience, however, will be acceptable to God and agreeable to men only if compliance with what is commanded is not cringing or sluggish or half-hearted, but free from any grumbling or any reaction of unwillingness. For the obedience shown to superiors is given to God, as he himself said: *Whoever listens to you, listens to me* (Luke 10:16). Furthermore, the disciples' obedience must be given gladly, for *God loves a cheerful giver* (2 Cor 9:7).

2. Chadwick, 151.

If a disciple obeys grudgingly and grumbles, not only aloud but also in his heart, then, even though he carries out the order, his action will not be accepted with favor by God, who sees that he is grumbling in his heart. He will have no reward for service of this kind; on the contrary, he will incur punishment for grumbling, unless he changes for the better and makes amends. (RB 5.17-19)

Cenobitic Community

Obedience has a special importance in cenobitic communities of monastics who pray and work together daily, as contrasted with hermits who are more alone during the week. Some of this is just functional. Without obedience the spiritual and physical work of the monastery cannot function. We all have to show up for prayers, work, meals, and conferences at designated times or monasteries would degenerate into anarchy and chaos. This is just common sense.

It is always interesting to me that those who are willing to be obedient to superiors in secular jobs are sometimes unable to be obedient in religious communities. What's the difference? Mother Mary Francis who founded the Poor Clare Monastery in New Mexico said that in the secular world you are obedient in order to keep your job and make money! If you are disobedient in secular jobs, you get fired. She was astonished at how young girls were willing to change their appearance and behavior patterns in obedience in order to make money, but complained when asked to do the same thing for God. She had a point.

So in cenobitic communities, we are obedient in order for the community to *function*. But we are also obedient in order to find real *humility*. It is interesting that the Rule of Benedict lists radical obedience in its chapter on the steps of humility. The desert fathers say much the same thing.

Saint Syncletica said that for those living in a more intense monastic community as cenobites, *obedience is even more virtuous than chastity*, however perfect. Chastity can carry pride, but obedience builds humility.[3]

The Cross

Obedience is not just about the practical functioning of a monastery. Monastic obedience is seen as a special way to embrace *the cross of Christ*. It always remains a spiritual reality, and only when we see it as such are we able to bear it with joy.

Hyperichius said, "*The monk's service is obedience*. He who has this shall have his prayers answered, and shall stand by the Crucified in confident faith. For that was how the Lord went to his cross, being made obedient even unto death' (cf. Phil. 2:8)."[4] So the entire monastic life can be summarized in one word: obedience. When properly understood it contains all the richness of monastic life in Christ.

New Members

Obedience is especially important for *new members* of monastic communities. Often in their zeal to be a monk, they become critical of older monastics. They are so fresh from the world that worldly patterns of competition and the need for self-glorification hide under their seemingly holy zeal for God. Obedience is a special way to expel that from their soul.

The old men used to say: "From those who have not long been converted to the life of a monk, God demands no virtue so much as earnest obedience."[5]

3. Chadwick, 152.

4. Benedicta Ward, ed., *The Desert Fathers: Sayings of the Early Christian Monks* (New York: Penguin, 2003), 143.

5. Chadwick, 153.

Imperfect Leaders

Sometimes we grow weary of obedience to a father or mother whom we think imperfect. So we consider retiring into the *seclusion of a hermitage*. This is a common trick of the enemy for most, especially the younger monastics. In reality we are just running from ourselves in order for our ego and pride to be left alone with no one to call us into account.

An old man said: "A brother who entrusts his soul in obedience to a spiritual father has a greater reward than the brother who retires alone to his hermitage."[6]

Difficult at Times

Sometimes obedience and the revelation of thoughts to a father or mother are *hard*. We sometimes find ourselves facing obedience to do a job that we might not like or that places us in contact with other temptations, so we want to change it. Are we to be obedient to our elders, or act on our own and run away? The following longer story describes the predicament of one younger monk.

A brother is given an obedience to go into town on business trips for his spiritual father. While in town he falls into temptation to commit fornication with a beautiful woman. He feels that he cannot go back to town, or he will sin. Yet he cannot disobey his spiritual father. What should he do? So he goes to another elder to try to get a different obedience. That elder tells him to return to his own spiritual father and lay out the case, and if he still asks him to go to town for the business of the monastery, God will supply the grace to resist the temptation. It is up to him to cooperate with the grace to resist or to give in. "Know, O my brother," the elder told him, "that Satan

6. Chadwick, 155.

is not so anxious to cast thee into fornication as he is to dismiss thee from obedience."[7]

This is kind of like the common syndrome of kids playing one parent off the other. We all know how it goes: The kids ask dad for something. Dad says no. So the kids go to mom! But when mom figures out that they have already asked dad, and dad's response is reasonable, even if she might have said something a bit different, mom will say to do whatever dad said. And if mom gives a different direction anyway, she undermines the authority of dad, and it creates division between the wife and the husband. A house divided cannot stand (see Luke 11:17).

This same syndrome happens in community when the abbot commands something to a monk, the monk doesn't want to do it, so he goes go to the prior or another leader to try to get a different outcome. But once the prior or other leader figures out that he has already received an answer from the abbot, he tells him to do what the abbot asked. Or the lower leader might advise not to follow the will of the abbot, and the community is in chaos (see RB 65).

The story of the young monk struggling with obedience concludes: "So, my sons, obedience is good, if it is for God's sake. Strive to win at least some trace of this virtue. It is the salvation of the faithful, the mother of virtue, the opening of the kingdom of heaven, the raising of men from heaven to earth. Obedience lives in the house of the angels, is the food of all the saints, who turn to it at their weaning and by its nourishment grow to a perfect life."[8]

7. E. A. W. Budge, ed. and trans., *The Paradise or Garden of the Holy Fathers*, 2 vols. (London: Chatto & Windus, 1907), 1:210.

8. Chadwick, 155–156.

Questions

1) Do you understand obedience as military-like or relational?

2) Do you really listen when others, especially leaders, speak, or are you constantly reacting in your thoughts?

3) Are you prompt in carrying out the direction of a spiritual father or mother?

4) Do you inwardly grumble while fulfilling an obedience from a spiritual father, mother, or elder, or are you joyful?

5) Are you willing to be obedient to secular bosses to keep your job, but not to religious superiors?

6) Do you see obedience as a way to joyfully embrace the cross of Jesus Christ?

7) Do you understand the importance of greater obedience for new members in communities?

8) Do you sometimes seek "solitude" in order to escape obedience?

9) Do you understand that disobedience is the devil's favorite trick?

18

Dying with Christ

"A monk cares for nothing but attaining the
goal of being crucified with Christ."

—Anonymous Desert Father, in James O.
Hannay, *The Wisdom of the Desert*

Everything in the preceding chapters—and in Christianity itself—is ultimately about personally dying and rising in Jesus Christ and our participation in that Mystery as a united people. It is God's eternal love in the Trinity being poured out in space and time in the incarnation of his Son and especially in his dying and rising in his Passion. It is about our personal love encounter with Jesus Christ as a united people in full communion with him and one another.

This teaching is offered by Jesus (Matt 10:33; 16:24; Luke 17:33), and it is fundamental in the early church (see Rom 6:6; Col 3:9; Eph 4:22; 6:24; Gal 2:20; and Col 4:18).

Every sacrament, every doctrine, and every church structure exist to facilitate that simple, but life-changing reality: the old self dying with Christ daily and our resurrection as a new person God originally created us to be. But we have often settled for a version of ourselves that is less than the person God created us to be. That is the old self. It doesn't make us, or anyone else, truly happy. That self must die. Then the person God created us to be can be born again in the resurrection of Jesus. Then we will be the person God intends us to be, we can be truly happy and free, and we will make others happier as well! So all that matters is that one is created anew. And we cannot be created anew unless the old self dies in order for a new self to be born again and rise up with Christ.

I often say that we have turned ourselves upside down through sin. Instead of being spirit, soul, and body, as described by St. Paul in 1 Thessalonians 5:23, we see ourselves and function with the body first, the soul second, and find our spirit asleep. Then we wonder why we are frustrated and unhappy! We must bring the old, incomplete, upside down, and frustrated self to the cross and let it die. Then we can be born again in the right order God originally intended for us. Then we can be "blessed," or truly happy again.

The desert fathers and mothers made this into a specialized way of life. They created what St. Benedict of Nursia would later call "a school of the Lord's service." But it is not a single event, though a single conversion point might start the process. It is really a complete way of life. This became the way of the desert fathers and mothers.

This complete monastic way of life is described in a rather long passage. It can be paraphrased, but it cannot be shortened too much for fear of missing its rich content.

The brothers once asked an old man, how is it possible for a monk to die daily with Christ, and like St. Paul, to say that "I no longer die, but Christ lives in me"? The old man answered that one can do this if he first does the "works of the body": contemplating in silence at all seasons, fasting, keeping vigil, reciting the psalms, saying the prayers, doing genuflections, and reading of the holy Scriptures. He must especially be careful concerning "the works of the mind": meditating constantly upon God. The old man continued, saying that such a person must pray "without ceasing" and without a wandering mind. He must keep the odious nature of the Lord's suffering away from his heart, and "he must suppress with keenness the thoughts of the devils which arise at their prompting." He must possess "the first and most important of all the spiritual virtues," more important than all the rest: death to "all the anxieties and cares of this world. And a monk must have no care, and no anxiety," and he must seek and desire only "the perfect love of God in our Lord Jesus Christ." He must fulfill at all times the command of St. Paul, "Love ye your Lord, rejoice in your hope, pray without ceasing, be fervent in spirit, endure your tribulations, be not anxious about anything, cast all your care upon the Lord; and let all your prayers, and all your requests, and all your petitions be made known unto God, to Whom be glory for ever and ever! Amen."[1]

Those Who Give Up and Leave

This is quite a tall order! And many fall from the path. The stories of the desert are filled with monastics who fall away. Some come back. Some don't. Any monastic who has lived any length of time in a monastery has seen this sad scenario. We watch some monastics gradually fall into a tailspin. We pray for them. We talk to them. We try to help them. But ultimately it is up to them to make the decision for themselves. No one can make that decision for them. The same is true in Christianity in general.

This is often very hard on the ones who stay. It is a bit like a divorce every time one whom they have loved decides to leave. The desert fathers and mothers were no strangers to this sad process and viewed it as a sharing in the cross of Jesus Christ. It

1. E. A. W. Budge, ed. and trans., *The Paradise or Garden of the Holy Fathers*, 2 vols. (London: Chatto & Windus, 1907), 2:327.

helps us die to our ego attachments to things and even people. Yet when done rightly it helps us to love everyone all the more.

A certain elder was once asked how the brothers could keep from being offended when one of them departs and returns to the world? He said to observe how dogs hunt rabbits. Some give up. Others keep going, despite the thickets and hills that scrape and tire their legs, and they catch the rabbit! So it is with the monk who seeks Christ and gazes steadfastly on the cross. He takes no notice of the things that trouble and offend him. He cares for nothing but attaining the goal of being crucified with Christ.[2]

The moral to this story is that we must chase the rabbit, and we won't be distracted or upset when others drop out of the race. We must have our "eyes on the prize." The prize is Jesus, and monastic life is a time-tested racecourse.

The Crucible of Community

Community can be a crucible of crucifixion in many ways. I have often said that after a decade or so in community, I felt much like a ragdoll with all its stuffing knocked out! That "stuffing" was my ego attachments to my own ideas, agendas, things, projects, and people. It was my old self. Only when my stuffing was knocked out could I really be free to be filled with the Spirit of God. Then Jesus became my "stuffing"!

The following story reflects such a process. Some brothers once asked Abbot Moses to speak a word. Moses asked his disciple Zacharias to say something. Zacharias took off his cloak and trampled it in the ground, saying, "Behold, unless a man is thus trampled on, he cannot be a monk."[3]

---

2. James O. Hannay, *The Wisdom of the Desert* (1904; repr. n.p.: Glass Darkly, 2012), 29–30. Citations refer to the Glass Darkly edition.

3. Hannay, 32.

As spiritual father and founder of our monastic community, I sometimes feel like a cloth that has been trampled into the ground. And I'm quite sure I'm not alone. This trampling hurts, then numbs. It can be either a curse or a blessing. How we face it is up to us. Monastic life specializes in this spirituality. If we allow our old selves to be trampled, then the new self in Christ arises. If we hang on to the old self, we are simply miserable, and monastic life becomes impossible.

Rest in Peace

St. Francis says that we don't experience peace until we die. This process helps us die to the old self so we can rise up anew in him. The following story from the desert fathers regarding the passive nature of a lifeless idol is not unlike those from St. Francis.

Abbot Anube went to a pagan temple with some brothers. He spent all day throwing stones at the idols and asking their pardon. The brothers asked him why he, as a Christian, would ask forgiveness of a lifeless idol? He said he did it as an example for them on how to live in community. When he threw stones at it, it did not get angry. It didn't get conceited when he asked forgiveness. He said that they could not live in community successfully without such an attitude.[4]

A similar story is told of Macarius about visiting the dead. He told the brethren, "You must be like these dead. You must think nothing of the wrongs men do to you, nor of the praises they offer you. Be like the dead. Thus you may be saved."[5]

Another story says simply: "If you wish to live, become dead, so that you may care neither for the insults of people nor for

4. Hannay, 33.
5. Hannay, 34.

their praise, for the dead care for nothing; in this way you will be able to live."[6]

For All Christians

All Christians must embrace the cross and resurrection daily. For those in different states of life, it is done in different ways. But we must all do it. For monastics it is done through seemingly more outwardly intense expressions of fasting, prayer, asceticism, community life, and ministry. For family members it is done no less intensely through the daily challenge of loving a spouse for richer or poorer, in good times and bad, in sickness and health for life. It is also done in raising children in the same way, in holding down a job we may or may not like to support a family, and in paying off mortgages and bills that pile up with each passing year. I joke with families when I say that most of us are just praying to follow Jesus faithfully as good Catholics, take care of our responsibilities in life, and get out as unscathed as possible!

The Cross Isn't Easy

This life of the cross isn't easy. The cross hurts, even though we know it leads to greater healing and resurrection. We meet with resistance from deep within our old selves at almost every step. We also meet with resistance from without—from the world, worldly Christians, and even from simple circumstances involving otherwise good monastics, Christians, and people in general. These are precisely the times when God sends us a cross for the sake of growth. But that growth through the cross is rarely easy. Otherwise, it wouldn't be a cross at all. But it is only through the cross that we really find resurrection.

6. Budge, 2:105.

On living the cross, Syncletica used the analogy of sailors meeting a headwind or storm. She said that at the beginning of a trip, sailors look for a favorable wind. But they often meet a headwind or a storm later. Just because the wind has turned, they do not throw the cargo overboard or abandon ship. No, they wait a while and struggle against the storm until they can set a direct course again. So when we run into headwinds and storms (and we all do), if we put up the cross for our sail we shall voyage through the world in safety.[7]

These crosses are daily occurrences for the experienced monastic or family member, and they no longer surprise one trained in the way of spiritual battle and victory. They might be big or small. But they are persistent. They are part of real life. This goes on from the moment we enter monastic life until the day we die. This is signified in our daily monastic garb, or the "habit." We wear it from the moment we enter monastic life until the day we pass to our Lord through death.

The Cross and the Monastic Habit

In the time of the desert fathers and mothers, each habit, or monastic clothing, had significance. There is a story that the devil kept tearing the cowl of St. Antony while he slept, so an angel told him to sew it with crosses, and the devil couldn't tear through it. Today, Coptic monks' hoods have crosses to remind them of Jesus, the twelve apostles, and spiritual warfare.

John Cassian and the desert fathers also say that the way of the cross is represented in the clothes of the monk. The habit is simple and poor. It is the garb of a common laborer but is distinct from the world. Each part is practical and symbolic. The monastic hood, or cowl, resembled the headdress worn

---

7. Owen Chadwick, ed. and trans., *Western Asceticism* (Philadelphia: Westminster Press, 1958), 87.

by infants in the fourth and fifth centuries; it was the symbol of being born again after dying with Christ. The scapular that covers neck and shoulders like a work apron is the symbol of a cross. The girdle is a symbol of courage. Monks are to live their lives based on the habit they wear. It is a silent reminder of the cross of Christ. It is a silent call to commitment and an assurance of victory in him. Like us, it speaks by being.

Questions

1) Do you see the reason for dying to the old self in Christ?

2) Do you see the reason for being dead to your ego attachments to self or the world?

3) Do you see crosses as a daily occurrence, or do you want them to happen once and then move on?

4) Do your crosses lead to resurrections, or are you stuck in the cross?

5) Are you childlike or childish in your approach to being "born again"?

19

Repentance and Mercy

After a couple of near-death experiences and seeing the other side at least from a distance, I was stunned with the fact that after all I have done in my monastic life, I am seemingly yet to begin really giving my life to Jesus. I have fallen desperately short. As Francis said at the end of his life, "Brothers, let us now begin, for up until now we have done nothing." I can certainly relate. I needed to repent.

Scripture

The first "sermon" of Jesus was to repent, to turn around. "Repent, for the kingdom of heaven is at hand" (Matt 4:17).

The Greek word used is *metanoia*. It comes from *meta*, or "with" or "against," and *nous*, or "mind," to "think" or "perceive." It basically means to change your mind. But we must do more than just think about a message. We must act upon it. John the Baptist said, "Produce good fruit as evidence of your repentance" (Matt 3:8). It must be a real, life-changing experience!

This repentance must also be heartfelt. It is certainly an objective decision, but it must be far more than that. It must come from deep within the heart and soul. God is close to the broken and contrite of heart (see Ps 51:17).

There is a difference between attrition and contrition. Attrition simply looks to the logic of turning back to God to avoid death. It just makes good sense. This is a good first step, but it isn't complete. We must also be contrite. It must include godly sorrow. We must have a personal *love encounter* with Jesus Christ. It's all about love. God doesn't want only our minds. He wants our hearts.

Broken hearts can feel again. In Psalm 51:19, the Greek word for *contrite* is *suntribo*, which means broken, bruised, crushed, shattered, or just worn down. Sometimes only when a heart is broken do the calluses that have encased it break away so that the heart can really feel again.

This heartfelt contrition is illustrated in the Gospel story of the Pharisee and the tax collector (Luke 18:10-14). The Pharisee did everything right theologically. He seemingly gave God all the glory for not being a sinner. But his heart was still self-righteous. The tax collector cried out only for mercy. Jews considered the tax collector a terrible sinner, the scum of the earth. He had become a traitor to his own people by collecting taxes for the Roman occupiers. But he knew he was a sinner and cried out from his heart for mercy. He was overwhelmed with contrition. And God heard his prayer and not that of the Pharisee.

Penthos

This idea is developed in later Eastern monasticism using the Greek word *penthos*. In Scripture it is *pentheo* and means sorrow with deep mourning and wailing (see, for example, 1 Cor 5:2). It is often translated as "compunction." It is a heartfelt compunction that produces many sighs and tears in the truly repentant Christian. *Penthos* is the simultaneous and overwhelming awareness of our own sin and of God's mercy for us in the gift of Jesus Christ that leads us to tears of sorrow and joy all at once. It is overwhelming and can lead to rapture.

The Desert

The desert fathers, mothers, and hermits lived lives that illustrated this rich gospel tradition. The flight into the desert was itself a radical illustration of changing one's entire way of life. They left the comforts of city and village life for a life of solitude, destitution, and complete reliance upon God and his angels in spiritual or human form in the desert. They did this through many struggles and tears. It is a life that at first glance seems nothing short of miraculous! But it also had a practical, or doable, side.

Many of the stories from the Coptic tradition bring out the repentance involved in *turning from often radical lives of sin* and pleasure to lives of self-renunciation.

Abba Kyriakos the Hermit said, "I have lived in the wilderness for many years and have always longed for solitude so that I may lead a repentant life and not die in my sin."[1]

Some *give up very successful lifestyles* to live as monastics in the desert. Arsenius was a senator. He gave up more than most other monks could imagine to live in the desert. Queen Annasimon the Hermit gave up a royal life as a beloved Christian queen and sought obscurity as a sort of fool for Christ in the lowest place in a female monastery. Once she was discovered and given great honor, she withdrew completely into total solitude in the desert.

Female hermits are often portrayed as turning from a life of harlotry, though some turn from a life of real royal opulence. One anonymous female hermit expressed her desire to give herself completely to the Lord. She said she would go to the place that God would lead her. She went seeking an elder in sackcloth. He was puzzled when he saw her, so she said, "I have left the world to be alone with my Lord, and I have come to you

---

1. Samaan El-Souriany, *The Hermit Fathers* (Putty, Australia: St. Shenouda Press, 2010), 41.

so that you may dress me in the holy 'eskeem' [monastic habit or clothing]." She gave him all that remained with her—money, jewelry, and clothes. When he saw her abundant tears of repentance and her earnest desire to follow the monastic way, he shaved her head, dressed her in the holy "eskeem" and clothed her in a garment made of loofa plant.[2]

The story of *St. Mary the Hermit* is legendary. She was a woman who, after a rebellious start with her parents, gave her life over completely to sexual excess and harlotry. For seventeen years the devil stirred within her disturbing and lustful desires of all kinds. She ended up selling herself as a harlot to some men traveling to Jerusalem. There, after being physically repulsed from the Holy Sepulchre, she had a conversion experience with Mary and Jesus. She repented and gave herself to a life in the desert as a hermit.

The trials and satanic wars that Mary the Hermit faced were severe, and she later said that she trembled when she remembered them. She would beat her chest remembering the day of her repentance, surrendering herself with tears of repentance before the Lord and asking for the intercession of his Virgin Mother St. Mary. After relentless spiritual struggles and many tears, a bright light surrounded her and immediately the devil fled. She then lived in the comfort and security of God's glory.[3]

Despite many profound examples of women, the stories are *mainly of men* who also went through conversion. Some of them repented, not only at the beginning of their monastic life but also after doing their monastic life badly. They came back and ended their lives in saintliness. There are too many such stories to include. But I will mention a couple.

Abba Moussa the Hermit lifted up his hands toward heaven and wept, then threw himself to the ground and rolled in the

2. El-Souriany, 51.
3. El-Souriany, 173–178.

dust. He prayed and cried grievously, "O my Lord Jesus Christ, have mercy upon me, my Lord Jesus Christ, have mercy upon me!" Then our merciful God heard his heartfelt prayers, saw his repentant tears, and heard his sincere confession of sin and humble repentance of life. Jesus Christ willingly accepts everyone who turns to him with sincere repentance.[4]

Abba Timothy the Hermit realized and regretted his sin even as a monk. He cried bitterly. At that moment he imagined death and the severe torment he would face. Jesus told him to escape to the wilderness and cry with tears of repentance over his sins, and he would forgive him! Immediately he got up and obeyed. Eventually the Lord led him to a cave that was situated beside a beautiful palm tree. That tree bore twelve baskets of dates a year, and for thirty years, this alone was his food. When his tunic wore out, God permitted his hair to grow long enough to cover him.[5]

Turning back now to *more mainstream desert father stories,* the tradition continues. The stories of *judging* a monk too harshly are common. Repentance should always be met with forgiveness.

While visiting a community once, Isaac of the Thebaid passed judgment on a sinful brother. When he was returning to his cell, an angel approached him and said, "God sent me to ask you, 'Where do you tell me to send that sinful brother whom you sentenced?'" Isaac repented of his sinful judgment and asked the angel for forgiveness. The angel said, "God has forgiven you. In the future, take care to judge no man before God has judged him."[6]

4. El-Souriany, 75–86.

5. El-Souriany, 191–194.

6. Benedicta Ward, ed., *The Desert Fathers: Sayings of the Early Christian Monks* (New York: Penguin, 2003), 84–85.

Though life in the desert was physically harsh and demanding, the examples of monks who knew how to *treat repentant monastics gently* is a sign of real spiritual fatherhood.

One account tells us that Abba Silvanus, "like a skilled physician," put on the soul of a sinful brother "a poultice made of texts from Scripture, showing him that repentance is available for them who in truth and in charity turn to God."[7]

The example of St. Antony is always paramount and shows how he valued a sinner who repented: A brother expelled from a nearby monastic community because of his sins fled to St. Antony. After spending some time with the monk for healing, Antony sent him back to his home monastery, but upon his return, the brothers immediately drove him out again. He went back quickly to Antony, explaining that his abbot would not receive him. Grieved at their behavior, Antony sent a message to the brothers at the monastery: "A certain vessel suffered a shipwreck at sea, and all her cargo was lost. Yet the sailors brought the ship to land with great labor. Do you wish to now put forth into the deep and sink the ship that has already been rescued?" Ashamed of themselves, the brothers at once welcomed back their brother who had sinned.[8]

Some brothers even went so far as to *feign committing the same sin in the past (usually fornication) as a fellow brother, so as to avoid preaching "down" to him* and to accompany him back to repentance without condescension.[9] Only mature and skilled brothers can do this, but it a powerful witness.

A story shows up more than once of brothers being attacked by thieves, and their peaceful nonresistance pricks the thieves'

---

7. Owen Chadwick, ed. and trans., *Western Asceticism* (Philadelphia: Westminster Press, 1958), 125.

8. See James O. Hannay, *The Wisdom of the Desert* (1904; repr. n.p.: Glass Darkly, 2012), 46–47. Citations refer to the Glass Darkly edition.

9. E. A. W. Budge, ed. and trans., *The Paradise or Garden of the Holy Fathers*, 2 vols. (London: Chatto & Windus, 1907), 2:121.

hearts to repentance.[10] This is not, however, an excuse to keep sinning. There is a difference between *enabling* sin through undue permissiveness and *empowering* the offender through a call to repentance.

Honest confession and true repentance are always preferred to a self-righteous inability to admit our own sins. Abba Poemen said, "I prefer a man who has sinned, and done wickedly, and repented, to the man who has not sinned and has not shown repentance; for the former possesses a humble mind, and the other esteems himself in his thoughts a just man."[11] And Abba Sarmâtâ used to say, "I prefer a man who has sinned, and who knows how to acknowledge his sins, to him that does righteousness, and who says, 'I do what is fair.'"[12]

Do It Today

We must not put off till tomorrow what we can do today. This is true especially of repentance (see Ps 95:7-8). One story recounts that a certain old man used to think, "Let today go by, and repent tomorrow." But another elder would say, "No, not so. I will repent today, and tomorrow shall be as God wills."[13]

Death

At the end of his life St. Francis said, "Brothers, let us begin, for up until now we have done nothing."

I can confess that the older I get and the closer I get to death, the more *I see two things*: first, how far short I have fallen in my Christian life, and my need to repent; and second, the glory we are all able to share through mercy both on earth and in heaven.

10. Budge, 2:42.
11. Budge, 2:23.
12. Budge, 2:140.
13. Budge, 2:140.

I am increasingly aware of how little I have done with the great things God gave me. This moves me to deep repentance and many tears. I am not alone in this experience. It is common to most serious Christians and was certainly the experience of the desert fathers and mothers.

When Abba Sisoes was about to die, his face was shining like the sun. He told the fathers with him that he had been visited by Antony, then the prophets, and then the apostles. "The angels came to take me away," he said, "and I begged them to leave me so that I might stay here a little longer and repent." His companions told him he had no need to repent, and he replied, "*I do not know in my soul if I have rightly begun to repent.*" Here the account notes, "and they all learned that the old man was perfect." Then suddenly his face beamed again like the sun, and all the fathers were afraid. And he said, "Look, look! Behold our Lord comes and says, 'Bring to me the chosen vessel which is in the desert.'" And then he delivered up his spirit, "and he became [like] lightning, and the whole place was filled with a sweet odor."[14]

Questions

1) What does repentance and *metanoia* mean, and how do you do that?

2) Can we repent by our own effort alone, or do we need grace?

3) What is the difference between attrition and contrition, and is one sufficient without the other?

4) What is *penthos*?

14. Budge, 2:177.

5) What are some of the good and bad things the desert fathers and mothers gave up in order to embrace monastic solitude, and how does that apply to you and me?

6) Does the requirement of repentance cause you to be judgmental or merciful?

7) How do you reach out to sinners, and are you willing to really identify with them in order to reach them?

8) Is your life in Jesus prompting others to repent and turn to Jesus?

9) What is the difference between enabling sin and empowering forgiveness?

10) Do you see each passing day of your life as an opportunity for greater repentance?

11) Are you ready to meet God if you died today?

Sorrow and Tears

20

I remember the first time I thought I was going to die. My blood pressure had dropped alarmingly, and a resident nurse took me to the hospital. On the way no one was sure if I'd make it. I remember crying gently as I relived my life. I wasn't sad. I was gently repentant for my shortcomings, and grateful for the many gifts God had poured out on me in my life. All I could do was to gently and quietly weep.

After my more recent experiences with illness, glimpsing the other side, and repentance, I was reduced beyond words or even objective thought before God. This time it hurt to think objective thoughts, and words were simply impossible. All I could do was mumble to myself and God in tongues and weep. This wasn't crying from pain alone. It was pure repentance before God. Afterward I found that tears best expressed what was in my heart.

These tears were for sins and shortcomings, but also that God would forgive me, and let me see his glory. But now the tears were far deeper than the first time. These tears were beyond sorrow or joy. They were both at the same time and more! They were tears of mystery. They were tears of paradox. They were tears of love.

It was with this more recent experience that the desert tradition exploded in my life again. I had read stories of tears and sorrow since the beginning of my conversion over forty years ago. But such tears eluded me, though I wept in my heart. Now the tears flow, and flow frequently, though I try not to make a display of them in public.

The desert fathers and mothers say that sorrow is an essential part of repentance. It is a sorrow that leads to the joy of mercy and forgiveness. Sorrow for sin against God reveals a love relationship between God and us.

As we have seen, *penthos* means a deep and heartfelt compunction for sin. Ironically, it brings both deep compunction for sin and an almost overwhelming joy for mercy that defies description. These are often experienced at the same time in a way that is mysterious and paradoxical. It can never be fully explained. It can be manifested only in tears. And only those who have experienced it know what is meant beyond the words.

Scripture

We find the word *penthos* in Scripture. "He will wipe every tear from their eyes, and there shall be no more death or mourning [*penthos*], wailing or pain, for the old order has passed away" (Rev 21:4).

There is good and bad sorrow. "For godly sorrow produces a salutary repentance without regret, but worldly sorrow produces death" (2 Cor 7:10). The Greek word used for "sorrow" here is *lupe* and really just means "regret." What is the difference between good and bad sorrow? For myself, I have narrowed it down to this: bad sorrow cripples, and good sorrow motivates us to repent and go forward in Christ.

Jesus felt great and almost overwhelming sorrow in the agony in the garden before the Passion, where he, though sinless, bore the sins of the world (see Matt 26:38). But this sorrow led to the joy of the resurrection! Godly sorrow leads to unspeakable joy (see John 16: 20). The word used for Jesus's sorrow is *peri-*

lupos (similar to *lupe*); it means an *exceeding* sorrow. It is not *just* to be filled with sorrow, but to be *very* sorrowful! Sorrow motivated even Jesus, who was without sin yet fully human, to move forward in his ministry. It also created divine empathy with human sorrow.

Joy is also traced back to the cross. "In contrast, the fruit of the Spirit is love, *joy*, peace. . . . Against such there is no law. Now those who belong to Christ Jesus have crucified their flesh with its passions and desires. If we live in the Spirit, let us also follow the Spirit" (Gal 5:22-25).

Through this paradox of finding life in death in Christ, we find the strength to keep going in the face of tough situations and adversity. "We are treated as . . . sorrowful yet always rejoicing" (2 Cor 6:8-10).

Godly sorrow begins in repentance and tears for our shortcomings and sins, and it ends in glory. "Begin to lament, to mourn [*penthos*], to weep. Let your laughter be turned into mourning and your joy into dejection. Humble yourselves before the Lord and he will exalt you" (Jas 4:9-10).

As I advance to the later years of my life, I am overwhelmed by both my sins and the undeserved glory God allows me to share. At every Eucharist I am overwhelmed that Jesus would give his life personally for me and for any sinner. I am reduced to tears of sorrow and joy, all at once. I am reduced to nothing, yet I am motivated to live my life all the more fully for him. The Eucharist can leave me both exhausted and exhilarated. For that reason, I can partake only a few times weekly. Daily is simply too much for me now, though I still recommend daily Eucharist for those who desire it.

The Desert

The desert fathers and mothers knew this far better than I can experience or feebly express. They especially valued the gift and way of tears. We can at least glimpse it.

It was said of Abba Arsenius that as he worked, he kept a handkerchief at his breast "because tears fell so often from his eyes."[1]

A brother asked Abba Ammon the classical opening request: "Speak to me a word." The old man told him to go and meditate "like the criminals in prison." A monk should always be like a criminal waiting for judgment, continually asking himself how he would stand before the judgment seat of Christ. How shall he account for his sins? "If you always meditate like this," Ammon concluded, "you will be saved."[2]

Motivational

But such meditation was not crippling. It was motivating. It made them better monks and disciples of Jesus. It made them better human beings.

Evagrius counseled, "While you sit in your cell, draw in your mind, and remember the day of your death. And then you will see your body mortifying. Think on the loss, feel the pain. Shrink from the vanity of the world outside. Be retiring, and careful to keep your vow of quiet, and you will not weaken. Remember the souls in hell. Meditate within on their condition, the bitter silence and the moaning, the fear and the strife, the waiting and the pain without relief, the tears that cannot cease to flow."[3]

Here, sorrow produces tears. These tears are *essential* to developed desert spirituality. Some fathers wept so much that it actually wore creases in their cheeks. Tears are not some peripheral aspect of desert spirituality. They are common and even essential.

1. Owen Chadwick, ed. and trans., *Western Asceticism* (Philadelphia: Westminster Press, 1958), 43.
2. Chadwick, 43–44.
3. Chadwick, 44.

But it was not all negative. We are also to mediate on heaven and glory. Evagrius continues that we should also remember the day of resurrection: "Bring before your eyes the good laid up for the righteous, their confidence before God the Father and Christ his Son, before angels and archangels and the powers, and all the people: the kingdom of heaven and its gifts, joy and rest."[4]

Evagrius concludes his counsel with a balance of sorrow and joy. He says to remember both, not just one or the other. "Weep and lament for the judgment of sinners, bring to life the grief they suffer; be afraid that you are hurrying toward the same condemnation. [But also] rejoice and exult at the good laid up for the righteous. Aim at enjoying the one, and being far from the other. Do not forget it, whether you are in your cell or abroad. Keep these memories in your mind and so cast out of it the sordid thoughts which harm you."[5]

St. Bonaventure spoke of this balance before St. Francis was stigmatized with the marks of Jesus Crucified in his hands, feet, and side. He spoke of a *mixture* of sorrow and joy. They happened all at once as a paradox and propelled Francis into a mystical rapture that culminated in his stigmatization in Christ. The desert fathers paved the way for this.

Essential

Sorrow is *essential* to being a monk. I will confess that I understood this as an *idea* when I was young. But it is only in recent years that this has begun to drop from my head to my heart. I am most blessed that God has allowed me this small experience of what the greats experienced more fully.

4. Chadwick, 44.
5. Chadwick, 44.

Abba Poemen told Abba Anub that unless a man puts to death all his self-will and possesses holy grief, "he cannot be a monk."[6] He continued, "Grief is twofold: it works good, and it keeps out evil."[7] Holy sorrow motivates us to do good, and spurn evil. It is motivational and positive, not negative and crippling.

Good and Bad Sorrow

St. Syncletica also addresses the two kinds of sorrow. She said that there is a useful sorrow and a destructive sorrow. Sorrow is useful when we weep for sin and for our neighbor's ignorance, so that we may not relax our purpose to attain to true goodness. These are the true kinds of sorrow. Our enemy sends sorrow without reason, which is called acedia, the noonday devil, or dejection that leads to boredom. But we can always drive out a spirit like this with prayer and psalmody.[8]

Not Automatic

Sorrow is not automatic or unceasing. It is something we *grow into*. Later commentators distinguish the *gift* of tears, which happens to us as an overwhelming grace, and the *way* of tears, which is maintained by meditation. The former is beyond our control and is overwhelming. Diodochus of Photike says that it is impossible to minister while under this first anointing. The second is under our control (see 1 Cor 14:32) and is a constant attitude and gentle experience.

For myself, I often now find myself overwhelmed seemingly out of nowhere. A line from the liturgy, receiving the Blessed Sacrament, or just sitting before the tabernacle can cause me to simply be overwhelmed and reduced to nothing. At these

6. Chadwick, 45.
7. Chadwick, 45.
8. Chadwick, 120.

times I cannot speak or keep my composure. It can be quite embarrassing. So I try to hide such things as best I can. This is more like the gift of tears.

Stable

But the *way* of tears produces a sorrow that should be *stable*, and not come and go based on external experiences alone. It is emotional, but not emotionalism. One young monk went to talk with an elder and said that when he was alone in his cell he was sorrowful, but the sorrow left him when others visited him. The old man said he was not yet stable in sorrow and only used it as a transitory and expedient feeling.[9] So deeper, godly sorrow is not just a feeling that comes and goes. It becomes a state of heart and mind.

But caution: When we have this state of heart and mind, it doesn't mean that we should never go out of our cells or entertain visiting monks. "When visitors come, we ought to welcome them and celebrate with them. When we are by ourselves, we need to be sorrowful."[10]

Sorrow Matures

This also *matures as we grow* over the course of many years. Syncletica said that Christians are like someone trying to light a fire. Initially, smoke gets into our eyes, and we begin to cry. But we succeed in starting the fire. Syncletica quoted the Letter to the Hebrews—"Our God is a consuming fire" (12:29)—and said, "and so we must kindle the fire of God with tears and trouble."[11] Only then can a roaring fire of enthusiasm and charismatic praise

9. Chadwick, 136.
10. Chadwick, 144.
11. Chadwick, 46.

be built up and hot coals of contemplation be established that calmly heat the house of our souls.

Many monastics and spiritual seekers *long for tears, but they do not come*. It is a way that comes for those who seek, but it may take time and experience to understand. I know that is how it has worked for me. One ancient account tells us, "A brother asked an old man: 'I hear the old men weeping, and my soul longs for tears: but they do not come, and my soul is troubled.' And the old man said: 'The children of Israel entered the promised land after forty years in the wilderness. Tears are like the promised land. If you have reached them already you will no longer be afraid of the conflict. For thus God wills that the soul be afflicted, that it may ever long to enter that country."[12]

Initial and Mature

So we must pass from *initial tears to mature tears*. Often this means an almost uncontrollable weeping for sins at the beginning of our conversion to Christ. This is followed by dryness, and we have to find a weeping of the heart that only occasionally manifests in external tears. Finally, we find a weeping heart that manifests in frequent tears that are gentle and controlled.

As we mature, initial tears alternate from sorrow to joy and merge into a paradoxical and indescribable weeping of sorrow and joy all at once. For myself, I think God has only gradually let me see both the enormity of my sins and the infinite abyss of his forgiveness and love that leaves me in indescribable tears of gratitude and joy. If I saw my sins all at once, I would have been overcome, given up, and been unable to make progress. If I saw the fullness of forgiveness for them all at the beginning, I would have been so awestruck that I would have been completely rapt and unable to stay in this world. So God allows us to grow in

12. Chadwick, 48.

our awareness of this mystery bit by bit, as we are able to process it and mature in Christ. Then we can move forward as we mature and are capable of perceiving such mysteries. This is all because of God's goodness, mercy, and love.

Questions

1) What is *penthos*?

2) How is sorrow and joy found in *penthos* for you?

3) Do you allow yourself to weep when meditating on Jesus?

4) Is your sorrow motivating or crippling?

5) Do you also meditate on the positive things of God and heaven?

6) Have you grown in a powerful experience of *penthos*?

7) Are you patient in growing in *penthos*?

21

Gluttony and Fasting

> "Abba Pambo asked Abba Antony: 'What shall
> I do?' The old man replied, '. . . Keep your
> tongue and your belly under control."
>
> —Quoted in Owen Chadwick,
> *Western Asceticism*

I've always been rather thin. But I have the propensity to eat too much simply because I love food! When that happens, I put on weight. And I have! This usually happens a pound or two a year as I slowly indulge my appetite. It is not until it is out of control that I notice. Only with the help of a strict, prepackaged weight loss system did I shed the weight. Like an alcoholic, I say that I am a *recovering* glutton, not that I am no longer a glutton! All that to say that I personally understand the struggle with food and being overweight. And when my body is thin, my spirit stays energetic and bright.

Gluttony is defined by the desert masters as eating more than you need at any meal and eating between meals without need. Most of us are guilty of gluttony under that definition! Gluttony is a little, almost unnoticeable sin. Even in a monastery, who's going to monitor a person's eating habits to such a point? Few will say anything about the extra food on the plate or going back for unnecessary second helpings. (But they might notice it!) The fact is, each of us must monitor ourselves about such things.

We saw in the chapter on Thoughts and Demons that the desert fathers adopted the Evagrian use of eight thoughts. Cassian modified it somewhat. Both Evagrius and Cassian begin the list with gluttony and call it one of the three that lead the way to the others. This surprises most Westerners today. Why is such a seemingly small temptation listed first? It is because small temptations give way to bigger temptations if left unchecked. Small venial sins give way to big mortal sins if left unchecked.

Specifically, the fathers link gluttony with temptations to sexual sin. They learned this from experience. When you cannot control your desire to eat and drink, this often stimulates the flesh and opens the door to sexual temptations and other sins of the flesh. Big carnality usually begins with small carnality. Control the small, and you can overcome the great.

Gluttony is eventually defined by Cassian as eating to the point of being completely full or overfull and eating between meals unnecessarily. The remedy for gluttony is simple: moderate fasting. Cassian doesn't recommend long fasting periods of complete abstinence. He says they discovered this also stirs up gluttony at the end of the more extreme fast. So Cassian recommends that the average monk eat daily but moderately. Only the advanced can fast more completely. But his definition of "moderate" would be considered "extreme" by most modern Westerners today.

The Rule of Benedict says there are one or two meals daily, each with two cooked dishes, fruit and vegetables if available, and a generous serving of bread (RB 39.1-4). In Lent there is only one meager meal daily. Today, few Benedictines adhere to this diet strictly and eat three square meals daily for health reasons.

The diet of the desert was far simpler. Scholars say that desert monastics ate bread that they allowed to harden, so it needed to be eaten after soaking it in water. They also ate dates, dried figs, olives, lentils, chickpeas, and herbs, depending on what was most available around their hermitages. They even ate salted fish. It was very simple. Only later would communities develop larger gardens. Today the monasteries of Egypt have rather extensive farms due to the government assistance after President Anwar Sadat allowed them to sink deep water wells. Since then the desert has truly blossomed. But they still maintain a simple diet.

After the establishment of more common rules, meals were eaten at the ninth hour, or three o'clock in the afternoon. A light snack might be allowed before bedtime. While this sounds radical to modern ears, it was not all that uncommon in the ancient past when food was less abundant. By the time of the Rule of Benedict, eating was simple but moderate. Indeed, some would argue that the monastic was guaranteed a regularity of food, clothing, and shelter that many poor folk in the world had to really struggle to maintain.

Modern Westerners love to eat and drink, and our epidemic of obesity and related health problems gives evidence to this addictive obsession. In our culture, we have access to varieties of food and delights that were unimaginable even to the royalty of ages in the not-so-distant past. We are bombarded by commercials about delicious food every time we watch TV or a movie. But don't be fooled. If you think it, and if you play with and entertain the thought, you will eventually do it unless you intentionally dismiss it. You can also just turn off the TV! You might discover better images and entertainment in the holiness of the Spirit of Jesus Christ!

Desert Specifics

The earlier desert fathers and mothers often fasted for days on end. The Spirit-bearing wanderers ate only what the meager grass and moisture of the desert provided. But this was not a goal or an end unto itself. It was only a tool to overcome gluttony and the greater lusts of the flesh it excited.

The exact regimen was originally left to the monk and his or her spiritual father or mother. We often hear the caution to be *moderate* and to stay focused on the spiritual life, rather than on fasting alone. Fasting was not viewed as a kind of athletic competition. *Discretion* was needed.

Abba Antony said that some wear down their bodies by fasting and other practices. But because they do not have discretion, it actually puts them further from God.[1]

Interconnected

Cassian brings out the classical connection between gluttony and sexual sin. The traditional teaching of the desert fathers for brothers is that too much food excites sexual lust and is manifested in lustful dreams or illicit sexual acts. He links this with too much variety and quantity in food that excites desire. So this involves not only quantity but variety. This is pretty tough in a culture like ours, where such a wide array of types of food from all around the world are availiable by a simple drive down the street or delivered to your door at the touch of a smartphone.

But after sounding radical to our modern ears, he returns to a pretty *moderate* teaching that is quite practical. Food is simply to support life. It is also a doorway to desire. In other words, we eat to live, not live to eat. Personally I believe we can enjoy food without getting lustful about it. We shouldn't be daydreaming about it between meals in a way that keeps us from our daily duties and relationships.

A clear and simple rule of the Fathers is to *stop eating while still hungry* and not to continue until you are stuffed. Such a clear solution is hard to beat. It would solve much of today's excesses by its comfortable and easy moderation. A good rule

1. Owen Chadwick, ed. and trans., *Western Asceticism* (Philadelphia: Westminster Press, 1958), 105.

is to push away from the table while still a bit hungry but full enough to sustain health.

Cassian emphasizes the *interconnectedness* of gluttony and lust. Self-control and fasting are especially important for bringing about the specific purity of soul that comes through restraint and moderation. He also says that no one whose stomach is full can fight mentally against the demon of unchastity.

Fasting

The fathers also get practical in a way more doable for most modern monastics and Christians in general. Some fast more extremely but recommend a *daily moderate fast* based on their experience as elders.

Abba Joseph asked Abba Poemen, "How should we fast?" And Abba Poemen said he would have everyone eat *a little less than he wants every day*. Abba Joseph asked if he fasted more when he was younger? And the old man said that he used to fast three days on end, even for a week. But, he said, the great elders had tested all these things and found that it was good to eat something every day, but on some days to eat a little less. "They have shown us," he said, "that this is the 'king's highway,' for it is easy and light."[2]

One desert mother said the devil sends a *severe fast that is too long*. The devil's disciples do this as well by appearing to be holy men and women. How do we distinguish the fasting of God from the fasting of the devil? Clearly the difference is moderation. "Throughout your life, then, you ought to keep an unvarying rule of fasting. Do you fast four or five days on end and then lose your spiritual strength by eating a feast" at the end of the fast? That makes the devil happy. Extremes are destructive. "So do not suddenly throw away your armour, or you

2. Chadwick, 115.

may be found unarmed in the battle and made an easy prisoner. Our body is like armour, our soul like the warrior. Take care of both, and you will be ready for what comes."[3]

Wine

The use of *wine* comes up regularly in monastic teaching.

Abba Poemen taught that wine is not for monks.[4] St. Benedict wrote later, "We read that monks should not drink wine at all, but since the monks of our day cannot be convinced of this, let us at least agree to drink moderately, and not to the point of excess, for *wine makes even wise men go astray* (Sir 19:2)" (RB 40.6-7). So, we may use it, but not abuse it.

Culinary Arts

Many monasteries have become famous for great cooking and bakery recipes that are sometimes marketed to the secular world with great success. We have our Little Portion Bakery. This isn't a bad thing unless the monastics give in to gluttony and avarice as a result. The desert fathers and mothers address monastics getting too caught up in preparing food and drink. I've seen our own monastics become almost obsessive about cooking food for the monks' table. Fasting helps control and settle the pleasures of the flesh that take us away from God.

Syncletica addresses this. She said that the pleasures of the wealthy world must not seduce us, as if they are actually necessary or useful. Because of this pleasure, she said, "honor the art of cooking. But by rigorous fasting, you should trample on those pleasures. Never be sated with bread, nor want wine."[5]

3. Chadwick, 120–121.
4. Chadwick, 53.
5. Chadwick, 55–56.

Abba Hyperichius said that just as donkeys are terrified of lions, so *temptations are terrified of a monk who fasts in moderation.* He said, "Fasting is the monk's rein over sin. . . . When the monk's body is dried up with fasting, it lifts his soul from the depths. Fasting dries up the channels down which worldly pleasures flow."[6]

One old man said, "Ever since I became a monk, I have never taken my fill of bread, or water, or sleep; and because I am tormented by desire for food, I cannot feel the pricks of lust."[7]

Judgment

But after extoling fasting as a remedy for the temptations of the flesh, Hyperichius qualifies this by *warning against those who scrupulously keep external fasting while not fasting from judgment of others.* He says it is better to eat meat and drink wine and not judge or disparage others than to fast and continue to do so. This places the authentic spiritual goal squarely before our eyes.[8]

Humility, Love, and Discretion

Humility and love are always the goal of one's spiritual life in Christ. Fasting isn't ignored or jettisoned in favor of the spiritual. It is simply kept in the *proper context* of the spiritual goal.

Jesus summarizes the general *problem of religiosity* when he says, "Woe to you, scribes and Pharisees, you hypocrites. You pay tithes of mint and dill and cumin, and have neglected the weightier things of the law: judgment and mercy and fidelity. But these you should have done, without neglecting the others.

6. Chadwick, 56.
7. Chadwick, 69.
8. Chadwick, 56.

Blind guides, who strain out the gnat and swallow the camel!" (Matt 23:23-24).

Discretion, or discernment and moderation, are the key in all of this. In one account we read: "An old man was asked by a brother: 'How do I find God? With fasts, or labor, or watchings, or works of mercy?' The old man replied: 'In all that you have said, and in discretion. Even if our mouths stink with fasting [bad breath], and we have learnt all the Scriptures, and memorized the whole Psalter, we still lack what God wants—humility and charity.'"[9]

If we are really on fire with the Spirit of God, we will fulfill the ascetical disciplines like fasting and even surpass the minimum requirements of church and monastic community, but always with joy and great love for others that *avoids judging* or speaking against those who are not able to do so themselves. As St. Paul says, "Live by the Spirit and you will certainly not gratify the desire of the flesh" (Gal 5:16).

Abba Joseph said, "If you will, you could become all fire."[10]

Questions

1) Do you tend to overly fast and then binge at the end, or do you eat moderately day in and day out?

2) Do you eat too much at a single meal and between meals?

3) How do you respond to advertisements about food?

4) Do you see the connection between temptation to a small sin like gluttony and the other greater ones?

9. Chadwick, 125.
10. Chadwick, 142.

5) Do you see the connection between external actions and inner dispositions?

6) Do you drink alcohol too freely?

7) Is fasting enough if we still carry inner judgments against others?

8) Are you on fire with the Holy Spirit who empowers us in fasting and virtue?

22

Sexual Sin

I am older, but I was once young. Just like anyone else, I struggled with sexual lust. But sexual lust doesn't haunt me like it once did. I am grateful. Now I can love people for simply being people, rather than for how sexually attractive or dangerous they are. This has been most liberating for me. But it still occasionally arises.

I heard a story in which an old monk was visited by the wife from whom he'd separated to become a monk and who had subsequently become a nun. Now that they were both very old, she wanted to visit her husband one more time before they died. When the brothers went and told the old monk that his wife had come to pay her respects one more time before they died, he refused to see her. This happened three times! Finally they asked why he would not see her. He said, "Brothers, you don't understand. The coals are still warm!" This story teaches us that we never completely outgrow the capacity to be tempted to sexual lust.

We live in a sexually promiscuous and perverse culture. Pornography bombards us through TV, movies, and the internet. Wrong is now right, and right is now wrong.

This brings us to our next thought, sexual sin. One of the Greek words used for this is *porneia*. It broadly means adultery, fornication, intercourse with animals, intercourse with close relatives (see Matt 19:9, and, for example, Lev 18 and Rom 1:26-27). It's the root of the word *pornography*.

There is a *connection between gluttony and sexual sin*. There is a logic to it. Indulging little temptations gives rise to bigger temptations. And when big temptations are not remedied, they give birth to sin. Little carnalities open the door to big carnalities, and big carnalities kill us both spiritually and physically (see Jas 1:14-15).

Scripture

Jesus is clear that the sexual immorality begins in the thoughts (see Matt 5:27-28). The battle for the soul is in the mind (see Matt 15:19-20). But he also encourages the courageous and energetic avoidance of the occasion for sin. He tells us metaphorically to gouge out our eyes or cut off our hands if they are occasions for sin (see Matt 5:29-30; also Rom 13:14).

Contrary to modern belief, the habitual surrender to sexually indulgent practices is not harmless or simply a private matter. These actions have *serious consequences*. They keep us from communion with God (see 1 Cor 6:9-10).

The Desert

The desert fathers and mothers were no strangers to battling sexual thoughts and demons. Some came from backgrounds of promiscuity and even prostitution. Once they renounced their old ways of life, they often had to fight for years with their thoughts as the place of demonic temptation.

Mary of Egypt fled a life of promiscuity and prostitution to live as a hermit in the desert by the shores of the Jordan River. Her memory was filled with tempting images of sexual pleasure for seventeen years! She cried out for mercy, and she was finally given an extraordinary mystical light by Christ.

This reminds us of St. Augustine in the West, who spoke of seeing dancing girls in his thoughts, dreams, and memories after giving up a life of sexual promiscuity. The truly great saints were never afraid to openly admit their faults and failings, and to ask for prayer from their brothers and sisters.

In the desert a brother asked an old man what to do to overcome his sexual thoughts. He answered that when the demons bring such thoughts and excite the feelings, "do not hold converse with your soul," that is, he should not respond or entertain their suggestion. "Though the demons are careful to send in thoughts," the old man said, "they do not force you. It is yours to receive or reject."[1]

The biblical lists of serious sins include fornication, along with other sins such as anger, slander, and lying. St. Paul tells us that those who give themselves over habitually to this behavior have essentially renounced God (see 1 Cor 6:10). But this should not confuse us. *Fornication is often more difficult to overcome than other sins.* It is primordial.

When a brother said that slander was worse than fornication, Abba Mathois responded, "Slander is bad, but it is curable quickly; the slanderer can do penitence and say, 'I have spoken ill,' and it is over. But lust is essential death."[2]

Thoughts

These temptations often come as *memories or fantasies* in the mind, even after we have renounced frequent social interaction with those to whom we are attracted.

A brother told an elder of his temptations by sexual thoughts, "memories of mine which trouble me with their pictures of women." The old man told him, "Fear not the dead, but flee the living—flee from assenting to sin or committing sin, and take a longer time over your prayers."[3] This sounds simplistic, but

---

1. Owen Chadwick, ed. and trans., *Western Asceticism* (Philadelphia: Westminster Press, 1958), 69.

2. Chadwick, 62.

3. Chadwick, 62.

prayer causes our minds to dwell on the holy, and you cannot think two things, the holy and the unholy, at once.

Acts

But sometimes this doesn't work, and even monastics fall into *acts of fornication*. Surprisingly, there are ample ancient stories about such falls by the desert fathers and mothers. Unfortunately, such occurrences are not uncommon in our own day. Compassion is needed.

Sometimes one who has not fallen into fornication feigns having done so in order to accompany one back to penance and forgiveness. This is extreme, but it is powerful! This happened in the case of two brothers who shared a cell. When the ruse was discovered, the elders said this was a way for one brother to lay down his soul for the other.[4]

Struggle

The battle against lust can be fierce and unremitting. Abbess Sarah struggled with lust for thirteen years. She never prayed to be released from the struggle, but only for the strength to battle successfully. She succeeded. Then the demon of lust tried to tempt her back into his grip through pride at winning the battle. She renounced this, saying "It is not I who have beaten you, but my Lord the Christ."[5]

Revelation of Thoughts

One of the greatest tools in the desert against the demon of lust was the *revelation of tempting thoughts* to one's spiritual

---

4. Chadwick, 67–68.
5. Chadwick, 63.

father, mother, or elder. One story tells of a brother who was troubled by lust. He told his temptations to an old man, and the old man consoled him. Tempted further, he returned to the old man again and again. The man encouraged him to keep returning to talk about his temptations, saying, "Nothing troubles the demon of lust more than disclosure of his [temptations]. Nothing pleases him more than the concealment of the temptation."[6]

In another story, a brother actually committed fornication with women during a trip to town. The father simply asks if the brother is repentant. He then does something that is part of good spiritual direction. He offers to *carry half the burden* with the brother. This helps to lighten the load for the brother.[7]

Pass the Thoughts By

We are also encouraged to simply let the tempting thought pass by, without giving it *too much unnecessary attention*. Sometimes obsessing about a temptation makes it far worse. It is like throwing gas on a fire. The old man in the above account concludes by saying that we cannot stop the tempting thoughts altogether. That is part of life. But we do have the power to fight them. So we shouldn't be overly concerned when they arise. Simply fight them and move on.

One father compared temptations to the enticing smells of cooking food wafting from a restaurant as we pass. We should learn to simply walk on by, ignoring the desire to go in and eat. "We cannot make temptations vanish," he said, "but we can struggle against them."[8]

6. Chadwick, 63.
7. Chadwick, 184.
8. Chadwick, 64.

Don't Dally

So we are *not to "dally" with thoughts*.[9] Having temptations is not sin. Entertaining them and dallying with them is. One old man saw a demon playing with the disciple as the disciple dallied with tempting thoughts.[10] Later fathers would develop this and say that the demons have the power to excite our flesh by actually touching it. The same old man also saw the disciple's angel frowning, because the disciple was not sufficiently fighting against the temptation.[11] There are unseen real spiritual forces at work all around us, and they are personal! Let's make sure that our angels are smiling and glorifying God because of our thoughts and actions in Christ.

Struggles against thoughts and demons of lust are harmful, but even they do not overcome the eventual good that God brings to us through all things when we approach them with faith (Rom 8:28). Also, the need to struggle against them is experienced not only by those beginning monasticism in the desert, but also by the advanced. Beginners couldn't deal with the more advanced battles. Only the advanced have the experience for such spiritual struggle.[12]

There are *no magical answers* to such temptations. We simply go through the process, using the tools at our disposal. One brother said that he fought temptations with the prescribed tools, but never felt any consolation at all. The father simply said, "Go on meditating."[13]

The reality is that such *thoughts have no power over us, unless we give into them*. Then they can get stronger. One old man said that when we push back against the lustful thoughts that

9. Chadwick, 65.
10. Chadwick, 65.
11. Chadwick, 65.
12. Chadwick, 65.
13. Chadwick, 70.

come at us, they are brittle as papyrus and break easily, but if we dally with them, they become hard as iron.[14]

The fathers say that the desire for fornication *never really goes away completely, but it can be imprisoned.*[15]

Cassian's Remedies

Cassian treats the cause and provides the remedy. He says that *bodily fasting is not enough.* It must be accompanied by contrition of heart, intense prayer to God, frequent meditation on the Scriptures, toil and manual labor, accompanied with great humility. One must constantly guard the heart from base thoughts.

The cure? *Rebuttal.* This is usually described as an energetic rebuke of the demon or thought with the name of Jesus. He uses the analogy of *cutting off the serpent's head* before its body gets in the house of the soul. In other words, nip sexual thoughts in the bud before they take hold and become more difficult to expel from our souls.

Cassian gets practical regarding how to fight the demon of fornication. His answer? Since most fantasies happen at night, get up and pray! If you need to, get out of bed, *go to the church, and keep vigil!* It's more difficult to sin there. Simple, but effective.

The other remedy is *manual labor.* Hard work for God during the day leaves little time or energy for the devil afterward. This is a time-tested remedy that works, at least most of the time. But it isn't the only remedy.

I add one other: an *enthusiastic, charismatic prayer life* that releases energy in our love for God in a way beyond objective thought or words. Sexuality involves the use of energy. When we use all our energy for God, there isn't much left for sin. We fight

14. Chadwick, 70.
15. Chadwick, 108.

fire with fire and passion with passion. The power of the Spirit simply expels all demonic foes if used rightly. I have heard that St. Symeon the New Theologian says that one who participates in the divine Spirit is freed from all passionate lusts.

But the Spirit must sometimes be stirred up beyond conceptual thought by praying in tongues. Plus, we overcome the body with holy uses of the body. Raise your hands to God either standing or on bended knee. It isn't automatic. It is an act of the will. When we get busy doing the dos, we simply don't have the time or energy to do the don'ts!

The Eastern fathers eventually employed *metanies, or prostrations*. This means prostrating fully on the floor and getting back up. A great schema monk, or the few who have entered the most advanced stage of monastic life in reclusion, do five hundred a day. Some do more! Well, this takes a lot of energy. It is literally a prayer calisthentic for Christ!

Cautions

But there is a healthy warning here as well. Evagrius warned that we must also be careful not to unintentionally "turn the very antidote of passion into passion."[16] This can become spiritual gluttony in itself. We first overcome one passion with the passionate use of religous practice. But in the long run it can stir up another passion, albeit under the guise of religous practice. This should be discerned with one's spiritual father, mother, or elder.

The Logic of Love

Sometimes it is *logic that conquers*. In the stark realization of what an action actually brings, the demon is defeated. With lust

---

16. Evagrius Ponticus, *The Praktikos and Chapters On Prayer*, trans. John Eudes Bamberger (Collegeville, MN: Cistercian Publications, 1972), 57.

and fornication, we should calmly consider what the church teaches about Christian sexual life. There are *three character-istics of holy sexual relations:* (1) they are mutually self-giving; (2) they happen in the context of marriage; and (3) they include the possibility of procreation under ordinary circumstances. This rules out many practices commonly espoused in modern culture today.

St. Francis suffered from a temptation of sexual lust that lasted several years. He tried all the ascetical disciplines. They didn't work. He finally reasoned that if he had sex with a woman, she would eventually have children. That meant he should get married. That meant getting a secular job. When he looked at the logic of it, he realized that this wasn't the life he wanted. Then the lust disappeared! There are similar desert stories.[17]

Sometimes we must simply think it through. What actually happens to us when we give in to sexual lust? Is this really what we want? For any serious Christian, the answer is "no!" Sometimes that is enough to defeat this demon.

Questions

1) Are you affected by the sexual immorality that is so com-monplace in today's media?

2) Are you aware of how giving in to small, almost unnoticed temptations can lead to greater ones?

3) Do you understand the connection between thoughts and actions?

---

17. E. A. W. Budge, ed. and trans., *The Paradise or Garden of the Holy Fathers*, 2 vols. (London: Chatto & Windus, 1907), 2:127.

4) Do you employ appropriate external discipline in relationships?

5) Are you inspired to action by the radical examples of those in the desert who repented from a life of fornication?

6) Do you understand that sins like fornication cut us off from a full communion with God?

7) Are you forgiving with those who fall into habitual temptation and sin?

8) Do you give up when sexual temptations seem relentless, going on for years and even decades?

9) Do you practice the revelation of thoughts with a spiritual father or mother in your battle against lust?

10) Do you dally or play with tempting thoughts of sexual sin?

11) Are you aware that temptation is a source of greater victory in Christ?

12) Do you use the traditional remedies of work and charismatic prayer against this temptation?

13) Do you dally with sexual thoughts?

14) Do you use the power of rebuke, or rebuttal, against such temptations?

15) Are you on fire with the Spirit of God when facing such temptations?

Avarice and Poverty

The third of the eight thoughts is avarice, or the need to possess and control. This involves things, situations, and people. It is remedied by living in a community under a rule and an abbot, or spiritual father or mother. For those who don't live in monasteries, it is overcome by living among one's family, in a parish community, or in what our community calls cell groups, or small groups and ministries under a pastor, spiritual director, or superior. If approached with the right attitude, even daily life in the workplace can cure it.

It is often thought that avarice is primarily connected to possessions and wealth as contrasted to gospel poverty. This is certainly the most common experience of it. I have written rather extensively about the practical reasons for simple living in my previous books.

But it also refers to possessiveness or control. That means control of things, people, and situations. So avarice is far-reaching indeed. It is applicable to those who live in communities of consecrated life and those who live in the world.

I have always been comfortable with simple living. We were not a well-to-do family and learned to live simply, but with fun. I can remember our "fun" gravy and bread nights when I was growing up. Little did I know that the reason for the "fun" night was because there was no other food in the house! But we kids didn't know, and mom and dad made it fun.

One hard lesson came on a day when I kept throwing baseballs over my dad's head and into the creek. Finally he took out his wallet, pulled out a dollar bill, and ripped it in two, saying that every time I lost a ball it was like ripping up money. Whoa! I knew my dad was angry. But that's the only time I saw his frustration and anger over money worries. My parents were far from perfect, but they were still amazing considering how poor we were. I will always love them for it.

This simple living became intentional when I began to follow Jesus in integrated monastic life. I have had the pleasure to generate millions of dollars for the poor and for our community, but I have never had the desire to live in more than a hermit's cell. Community life requires the sacrifice of possessions and simple living.

Before I encountered monastic and Franciscan ways of life, I always desired a simple life in a small cabin or old farmhouse. The rock 'n' roll life of opulence and fame I encountered in Los Angeles always turned me off. I saw it as empty and witnessed the futility of it in the personal lives of many friends who opted for it. I was more interested in spirituality. I was curious about the Mennonite and early Quaker traditions. I was especially interested in the Old Order Mennonites and Amish, and I enjoyed visiting what I could see of their communities in northern Indiana. Plus, they made some really great baked goods!

But I also got rather scrupulous. I was an avid environmentalist and organic gardener. While these are good things and still interest me, they boomeranged and had a negative effect on me. Soon I was so concerned about the environmental and social consequences of even the most basic things of life, I couldn't really enjoy much of anything.

Then I met the Franciscans, who knew how to make gospel poverty fun. They taught me that we could still go to the dollar matinees down the street from the friary on Saturdays as a community and really enjoy ourselves. One friar even, God forbid, humorously confessed to me that he snuck in sodas and chips because he refused to pay the outrageous prices at the concession stand! And no, I didn't follow suit. But I had to learn how to lighten up again, and the friars taught me how to balance a real commitment to simple living with the joy *of* living. I am most grateful for that gift!

Later in my role as a founder, I also had leadership thrust upon me. It was a responsibility and duty that I simply could not evade. This occurred in ministry and in community. This changed my purely personal approach to poverty to meeting the physical and spiritual needs of an entire community. Therefore, I had to grapple with the balance between good stewardship and the apparent need to control things and people. This was especially tough for me.

By nature I am withdrawn and isolated. I had to learn these skills, and it took me decades to even minimally get the hang of it. The trick is to completely let everything go to God and to become a good steward at the same time. For myself, I learned this only after repeated failures, many tears, and getting the ego-stuffing knocked out of me repeatedly, usually through failed community projects and relationships. These are tough lessons indeed. And at older age, I still don't believe I have the hang of it. But I'm still trying!

We live in a consumerist culture. We enjoy more materialistic comforts and pleasures than dreamed imaginable by even the royalty of past generations. Electricity, transportation, and mass production changed everything. Ice cream and iced drinks alone were unheard of for the average person until the recent age of refrigeration. Central heating and air conditioning are now taken for granted, and the ability to travel the world is only now becoming commonplace. I remember how at the beginning of my ministry only the richest of the rich got to travel by air to far-off places. Now it seems like almost everyone does it.

Some of this is a blessing. Some is a curse, for it comes with a price tag that is both subtle and beyond what most of us are ready to pay. This is true on a global, environmental level, and personally. We are often consumed by what we consume. We are often possessed by our possessions. And the more things we possess, the more we can become objects ourselves. We are robbed of our true humanity.

We are also a people who try to control people, situations, and things. This includes other people, corporations, and even nature. We try to control our bodies by sheer ego. The need to control works sometimes, but most of the time it does not. We are not God! This leads those who egotistically still want to be God into frustration, anger, and the other thoughts that follow.

Scripture

There are three basic paradigms of gospel poverty in the New Testament. One is complete renunciation of all goods; we find calls to this in Matthew 10 and 19. Another is holding all things in common, as we see in Acts 2 and 4. And a third is using our right to private property in a way that brings equality to all; we are exhorted to this in 2 Corinthians 8. The first was lived by St. Antony of the Desert and St. Francis; the second was lived by St. Augustine, St. Basil, and St. Benedict; and the third is lived by the average Christian. All three challenge our status quo to the core. They are all designed to free us from avarice in a way proper to one's state of life.

Community, Rule, and Abbot

John Cassian said that avarice is overcome by living in community under a monastic rule and spiritual father or mother. There is a reason for this. You cannot hang on to possessions or control situations or people in a monastery. In monastic life everything is for God and others. And we come specifically to relinquish our self-will, the old person who wants to control possessions, situations, or people. In community we let go of all that on purpose, by an act of our will. When we join a monastery, we freely choose a community where this transformation can happen and a spiritual father or mother who guides us in the process. So it is undertaken freely and with trust. It is an act of faith.

Personal Possessions

The desert fathers demanded relinquishing personal possessions to become part of a colony of hermits or community of monks. Hermits had to have a few basic things in their cells in order to work with their hands, prepare frugal meals, and pray. But it was minimal even by their own culture's standards. Food, clothing, and shelter for the first monks of desert were poor, but they met their basic needs. Gospel poverty is foundational to overcoming avarice.

This reminds us of saints of the West like St. Francis, who has become legendary for his poverty. There are many stories of his giving away his religious habit, his mantle, or wraparound coat, or even Gospel books and altar dressings to the poor. He said that giving away the Gospel speaks more loudly of its contents than hanging on to a Gospel book and not living it. The desert fathers agree.

Books

Abba Evagrius said that there was a brother who had no possessions but a Gospel, which he sold to feed the poor. And he said, "I have even sold the word which commands me to sell all and give to the poor."[1]

Abba Theodore had three good books. He went to Macarius, and explained that he benefited from reading them, and the

---

1. Owen Chadwick, ed. and trans., *Western Asceticism* (Philadelphia: Westminster Press, 1958), 78.

brothers also borrowed them and also benefitted. But he felt guilty about possessing them and asked Macarius what he should do. Macarius told him, "Reading books is good, but possessing nothing is more than all."[2]

Books are a perennial problem with monastics. I admit that I love to read and study. But it is all too easy for me to cross the line between reading and learning for the sake of God and others, and wanting to be thought well educated and important or to "own" the books I use for study. I am not alone in this. Love of learning and even holy books can easily become an unholy thing.

Monks and family members must renounce personal possessions in order to freely give to their communities, spouses, and family.

Monastic life is absolute in having each member renounce personal possessions. The Rule of Benedict says quite strongly, "Above all, this evil practice [of monks having private possessions] must be uprooted and removed from the monastery. We mean that without an order from the abbot, no one may presume to give, receive or retain anything as his own, nothing at all—not a book, writing tablets or stylus—in short, not a single item, especially since monks may not have the free disposal even of their own bodies and wills" (RB 33.1-4). Lest this sound too harsh, however, he immediately adds, "For their needs, they are to look to the father of the monastery, and are not allowed anything which the abbot has not given or permitted. All things should be the common possession of all" (RB 33.5-6).

Along this moderate vein, Benedict continues, "It is written: *Distribution was made to each one as he had need* (Acts 4:35). By this we do not imply that there should be favoritism—God forbid—but rather consideration for weaknesses. Whoever needs less should thank God and not be distressed, but whoever

2. Chadwick, 78.

needs more should feel humble because of his weakness. . . . In this way all the members will be at peace" (RB 34.1-5).

So monastic renunciation of property and control does not lead to imprisonment. It leads to freedom and joy if one embraces it freely and for the right reasons. Otherwise it is intolerable.

We read, "Abba Cassian said that Syncleticus renounced the world, and divided his property among the poor. But he kept some for his own private use, and was unwilling to accept either the poverty of those who renounced everything or the normal rule of monasteries. Basil of blessed memory said to him: 'You have stopped being a senator, but you have not become a monk.'"[3]

Process

Cassian tells the legendary and tragically humorous story of the avaricious monk who finds seemingly innocent and justifiable reasons for keeping back for himself a little of what he generates for the monastery. He says it is to provide for health issues in later years. This is not so bad, and we have all had similar thoughts. But such private property is against the rule and the teaching of the abbot, so he is forced to conceal it from the abbot. This gives rise to guilt. But it is guilt without repentance. So inner paranoia, self-justification, and sin grow. He convinces himself that the abbot dislikes him, though the abbot doesn't have a clue about his private possessions and likes him as well as he likes the other monks. But the monk's inner illusions turn to delusion. So he convinces himself that he must leave in order to keep his now precious possessions, though they probably didn't amount to much. And to make matters worse, once he decides that he is leaving, he tries to convince others to come with him in order to confirm his delusional self-justifications! But the

3. Chadwick, 79–80.

bottom line is that he just liked his "stuff"! He left because of a pittance of personal possessions of which he was unwilling to let go. Unchecked avarice always leads to tragic conclusions in a monastery. But this tragic scenario is not uncommon to anyone who has lived in a monastery long enough to see various folks come and go.

Living in poverty is hard work! You have to work for your daily keep, because you aren't storing up treasures for future days on earth.

Connected

Avarice also paves the way for other tempting thoughts and demons. As we shall see, it also leads to anger and bitterness, which leads to boredom, self-glorification, and pride.

An old man, asked why we are troubled by demons, answered: "Because we throw away our armor—humility, poverty, patience, and men's scorn."[4]

Insatiable

Abbess Syncletica speaks of the all-too-common phenomenon of "the more we get, the more we want." She spoke of merchants who sought more wealth no matter how much they had and who saw little value in what they already had. The monastic, she said, renounces all for God.[5]

4. Chadwick, 169.
5. Chadwick, 120.

Questions

1) Are you possessed by possessions and consumed by what you consume?

2) Do you see simplicity as a means to freedom or imprisonment?

3) Do you try to control people, situations, and things?

4) Do you embrace family and community as a means to overcome avarice?

5) Do you sometimes try to possess religious things and contradict our religion by doing so?

6) Do you think that merely possessing and reading books about saints and Christianity make you a better Christian and saint?

7) Do you renounce all personal possessions in order to better serve your family and community?

8) Are you aware of the subtle process of controlling and how it destroys families and communities?

24

Anger and Bitterness

I don't get angry very often, but when I do, it's serious! My parents said that I had a temper. I mostly tend to just get frustrated in the monastery. But I still have times of anger. And I've noticed that there is a residual anger that can build up deep inside of me and poison much of my other work for Jesus if I don't let Jesus really heal it.

Monasteries can also be places of repressed anger and bitterness under the guise of holy silence or false humility. It can slowly permeate every relationship and poison the whole place. It's oppressive. It rarely raises its ugly head in an overt way, but angry monastics slowly quarantine themselves off into their respective corners and stop really relating to those with whom they otherwise share such a beautiful common call. We can become the proverbial "ships passing in the night." It's always tragic.

Anger isn't unusual. We all have it. It happens at work and in families. It happens in parishes and dioceses. I've even heard stories that the likes of St. John Paul II had a temper. But his love for Jesus and people was stronger than his natural tendency to anger, and the love of God won. That's why he is a saint!

But we live in an unusually angry and polarized culture today. It seems somehow beyond the more ordinary anger that accompanies humanity. Today it is constantly fueled through our corporate and biased media and unfiltered social networks. Anger has become the new normal for the tone of our culture nowadays. It disturbs the peace of our culture, of families and churches, and of individual people who live in it. So we often walk around agitated and angry.

Anger is nothing new to the human experience. Scripture addresses it. The spiritualities of all major religions address it. The desert fathers address it too.

In Cassian, anger comes right after gluttony, sexual sin, and avarice. The logic is obvious. When you don't get the food you want, the sex you want, or the control you want, you first get frustrated, and then you get angry. Simply put, when we don't get what we want, we get mad. And this anger always leaves us, and those around us, wounded and worn out. This, in turn, leads to bitterness, which poisons everything and everyone we touch. It poisons our entire lives.

Scripture

Jesus says, "Whoever is angry with his brother will be liable to judgment, and whoever says to his brother, 'Raqa [empty headed],' will be answerable to the Sanhedrin, and whoever says, 'You fool,' will be liable to fiery Gehenna. Therefore, if you bring your gift to the altar, and there recall that your brother has anything against you, leave your gift there at the altar, go first and be reconciled with your brother, and then come and offer your gift" (Matt 5:22-24). St. Paul says, "You must put them all away: anger, fury, malice, slander, and obscene language out of your mouths" (Col 3:8).

But Paul also says, "Be angry but do not sin; do not let the sun set on your anger, and do not leave room for the devil" (Eph 4:26, 27). And Jesus was apparently angry at times. When the religious leaders judged him for healing on the Sabbath, he "[looked] around at them with anger" (Mark 3:5). And I would imagine he was a bit angry when he overturned the money changers tables (Matt 21:13)! There is a righteous anger.

But James balances this by telling us that "the wrath [*anger* in some translations] of a man does not accomplish the righteousness of God" (Jas 1:20).

The most common Greek word for *anger* and *wrath* is *orge*, from which we get the English word *orgy*. It implies letting something go way too far. Emotions alone aren't good or bad. It's what we do with them that make them good or bad. When we give into the bad, they go from bad to worse. They grow their roots deep into our sense of self and become a habit that is destructive to relationships and even to ourselves. Instead of emotions empowering the good, they enable the bad.

The fact is that most human anger is not godly. We often try to say that it is godly and "just" anger. But most of the time we are only trying to justify our ungodly anger. We say that we want justice, but we usually seek only justification. Sometimes this is regarding outright sin. But it can also hide under the guise of seemingly godly opinions, agendas, or programs. Only after we have extinguished the flames of human anger that burn in our hearts are we even remotely justified in an anger that is like Christ's.

Where does this anger come from? In my life I've discovered that it comes from attaching my ego, my sense of self-worth, and enjoyment to objects, people, or projects. Only by letting go of the old self through the cross of Christ can we be born again as the person God really created us to be and be free of such anger.

The Desert

This is the anger the desert fathers and mothers addressed. And ultimately they concluded that the only justifiable anger is against our own sin, not someone else's.

We are sometimes angry when we correct others. Even if we appear calm, the anger may still be there. We know it. And usually the other person knows it as well. When we do this, it causes anger to increase as a pattern. Correction should be done with genuine love for the other, not to justify our own sense of being right or in reaction to being wronged.

Abba Macarius said that when you reprove someone in anger, you are pandering to your own passion. Don't lose yourself to save another.[1]

Evagrius addresses the cause of anger. He specifically mentions sense gratification. He advised that we "cut away . . . fleshly pleasures, to remove the opportunities of anger. . . . It is because of pleasure that [we] have to struggle with anger, and trouble [our] mind, and throw away [our] understanding."[2]

When we see the destructive nature of most of our anger and do something to combat it, the demons are put to flight. One of the brothers asked Abba Isidore, the priest of Scete, why the demons were so violently afraid of him? He replied that since he had become a monk, he had been trying not to let anger rise as far as his mouth.[3] He never spoke out of anger.

Change Residence?

Changing our residence or community will not usually solve our problem with anger. Anger is our problem. We must change our attitudes. Once we start the pattern of running from the real cause, anger might seem to get better initially, but it will again rear its ugly head when we get angry at other people, situations, or even things. Even if we retire into solitude prematurely, anger is not really cured, and we end up getting angry at objects.

A brother was restless in the community and often moved to anger. So he went to live alone in a cave. "I will go live somewhere

1. Owen Chadwick, ed. and trans., *Western Asceticism* (Philadelphia: Westminster Press, 1958), 53.

2. Chadwick, 50.

3. Chadwick, 51.

by myself." He figured that since he wouldn't be able to talk or listen to anyone, he would be at peace. But one day when he filled his jug with water and put it on the ground, and it fell over suddenly, then fell over again after he picked it up, he became filled with rage and broke the jug. Returning to his right mind, he knew that the demon of anger had mocked him, and he said: "Here am I by myself, and he has beaten me. I will return to the community." And he went back.[4]

Ministry and Anger

We might be very successful in other areas of ministry, but anger might still be keeping us from personal holiness. Abba Agatho said that even if an angry man raises the dead, God is still displeased with his anger.[5]

Remedies

Abba Evagrius said *reading* and *prayer* focus and strengthen a wandering mind. Passion is dampened by *hunger* and *work* and *solitude*. Anger is repressed by psalmody, long-suffering, and mercy. But all these should be at the proper times and in right measure. If they are used at the wrong times and to excess, they are useful for only a short time. And what is useful for only a short time is harmful in the long run.[6]

No Excuses

The fathers didn't allow excuse for anger under any pretext. They were rugged and unflinching in this stand. This is radical in today's angry and polarized environment of self-justification.

4. Chadwick, 92.
5. Chadwick, 107.
6. Chadwick, 109.

Referring to the text of Matthew 5:22, in which Jesus warns against anger and which in several ancient manuscripts refers to one who "is angry with his brother without a cause," Abba Poemen commented, "If you are angry with your brother for any trouble . . . he tries to lay upon you—that is anger without a cause, and it is better to pluck out your right eye and cast it from you." But you can be angry if anyone wants to separate you from God.[7]

The fathers and mothers also caution against giving a command while angry. They were first tested themselves before they dared to direct another. They learned humility through their own obedience to God and a superior, and through their own experience of dying to anger. Only then could they safely direct others.[8]

Four Causes

The elders also taught about the causes of anger, as mentioned above. One elder mentions a series of four that is quite profound. He concludes by describing three kinds of people. These are most thought provoking, and helpful:

> A certain elder said, Anger arises through four things— through the greed of avarice, whether in giving or receiving; also through loving and defending one's own opinion; through a desire of being honourably exalted; also through wishing to be learned or hoping to be wise above all others.
>
> In four ways anger darkens the nature of a man—when he hates his neighbor, when he envies him, when he despises him, and when he belittles him.

7. Chadwick, 116.
8. Chadwick, 171–172.

In four places anger finds scope—first in the heart, second in the face, third in the tongue, fourth in the act. Thus if a man can bear injury, so that the bitterness of it does not enter into his heart, then anger will not appear in his face. If, however, it find expression in his face, he still may guard his tongue so as to give no utterance of it. If even here he fail and give it utterance with his tongue, yet let him not translate his words into acts, but hastily dismiss them from his memory.

Men are of three kinds, according to the place which anger finds in them. He who is hurt and injured, and yet spares his persecutor, is a man after the pattern of Christ. He who is neither hurt himself, nor desires to hurt another, is a man after the pattern of Adam. He who hurts or slanders another is a man after the pattern of the Devil.[9]

The fathers are clear that escaping or avoiding situations that cause anger does not cure us of our anger. One writes that anger is like poisonous serpents: just because they are not actually hurting anyone when they are alone does not mean they are harmless; when the opportunity arises to use their poison, they will use it.[10]

Inanimate Objects

Our anger often reaches beyond people, extending as well to situations and objects. How many of us haven't let out even the mildest expletive when we drop something, or a lid won't open, or the like? I know I have, though by God's grace my private use of foul language and thoughts substantially disappeared long ago.

9. James O. Hannay, *The Wisdom of the Desert* (1904; repr. n.p.: Glass Darkly, 2012), 105. Citations refer to the Glass Darkly edition.
10. Hannay, 105–106.

In one story, a monk dwelling in solitude felt irritation about little things like a pen that no longer worked well or a knife that was dull. He cursed the objects or the devil. It is not enough to live in solitude, where no one is around to bother us. If we don't first find patience, the passion of anger still dwells within us, and we haven't accomplished anything.[11]

Root Causes and Avoiding

The fathers and mothers advise avoiding anger by recognizing the deeper, spiritual reasons that a person has done something that makes us angry. Surprisingly, this has little to do with understanding her or his background, upbringing, and so on. It is more about what God is doing in us through the event. God is actually getting us to see our anger and to let God heal it.

If one is a slave to anger, he or she is not likely to conquer other sins. An elder said if we can't bridle our tongue in a moment of anger, we won't be victorious over any lust of his flesh.[12]

Bitterness

Unhealed anger gives birth to bitterness. The fathers call it "dejection." It comes when anger isn't really healed, but simply hides while there is no occasion for conflict. Anger is tiresome to maintain. So sometimes we just let it go for a while, but we don't really heal the inner anger that fuels so many of our conflicts and problems.

Hebrews calls this a "bitter root": "See to it . . . that no bitter root spring up and cause trouble" (Heb 12:15). Bitterness poisons everything it touches. Instead of praising God for all things, we complain about everything. We are negative, not positive. The

11. Hannay, 105–106.
12. Hannay, 107.

proverbial glass is always half empty, never half full. This bitterness blinds us to the good and miraculous things God does daily all around us in our lives. Plus, as the old adage says, like attracts like. Negative people attract negative people. Negative attitudes attract negative things.

Dejection and bitterness are the result of unhealed anger. Their cure is praise of God and both accepting and receiving forgiveness. They are also healed by not giving in to the preceding temptations.

Small carnal sin in gluttony gives birth to serious carnal sin in sexual sin. Avarice gives birth to anger. If left unhealed, it gives birth to bitterness. They are all connected. Healing anger heals bitterness. This is done through forgiveness. It is also healed through intentionally choosing hope and optimism. This comes from faith in the promises of God. Belief in those promises comes from humbly accepting them and not resisting such promises though pride.

Questions

1) Does your use of social and mainstream media create a sense of anger within you?

2) Do you understand that anger comes from ego attachment to ideas, opinions, and senses?

3) Do you correct others out of anger, or are you able to do so with love and patience?

4) Do you think that simply changing your residence, spouse, or community will heal your anger?

5) Do you try to justify your anger?

6) Do you get angry when you are corrected, or do you learn a spiritual lesson through it?

7) Do you see the connection between anger and sadness or bitterness?

25

Forgiveness

One of the best cures for anger is forgiveness.

Forgiveness is often misunderstood today. Does it mean accepting or condoning all bad behavior? If not, how do we avoid becoming judgmental? It is a hard balancing act and can only be done when we let go of our old selves through the cross of Christ and rise up as a new creation in him. These are easy words to say. It takes a lifetime to understand and live.

I have struggled with it too. As a founder of a community, I have certainly not met everyone's expectations, much less my own! Others have sometimes gotten angry and said some pretty terrible things about me or the community I founded. That always hurts. In the beginning, I had a tough time with it. I would say that I forgave them, but deep inside I carried some hurt and even resentment. But as I said before, after the passing of some years in community, I pretty much had the stuffing knocked out of my sense of self-importance. Only then did I really forgive. When there is little self-will left to get offended, I can forgive offenses much more easily. I can more easily confess my own sins and shortcomings too.

The English word *forgiveness* comes primarily from a variety of European languages. It literally means to give up the power to punish or judge in advance. For me, it means to "give in advance." One forgives even before the other person is ready to repent or reconcile.

The Greek word for forgiveness in Scripture is *aphiemi* and means to send forth, leave, let go, or divorce. So forgiveness is a letting go of, a sending away of our need to judge. It literally divorces the tendency to punish. This is radical!

Offering forgiveness is constant and unconditional. But actualization of forgiveness by the person being forgiven isn't unconditional. It is conditional. We must receive forgiveness to actualize it. Forgiveness in Scripture is often portrayed as being dependent on repentance, or a person turning back toward God.

Scripture

Jesus taught, "If your brother sins, rebuke him; and if he repents, forgive him. And if he wrongs you seven times in one day and returns to you seven times saying, 'I am sorry,' you should forgive him" (Luke 17:3-4). Even John, the beloved disciple said, "If we acknowledge our sins, he is faithful and just and will forgive our sins and cleanse us from every wrongdoing" (1 John 1:9). The word *if* in these passages suggests that forgiveness is conditional upon the repentance of the sinner.

But we also hear that God loves sinners and that his love for us is unconditional. He loves us even while we are sinners. "But God proves his love for us in that while we were still sinners Christ died for us" (Rom 5:8). Like forgiveness, love is activated, outwardly proved. "If you love me, you will keep my commandments" (John 14:15).

How do we balance these two ideas in Scripture? One on hand, should we only forgive someone if they repent? One the other, should we love others unconditionally? The latter can degenerate into enabling bad behavior. The former can turn us into a bunch of judgmental religious dictators who demand that folks become just like "us" before offering forgiveness.

I believe that forgiveness is like a rain that falls constantly from God. We are like cups or vessels left lying upside down outside. The rain of God's forgiveness and love is constantly falling upon us. But we cannot benefit from it as long as we are still upside down. In order to fill up with that forgiveness and love, we must turn our cups right side up. That is repentance. So God's forgiveness falls constantly from heaven for even the worst of sinners. But we must cooperate with that forgiveness by repenting in order to benefit from it.

But the burden isn't all on those who need to repent. It is also on us who are called to bring God's forgiveness to everyone. Sometimes in today's world, where truth has been so confused and distorted, we Christians find ourselves in the situation of proclaiming truth. As I often say, today right is wrong and wrong is right! Christians must proclaim the truth whether convenient or inconvenient (see 2 Tim 4:2). But we must speak the truth in love (see Eph 4:15) and learn to season our words with a little salt and humor (see Col 4:6), speaking at the right time (see Sir 20:19), often when actually asked about our faith (see 1 Pet 3:15) and in the right way. Otherwise we become moral rigorists and mere philosophers instead of followers of Jesus Christ. While a hard word works at certain times at a certain point in some lives, this usually pushes sinners further away in fear. It rarely works.

St. Francis gives us an answer. He said in a letter to a superior that there ought to be no brother anywhere in the entire world who could not find forgiveness by looking into his superior's eyes. Are we calling sinners to judgment, or are we offering forgiveness when they look into our eyes? That's quite a challenge for me and probably for you too.

Christian forgiveness and judgment bind or loose. While this is primarily given to St. Peter and the apostles in their role of leadership in the first Christian communities (see Matt 16:16; 18:18), it also applies to all of us. When we don't forgive someone, it binds up him or her spiritually and emotionally. This can even cause sickness, and kill.

But it doesn't just bind up others. It binds us up as well! Sometimes individuals or entire communities feel it. It permeates the spirit, or air, of entire communities. It suffocates. It's like a slow, seeping sludge that binds the free working of the Spirit in our midst. It kills communities.

The Desert

The desert fathers and mothers were radical when it came to the notion of forgiveness. While we often think of them as stern and ascetical, we are often surprised to discover that this was often their attitude toward themselves, but rarely toward others. The tradition of the desert is one of radical mercy and forgiveness. It is sure to challenge us.

Forgiveness and avoiding judgment of others are essential parts of what it means to be a monk. One hermit put it succinctly: "This is the life of a monk: work, obedience, meditation, not to judge others, not to speak evil, not to murmur."[1]

Abba Joseph asked Abba Poemen, "Tell me how to become a monk." Abba Poemen replied, "If you want to find rest in this life and the next, say at every turn 'Who am I?' and judge no man."[2]

Scripture also tells us to forgive as the Lord has forgiven us (see Col 3:13; Eph. 4:32). Well, that's quite a showstopper for me! Jesus has forgiven me and continues to forgive me more than I can now know.

Abba Moses gives us the classic desert father example of this. In Scete a brother was once found guilty of something. The elders asked Moses to come and judge him. But he would not come. The leading presbyter sent another message that the monks were waiting. So Moses went, carrying on his back an

---

1. Benedicta Ward, ed., *The Desert Fathers: Sayings of the Early Christian Monks* (New York: Penguin, 2003), 6.
2. Owen Chadwick, ed. and trans., *Western Asceticism* (Philadelphia: Westminster Press, 1958), 103.

old basket filled with sand. As he walked, the sand spilled out between the weaves. When the brothers asked him why he was carrying the basket, the old man said, "My sins are chasing me, and I do not see them—have I come today to judge the sins of someone else?" So the monks repented of their tendency to judge and pardoned the brother.[3]

There are many other similar examples. Abba Pior is also mentioned in a story. He carried sand on his back as a reminder to himself and to others that his sins weighed him down without the forgiveness of Jesus, and that he therefore should not judge another.[4]

A brother who had sinned was ordered to go to church for judgment by the leading presbyter. The great and holy Abba Bessarion rose up and went out with him, saying: "I too am a sinner."[5] This reminded the brothers that all had sinned and been forgiven, so all should be quick to forgive.

I must confess that, while I have spent many hours confessing my sins, memories of old sins I had forgotten still come to my mind on occasion. I am always struck that when I stand before God in Eternity, I will finally know myself as God knows me. And "I shall know fully, as I am fully known" (1 Cor 13:12). And everyone in God will know everything about everyone. This will be a *knowing* of *mercy* and love, not of judgment. But I will certainly be purged in that infinitely loving gaze of God. So while still on earth, I tend to walk with a constant awareness of this awesome mystery of forgiveness and love. How can I become judgmental of others on earth when I am aware of his forgiveness of me in heaven?

How To

The words of one ancient hermit tell us much about forgiveness and how to speak to those who disagree with us: "Ask God to

3. Chadwick, 102.
4. Chadwick, 104.
5. Chadwick, 102.

give you inner grief of heart and humility. Always look at your own sins, and do not judge another's. Be the servant of all. . . . If anyone speaks to you on a controversial matter, do not argue with him. If he speaks well, say, 'Yes.' If he speaks ill, say, 'I don't know anything about that.' Don't argue with what he has said, and your mind will be at peace."[6] They also reflect a mind that is nourished in *hesychia*, or peace and sacred stillness.

Antony said that judgment destroys people. It makes a shipwreck of our lives and can wreck entire communities too. We are to be about salvaging wrecks, not causing them! We do that through mercy and forgiveness for the repentant sinner.[7]

Should We Correct Others?

If we see others in sin, should we correct them? Yes and no. Actually, the answer is "sometimes." Sometimes it isn't our responsibility, but that of the spiritual father or mother. If we are still angered by their sin, we shouldn't correct them until we find a place of dispassion. Sometimes it is plain charity, remembering that we also have many small sins that people tolerate out of love. We must learn the time and place. As St. Paul says, "Let your speech always be gracious, seasoned with salt, so that you know how you should respond to each one"(Col 4:6).

A brother asked Abba Poemen whether he ought to tell anyone when he sees a brother sin. The old man said, "Whenever we cover our brother's sin, God will cover our sin. Whenever we tell people about our brother's guilt, God will do the same with ours."[8]

We should also remember the old expression, "There, but for the grace of God, go I." Seeing the sin of another, one holy man wept bitterly and said, "He today: I tomorrow." However grave a

---

6. Ward, 6–7.
7. Chadwick, 102.
8. Chadwick, 103.

sin we may see committed, we must not judge the culprit, but consider ourselves to be the worse sinner.[9]

Only when you really find this attitude as a lived experience in your life can you dare to correct someone without self-love and self-justification. God's love is always self-emptying. As St. Paul says, love "does not seek its own interests" (1 Cor 13:4-5).

Conversion

Besides being virtuous, nonjudgmentalism and forgiveness also converts people. It calls us all to the love of Jesus. After we have initially entered into that personal encounter with Christ, then Jesus begins to cleanse us from our sins, one by one. I know for myself that Jesus has done so throughout my monastic life in Christ. And I am still a work in progress! If I were expected to repent of all my known and unknown sins before being a Christian, I would never have been able to make that choice. Jesus meets us where we are and both reveals and forgives sins, as he knows we are ready and able to process them. It is a lifelong process. I am still just beginning.

Abba Apollo in Scete was originally a rude and brutish herdsman. He callously ripped open a pregnant woman's belly just to see what the child looked like. Both died. Realizing the terror of what he had done, he repented with a purged heart. He went to Scete and revealed to the fathers the abhorrent thing he had done. When he heard them singing the Psalms— "Seventy is the sum of our years, / or eighty, if we are strong" (90:10)—he said, "I am forty years old this day, and I have never really prayed. Now, if I live for forty years more, I will never stop praying to God that He may forgive me my sins." And from that time on he lived up to this declaration. He was always begging God, "I,

9. Chadwick, 105.

O my Lord, like a man, have sinned, and You, as God, please forgive me." He prayed this prayer night and day.[10]

I, somehow, think that if God forgave him his terrible double homicide, he will forgive us our sins too. No sin is too small or too great for God's mighty mercy, as we learn from Jesus Christ. All we need do is to turn back to him in sincere love. Will you turn today?

Questions

1) Do you offer forgiveness conditionally or unconditionally?

2) Do you know how to activate forgiveness in your life through the condition of repentance?

3) Do sinners find forgiveness simply by looking into your eyes?

4) Are you aware of your own sins before you judge others?

5) Do you forgive as you are forgiven, and do you see your own sins before judging others?

6) Do you correct others with love and without judgment?

10. E. A. W. Budge, ed. and trans., *The Paradise or Garden of the Holy Fathers*, 2 vols. (London: Chatto & Windus, 1907), 1:270.

26

Nonresistance

n my life as a Christian, I have always espoused nonresistance. I've even had it tested in some big ways. By the grace of God, I have always responded without anger or violence. But those were the big instances. The daily, little occasions of life are much tougher.

We Christians believe in Jesus. But often we get very upset by those who do not share our belief. And this betrays our hypocrisy. Indeed, sometimes we Christians are portrayed as angry and uptight. And sometimes we are! We can be hypocritical.

The Greek word for hypocrite is *hupokrites*. It is the word for an actor on a stage. Are we often acting or putting on a false front in our religion?

I can remember early in my life as a founder of a new religious community, I really wanted to be peaceful, die to my old self, and lead by spiritual maturity. But I was still immature. I would often feel frustration and even anger when those who said they wanted to follow Jesus completely in the monastic tradition would stubbornly hang on to their self-will and worldly attachments when challenged by that same tradition. I understood it on a cultural and human level, but on an ideological level I couldn't understand it. It frustrated me. But I hated this reaction in myself, and I realized that it was just as bad as the self-will of those who frustrated me.

It took me a couple of decades to mostly outgrow it. This came by simply having my ego worn down. But it was good for me. At every step my ego was being "beaten" out of me by circumstances beyond my control. After a while there was little of my old self left. I simply gave up. I stopped resisting.

After two decades of leading, I went into more intense solitude. I still did a few concerts annually and went up from my hermitage to the monastery for community meetings and for Mass on Sundays and holy days. But I spent the rest of my time in my cell. I prayed my office and private prayers, ate, and worked there. What I learned about myself before God there is frankly beyond my abilities of description. It was both painful and revelatory. It melted me. It brought down old walls and illusions regarding spirituality, God, and myself. It opened up an entirely new part of my spiritual life and set me truly free for ministry. This is sometimes called reclusion.

After about five years in strict reclusion, my old self gradually fell away like an old set of clothes that simply didn't fit the person Jesus wanted me to be. I quit resisting. I let my ego die. And then I discovered who I really am in Jesus. Contrary to what I first thought, I actually became happier and unafraid either to be silent or to share my thoughts. That's because they were no longer coming from me alone. Jesus had somehow become my life. I was still alive, but only because I had largely, if not completely, died with Christ. I was free, because the shackles of my old self had been broken through the cross of Jesus Christ. But I must readily admit that I am still very much a work in progress. The more I travel this road of Jesus, the more I realize that I have barely begun to travel it. As some say, I am a practicing Catholic because I am still practicing!

Dispassion

This brings us to another remedy to anger, or perhaps better stated, a fruit of being free of anger: *nonresistance*. In the Eastern fathers, this is sometimes called dispassion, or *apatheia*, which is borrowed from the philosophical tradition of the Stoics. But this isn't the same as apathy, or not caring. It is an equilibrium that accepts blame or praise equally. It gives birth to nonresistance. It sees everything and is upset by very little.

Such dispassion and nonresistance come only when we really let our egos die through the cross of Christ, be born again in the Spirit, and rise up as a new person in the resurrection of Jesus Christ. It gives birth to a certain equanimity regarding the good or bad things that happen to us. It gives us a peaceful response in any situation.

St. Theodoros the Great Ascetic (not earlier than seventh century, not later than eleventh century), in *A Century of Spiritual Texts*, says of dispassion in general, "The monk, therefore, must be detached from material things, must be dispassionate, free from all evil desires, not given to soft living, not a tippler, not slothful, not indolent, not a lover of wealth, pleasure or praise. Unless he raises himself above all these things, he will fail to achieve the angelic way of life. For those who do achieve it, the yoke is easy and the burden light (cf. Matt 11:30). . . . This life and its activities are full of delight."[1]

Nonresistance is perhaps one of the most "resisted" teachings of Jesus. Today, we often prefer the "passive resistance" of Gandhi. Good as that might be, it isn't the nonresistance taught by Jesus. In the face of violence, squaring the rather clear and demanding teaching of Jesus on nonresistance isn't easy.

Today the average Christian must also differentiate between the use of *violence and force*. Force is acceptable under certain circumstances by the police, the military, or in defense of one's loved ones or life. Violence is not. This is just hair-splitting until it is put into practice when facing real conflict. I've had

---

1. G. E. H. Palmer, Philip Sherrard, and Kallistos Ware, trans. and ed., *The Philokalia*, vol. 2 (London: Faber & Faber, 1984), 49.23.

that tested only a few times in my life. Praise God, I was able to practice nonresistance and nonviolence by God's grace, which almost miraculously took over. And God protected me. Left to myself, I'd have been lost!

Jesus taught, "You have heard that it was said, 'An eye for an eye and a tooth for a tooth.' But I say to you, offer no resistance to one who is evil. When someone strikes you on your right cheek, turn the other one to him as well. If anyone wants to go to law with you over your tunic, hand him your cloak as well. Should anyone press you into service for one mile, go with him for two miles. Give to the one who asks of you, and do not turn your back on one who wants to borrow" (Matt 5:38-42).

The Desert and the Saints

The desert fathers, and many saints before and after them, took these words quite literally. For some, it cost them their life. For others, it cost them comfort or reputation.

Probably the most extreme desert story in this regard involves the great Macarius, who was falsely accused by the townspeople of fathering a child by a promiscuous woman who lived nearby. Instead of resisting or trying to get true justice, he passively accepted the blame and prepared to care for the rather promiscuous girl and the coming baby. The birth was a troubled one. There was much pain and tribulation. The girl saw this as a sign from God, repented, and cleared the monk's good name. The townsfolk also repented. But he didn't gloat in his righteousness. He simply went back to his cell as if nothing much had happened, clearly unruffled by the whole thing.[2]

We've already seen the famous story of Anub, who threw rocks at pagan idols, asked them forgiveness, and then praised

---

2. E. A. W. Budge, ed. and trans., *The Paradise or Garden of the Holy Fathers*, 2 vols. (London: Chatto & Windus, 1907), 1:271–273.

them for their nonresistance. We also saw a similar story of Poemen.[3] Indeed, I've found that the only way to practice nonresistance is when I die to myself through the cross of Jesus Christ and am able to rise up a new self according to the teaching of Jesus. If I hang on to my old self, nonresistance is virtually impossible for me.

Later monasticism is also filled with stories of monks who didn't resist robbers and sometimes ended up converting them through their Christ-like witness of nonresistance. The Franciscan stories are similar, and challenging.

Jesus taught, "If anyone wants to go to law with you over your tunic, hand him your cloak as well. Should anyone press you into service for one mile, go with him for two miles. Give to the one who asks of you, and do not turn your back on one who wants to borrow" (Matt 5:40-42). While this had some historical context in the practice of Roman soldiers requisitioning the services of citizenry and speaks specifically of a legal process, it held a special example for desert monastics.

In one story Macarius assists robbers by helping them load his few belongings onto their horses![4] I'm not sure I would be so accommodating! We have had petty thievery at our monastery. We've never reported the petty stuff, but we did report the theft of a monastery vehicle, and we did install a security system afterwards!

Then there are the clearly biblical patterns in the desert fathers of blessing those who injure them. Jesus says, "But I say to you, love your enemies, and pray for those who persecute you, that you may be children of your heavenly Father"(Matt 5:44-45). And Paul teaches, "Bless those who persecute you, bless and do not curse them" (Rom 12:14).

---

3. Owen Chadwick, ed. and trans., *Western Asceticism* (Philadelphia: Westminster Press, 1958), 159.

4. James O. Hannay, *The Wisdom of the Desert* (1904; repr. n.p.: Glass Darkly, 2012), 41. Citations refer to the Glass Darkly edition.

One story tells of one monk stealing from another monk! (I must confess I've never seen this in my community, and it would surprise me. But I have seen things "disappear" or be "moved" when one monastic wanted something for his own, and we have had theft from outside of the community. Sometimes when *everything* is *everybody's*, *nobody* takes responsibility for *anything*!) In the story the wronged monk simply said that he was sure that the thieving monk really needed the food he had repeatedly stolen. The wronged monk suffered terribly from hunger and eventually fell sick from starvation. As the other monks gathered at his deathbed, he called the monk who had stolen his food to come to him. The account continues: "Then taking his hands and kissing them, he said to those who stood around, 'I pay my thanks to these hands, brethren, for because of them I am going, as I trust, to enter the kingdom of heaven.'" The thieving monk saw this, and struck with guilt, repented heartily and became a most eager monastic follower of Jesus.[5]

One brother asked an elder to offer "one commandment, such that I may keep it, and thereby attain unto salvation." The old man replied, "When men do wrong to you and revile you, endure and be silent. To do this is a very great thing. This is above all other commandments."[6]

How
The following story of Abbot Poemen gets to the "how" of living nonresistance.

> A certain brother once questioned the abbot Poemen, saying, "What is this word which the Lord says in the gospel, 'Greater love hath no man than this, that a man lay down his life for his friend'? How may one do such a

5. Hannay, 39.
6. Hannay, 40.

thing?" The old man answered him, "Perhaps a man may hear from his friend some word which insults and angers him. Perhaps it is in his power to speak back to his friend in like manner. If then he chooses to endure in silence—if he does violence to himself, being fully determined to speak no angry word, nor any word to hurt or vex the other—then, verily, this man lays down, in sacrifice, his life for his friend."[7]

Questions

1) How do you understand nonresistance and dispassion?

2) Do you understand the difference between *apatheia* and apathy, dispassion and detachment with attention?

3) Are you dispassionate from your ego and from things?

4) How do you respond to unjust accusation?

5) Are you able to turn the other cheek without interior anger, bitterness, or judgment?

6) Do you really bless your persecutors?

7) Do you see the connection between nonresistance and justice?

8) Do you spiritualize persecution by embracing the cross and resurrection of Jesus Christ?

7. Hannay, 40.

Boredom and Listlessness

One of the fiercest demons that faced the desert fathers and mothers was acedia, the noonday devil, or listlessness. I simply call it boredom.

We all get bored. I often get bored with the daily turn of events. For me daily monastic life is a predictable turn of rising, prayers, meals, and work. Even life in itinerant ministry can become a predictable round of hotels, diet food, churches, and constant driving from place to place. Only the time on the platform in ministry and meeting the delightful folks who sponsor and attend my ministries are actually enjoyable for me. Family life also has its own routine. We all get bored with the routine of daily life.

It isn't whether or not we get bored on occasion. It's what we do with it that makes all the difference. Routine can comfort and direct us or bore us. The choice is up to us. Like with a living human body, the very routine that sometimes bores us can be like the stable skeletal system upon which we can hang the rest of the sinews, muscles, heart, and soul of a living body. Without it, we lack form and direction. We can end up a directionless blob of well-meaning intentions that cannot fully function. No.

We need the skeletal routine in order to be a fully functioning human person. But we must also flesh it out to really live.

If left unchecked, this ordinary boredom can gradually lead us to a full-on life of godlessness. Big consequences start in small ways. I've seen this in monastic life with many who cannot make a go of their vocation once the novelty wears off. For most of us, we get bored with a spiritual exercise or way of life. We get bored with ideas or people. We get bored with jobs, ministries, communities, or even spouses and children. This is nothing new.

I've also seen it with the proverbial "I'm spiritual, but not religious" syndrome. I have friends who get bored and disenchanted with organized church. Then they start having home Bible studies and prayer or meditation groups in their homes instead of going to church. When those break up, they settle for personal prayer alone. Then they lose that and end up not praying much at all, their relationship with God dwindles, and their lives become aimless and unhappy. Others simply lose their faith and live in blissful delusion. It all started with boredom with their local church.

This is especially pronounced with the routine of ordinary things and people in monastic life. I often say that monasteries are extraordinary places made up of very ordinary people. If you can't find the extraordinary in the ordinary, you will probably find monastic life very difficult, if not outright impossible!

The early desert fathers treat the workings and remedies for this demonic thought of boredom very basically at first. By the end of the first generation, they have already started to develop it in some detail in the context of monasticism. But these lessons are applicable to us all.

For the desert fathers this demon came in the middle of the unbearably hot desert days. The desert is a place of extremes. During those unbearable hours, many monks could only sleep. While this might be understandable, and even tolerated at times, it could be the kiss of death to the serious monastic.

I know that when I first moved into my hermitage, I would sometimes get bored and ended up just dozing off to sleep. It was easier to overcome when I was at the height of my recording ministry and was almost always spending part of my day working on new music. I would also have a concert tour to get ready for. Nowadays, as I spend more time in hermitage at the monastery, I am facing what anyone of retirement age faces. After a life of accomplishments, retirees are more inactive on the professional level. At this point we must do a serious self-assessment before God. How we deal with boredom makes all the difference.

For myself, I have chosen to dive deeper into monastic spirituality. I have already spent a lifetime studying the main sources. I tend to pick up a book and think, "Yep, I've heard all this before." So, I'm going deeper into the unwritten things of spirituality and just "being" in the presence of God's Being. When I do this, I might be less active, but I am far from bored!

Cassian

Cassian says that this demon *always* attacks the monk. None are exempt. "What am I doing here? I don't even like these people! What will happen to me when I am sick and old and unable to care for myself?" These and other similar thoughts stream almost endlessly unless confronted. Unchecked, they cause us to hate the monastery and the monks, the abbot, and even the Scriptures. They suggest to a monk that he should go elsewhere. They end in the destruction of one's precious vocation.

For most of us, it comes when the newness of monastic life begins to wear off. It also eventually comes to every ministry and to every couple in marriage. It comes when the honeymoon is over, the proverbial "seven-year itch"! It happens to all of us. That's not the issue. What is at issue is what we do with it. That is a choice. Those who choose to give in will lose their monastic, clerical, or family vocation, even if their body stays in the monastery, parish, or family house and job. Those who resist it will eventually break through to discover a whole new life!

Cassian, writing at the end of the first generation of the desert fathers, goes on to describe the agonizing process of this demon in more detail. He says that it produces in the mind feelings of extraordinary hunger, so that we cannot think of anything else but food. It suggests that we cannot be free of this demon unless we go and visit the other monks more often. Seeking others during times of solitary prayer is a distraction that can lead away from the deeper things God is trying to usher us into. When these tactics don't work, it simply makes us sleepy. When boredom is not overcome, how easy it is to just go to sleep!

When a monk finally succumbs to the demon of boredom, he begins to roam idly from monastery to monastery, thinking only of which monastery has the best food. In monastic tradition these are called "gyrovagues," or those who wander in physical and spiritual circles and are the bane of monastic life and real obedience to a spiritual father or mother and a specific community.

We still see many would-be monastics wandering from monastery to monastery today. These always find something wrong with every monastery they visit. So they move on. But the problem isn't so much in the monastery, though no monastery is perfect, but in themselves. The same is true of parishes, spouses, families, jobs, or ministries. Boredom in little things leads to the destruction of a bigger vocation if left unchecked. Acedia is dreadfully dogged!

Sometimes we are tempted to different ministry. The temptation to engage in active ministry is all too common in monastic life. The devil uses otherwise good things to accomplish something bad in our monastic vocations. Often, what God wills is for us to break through to a whole new level of prayer. And mystically, that prayer is what really changes the world spiritually.

Cassian describes the mental process of such ones and their eventual outcome. He says that the mind becomes filled with a constant flow of vain distractions once we initially give in to boredom. These distractions are religous in nature at first. But they prep the mind for the habit of mental wandering that leads to worse things. Finally it is ensnared by worldly things and gradually abandons the monastic life altogether.

St. John Climacus (of the Ladder) says similarly that at prayer this demon fills the mind with some job to be done and suggests any plausible excuse to drag us from prayer. The irony is that outside of the singing of the Psalms during prayer, this demon does not arise! When the Office is hardly over, we are wide awake again. Haven't we all had a bit of this experience? During the Divine Office or Mass we just can't stay focused or awake. Our minds wander like an undisciplined mule. But as soon as we are out of church, we are focused on our next task and wide awake again!

John of the Ladder continues. Again, it suggests leaving monastic solitude to be involved in a ministry like hospitality. It urges the hermit to do some kind of manual labor so he can produce something to give to the poor. Or it suggests visiting the sick, even quoting the words of Jesus, "I was sick and you came to visit me" (Matt 25:36). Notice that this is during prayer and solitude. There are times for legitimate work and ministry in a monastery, but not during times set aside for prayer and sacred reading.

Remedies

How do we resist? There aren't any magic answer pills in the desert. The fathers often say that the answer is simply to rise up and do something, but do something appropriate to the monastic vocation and call. If your mind is wandering during prayer, rise up and pray harder. *Stand up* and pray. Do some *prostrations* or stand up. Pray the Divine Office. Read the Scriptures.

Do a mental inventory of the good and bad things of the day, and praise and thank God for everything on purpose! If you are sleepy and lazy, do some constructive work. Clean and straighten your cell, inside and out. Do the labor assigned to you by your abbot. There's an old saying that if you are bored, it's because you are boring! When you are bored, get up and do something for God. You will soon find yourself free of boredom. You can defeat the noonday devil!

John Climacus recommends *mourning*, or *penthos*. Boredom can be overcome by the remembrance of past sins, battered by hard manual labor, and encouraged by the thought of the blessings to come.[1] Putting boredom into the first person he writes, "The singing of *psalms* and manual *labor* are my opponents by whom I am now bound. My enemy is the *thought of death*, but what really slays me is prayer backed by a firm *hope* in the blessings of the future." And he concludes, "*Unremitting prayer* is the death of despondency."[2]

The earlier desert fathers and mothers are a bit less developed, but no less challenging.

One old monk, asked why he never gave in to boredom said it was simply because each day he hoped to die.[3] Another used to say, "The man who constantly sets the *remembrance of death* before his eyes beats the demon of Boredom."[4] Another old man said that the fear of God drives away all evil things, but dejection drives away the fear of God, and the wandering mind drives away good works from the soul.[5]

---

1. Vassilios Papavassiliou, *Thirty Steps to Heaven: The Ladder of Divine Ascent for All Walks of Life* (Chesterton, IN: Ancient Faith Publishing, 2013), 111.

2. Papavassiliou, 113.

3. E. A. W. Budge, ed. and trans., *The Paradise or Garden of the Holy Fathers*, 2 vols. (London: Chatto & Windus, 1907), 2:195.

4. Budge, 2:217.

5. Budge, 2:277.

St. Makarios of Egypt said that one who cultivates a life of prayer must "fight with great diligence and watchfulness, all endurance, all struggle of soul and toil of body, so that he does not become sluggish and surrender himself to distraction of thought, to excessive sleep, [or] to listlessness."[6]

Eight Thoughts

St. John of Damascus also places the battle with acedia, or boredom, in the *list of eight*. He said that it does not lay within our power to escape these thoughts. But it is within our power to choose whether to entertain or act on them. He goes on to outline *seven stages*, from suggestion of the thought to full acting upon them.[7] St. Augustine reduces these to *three* in the West: 1) the suggestion of the thought, which is common to everyone and not sinful; 2) entertaining the thought, which is sinful; and 3) acting on the thought, which is the fruit of the sinful entertainment of the thought. I like the list of seven for its subtlety and completeness. I like the list of three simply because it's easier to remember! It works for me.

St. John of Damascus continues. *The eight passions are destroyed by these means*: "gluttony by self-control; unchastity by desire for God and longing for the blessings held in store; avarice by compassion for the poor; anger by goodwill and love for all men; worldly dejection by spiritual joy; listlessness by patience, perseverance, and offering thanks to God; self-esteem by doing good in secret and by praying constantly with a contrite heart; and pride by not judging or despising anyone in the manner of the boastful Pharisee (Luke 18:11-12), and by considering

6. Allyne Smith, ed., *Philokalia: The Eastern Christian Spiritual Texts: Selections Annotated and Explained*, trans. G. E. H. Palmer, Philip Sherrard, and Kallistos Ware (Woodstock, VT: SkyLight Paths Publishing, 2012), 96–97.

7. Smith, 152–153.

oneself the least of all men." He concludes that once we are free of these eight thoughts, we can fly unencumbered in God through Jesus.[8]

Questions

1) What is acedia?

2) Do you experience boredom in your spiritual life, in the church, or in your monastic community or ministry?

3) Do you understand the progression of acedia in your spiritual life?

4) Do you use good, old-fashioned work to balance your prayer in order to cure your boredom?

5) Do you see boredom in context of the eight thoughts and the remedies for overcoming them?

8. Smith, 154–155.

28

Self-Glorification and Pride

I have been involved in public life since I was ten years old. After my conversion, I used my talents for God and was again immersed in public ministry. During that time, I've paid my proverbial dues and experienced some degree of success and even fame. For me it is nothing particularly special. It's just what I do for a living.

That being said, I cannot help but have my ego stroked when people thank or praise me for my musical gifts or teaching abilities. I try to follow the example of St. Francis and offer all praise to God immediately. I tell myself that all the thanks and praise belong to God. But, truth be known, some of it rubs off onto me. And I like it! That's always a problem. It reveals my ego and pride. It reveals that my old self is climbing out of the grave and trying to control my life again.

We all experience it. You know, that little *need to be noticed*. We want others to notice our acts of kindness in order to be validated. We want to do works of holiness so that others will think us holy. It seems harmless enough. We can even say it is for witnessing Jesus to others. But it can also be a sham!

We also justify it under the virtuous practice of *affirmation*. But we demand it from others, rather than offering it to others.

Instead of a virtue, it can become a vice. We say to ourselves, "Aren't we supposed to affirm one another?" And then feel bad when we are not affirmed. Affirmation of others is part of Christian life. But demanding it for ourselves is the first step in a deadly slide toward pride.

Self-glorification is the seventh of the eight thoughts. It is that little need to be noticed. It is the need to be affirmed and praised most all the time. It wants to hang on to praise and glory for itself without giving praise and glory to God. It is considered the doorway to pride, the eighth and final thought.

We all *like* to be affirmed and noticed. We like to be praised. Part of this is understandable as our desire to belong to a family or group. It is natural. But when we get ego attached to the need to be noticed, it can be dangerous.

Scripture

Jesus says, "But take care not to perform righteous deeds in order that people may see them; otherwise, you will have no recompense from your heavenly Father. When you give alms, do not blow a trumpet before you, as the hypocrites do in the synagogues and in the streets to win the praise of others. Amen, I say to you, they have received their reward. But when you give alms, do not let your left hand know what your right is doing, so that your almsgiving may be secret. And your Father who sees in secret will repay you" (Matt 6:1-4).

St. Paul says, "For you have died, and your life is hidden with Christ in God. When Christ your life appears, then you too will appear with him in glory" (Col 3:30).

At the same time, such a life of humility will shine the light of Jesus before others. Jesus says, "You are the light of the world. A city set on a mountain cannot be hidden. Nor do they light a lamp and then put it under a bushel basket; it is set on a lampstand, where it gives light to all in the house. Just so, your light must shine before others, that they may see your good deeds and glorify your heavenly Father" (Matt 5:14-16). But if you think you are humble, you're not!

It's said of St. Francis that every time he was praised as a man of God, he would give all praise and glory to God. I try to do the same thing. Anytime someone praises me for my gifts of music or preaching, I either silently or out loud transfer all glory to God. I try not to hang on to any of the praise for myself. St. Francis says that anything good in us comes from God and all glory is to be given to God. Our creation and natural gifts, and our redemption and spiritual gifts all come from God the Father through Christ and in the Spirit. We can really claim nothing for ourselves, except our decision to sin. Thinking of that humbles us right away.

The Buddhists aim for the gift of *equanimity*. Christians do too. That means being equally happy with praise or blame, good things or bad. When we can retain our peace and our joy in blame as well as praise, then we are truly free.

This isn't an excuse not to thank or praise others for their natural or spiritual gifts and talents from God. But, when we are free from the need to be noticed and praised, then we can genuinely notice and praise others with no hard feelings at all. This is real freedom.

As St. Paul said, "Do nothing out of selfishness or out of vainglory; rather, humbly regard others as more important than yourselves" (Phil 2:3). That's a tall order! How can we do it? Again St. Paul offers some help: "If one part suffers, all the parts suffer with it; if one part is honored, all the parts share its joy" (1 Cor 12:26). We are the body of Christ. If someone else is honored, then all are honored. I am complete only when others succeed. And I am fully Christ-like only when I share in his sufferings.

The Desert

The desert fathers give ample examples of this teaching. They said of Arsenius and Theodore of Pherme that they hated fame and praise more than anything. Arsenius avoided people likely to praise him. Theodore did not avoid them, but their words were like daggers to him.[1]

A brother spent three days asking Theodore of Pherme for advice. Theodore would not offer any, and the questioner went away sad. Theodore's disciple asked him why he didn't answer the questioning monk. He answered that the monk was interested in getting credit only for himself by repeating what others had said.[2]

Talking about the sayings or lessons of others before we have learned them ourselves is a great danger. The *Philokalia*, a title that means "the study of the beautiful," includes some teachings about monks who become spiritual fathers *prematurely* and end up doing great harm to themselves and others. As a monastic founder, I have always been challenged by that and have no doubt been guilty of doing the same, especially in my earlier years.

Another brother spoke with the same Theodore. He began talking about things that he had never really experienced for himself. Theodore answered him by offering a tough analogy. He told him that he was like a man who had not yet found a ship to sail in, not put his luggage on board, or even not put out to sea, yet was already acting as if he had arrived at his destination. Theodore told the brother to make at least some attempt to experience for himself some of the things he was talking about, or he would have no authority from which to speak.[3]

Practice What You Preach

The teaching of the fathers offers the lesson that is summarized in modern times by the well-known adage, "practice what you preach." When we don't, our words are empty.

1. Benedicta Ward, ed., *The Desert Fathers: Sayings of the Early Christian Monks* (New York: Penguin, 2003), 77.
2. Ward, 79.
3. Ward, 79.

Poemen advised a brother to teach his heart to follow what his tongue says to others. He also said that monks often try to appear excellent in preaching, but they are less excellent in practicing what they preach.[4]

We aren't supposed to advertise our own wisdom by sharing it too freely, unless it is really for the genuine good of others. St. Paul tells us to say "only such as is good for needed edification, that it may impart grace to those who hear" (Eph 4:29). That word *edification* is from the Greek *oikodome* and means "to build up." It comes from *doma*, which means "to cover roof, or put a dome of protection on a house." Is our speech really building up and protecting those to whom we speak?

Syncletica used analogies to teach the same lesson. She said that an open treasury is quickly spent; any virtue is lost if it is published everywhere too freely. If you put wax in front of a fire, it melts; and if you pour vain praises on people, their soul gets soft and weak in seeking more praises.[5]

There is a danger in public ministry and the praise that goes with it. As one who has been in the public eye since I was ten years old, I have some experience with this. Public singing or speaking is kind of second nature for me. In one sense it's no more special to me than any other kind of work that one might do. But since anyone can get attached to the gratification of one's ego, I have fought to make sure that public ministry first flows forth from a private monastic life that is happy whether doing ministry or not. However, that is easier said than done! I say that my ministry must be focused on my being, not my being on my ministry. Otherwise I limit my ministry and kill my being.

Syncletica also said that a person cannot be both a seed and a full-grown bush. Likewise, people with worldly and secular fame cannot really bear heavenly fruit. We must find our reputations

---

4. Ward, 81.
5. Ward, 82.

in genuine holiness that is self-emptying. Only then can we edify others.[6]

Pride

In the Eastern list of the eight thoughts, self-glorification gives birth to pride. Self-glorification is listed as one of the three thoughts that lead the way to the other five. It opens the door to pride. And pride is the mother and culmination of all vices. That's why pride is first in the seven capital sins in the West.

In Cassian, pride is overcome by constant remembrance of what Jesus did for each of us on the cross. We are to envision his sufferings in detail. See the blood. Feel the pain and the anguish. And this was all done out of self-emptying love for each of us. This is personal. This is powerful. I don't think Jesus, in his humanity, knew my name personally. But in his divinity, the Son of God did and does, and the Son of God took on flesh to rescue *me*. This is powerful, and it is personal. We simply cannot remain filled with pride in the face of such love by God for my little life. It reduces me to tears of humble gratitude and raises me up to praise. It reduces my pride to pure love.

Questions

1) Do you have a need for praise? What's the difference between a healthy and an unhealthy need to be affirmed?

2) Do you understand the difference between keeping our works of mercy secret and shining the light of Jesus for others?

6. Ward, 82.

3) Do you confuse quoting the wisdom of the fathers and mothers with living it?

4) Do you give all glory to God for any praise you receive for your work?

5) Do you anticipate others in showing respect and appreciation for the work and life of others?

6) Do you see that the little need to be noticed can lead to pride?

29

Self-Accusation

In considering self-glorification, we saw that many of us have a need to be right. Some of this is from a genuine desire to do the right thing for God or just from a healthy sense of right that comes from a well-formed conscience. But it can often be unhealthy and bad.

After many years as spiritual father of a monastic community, I have come to believe that this ultimately comes from a poor self-image and trying to compensate for it by building ourselves up by just about always being right. But this is usually not a genuine building up of a good self-image in God. Egoism usually stems from a poor self-image and not knowing one's authentic place in Christ. The desire to always be right is often just a desire to be worth something or to be important by being right. It's trying to accomplish something good in a bad way.

I am reminded of the humorous Paul Simon lyric that says, "I remember once . . . I was wrong, and I could be wrong again."[1] Often we need to just admit that we can be, and often are, wrong about a great many things. We serve God, but we

1. Paul Simon, "Sure Don't Feel Like Love" (Universal Music Publishing Group, 2006).

are not God. We aren't always right. It is an illusion to think otherwise. Newsflash: God is God, and we are not!

If we really know who we are in Christ, we do not have a poor self-image. First, we are created in God's image and likeness. That's pretty amazing. Other creatures are created by God and loved by God. But only humans bear his image and likeness. God literally loved us into existence! And when we lost that likeness through sin, God loved us so much that he sent Jesus to rescue us by laying down his own life. From eternity, the Son of God knows us better than we know ourselves. He knows each of us by name and knows that we need to be rescued. Jesus came to rescue us, and he literally died for each one of us! That means we are worth a *lot* to God. We are loved! When we really discover this, we can rise from bad self-images into a positive one. But here's the kicker: We are only one of billions of humans who also bear this gift. Plus, in the church we are complete only when we recognize other people's gifts. And we recognize them even before our own. Love is self-emptying. So the need to be noticed and praised for everything we do disappears in the light of a solid sense of self in Christ and in his love that pours out to another at all times.

I've been in monastic and ministry leadership for decades now. I'm used to teaching and being listened to. Sometimes I can get a big head, and think that I somehow deserve to be respected and that others should almost automatically learn from my lessons. After all, "I'm John Michael Talbot!" But I am next to nothing. I make plenty of mistakes. Sometimes, I make big ones! Also true is the old saying that the higher the monkey climbs up the tree, the more you can see its bottom side. So at various times my bottom side has been pretty exposed!

There's an old lesson in public life that when you make a mistake in a song or speech, you just learn to cover it and keep on going. While helpful for the flow of a presentation, or even in liturgy, it can also produce a negative effect when we stop realizing that we really do make mistakes. I've learned the hard way that it's usually easier to just stop and say, "oops, sorry," confess it, ask forgiveness, and then continue. Confession is good for the soul. And it's good for those who follow our example.

I remember at a concert, somewhere in the Midwest, the guys in the band complained that the volunteers before the concerts were eating all of the musicians' food. These weren't just snacks. That was our supper! So the complaint was justified. At the next concert I noticed the volunteers eating the band's supper. I stepped in and nicely but clearly asked them to leave the food for the band. They looked a little shocked and quietly left. I did not like having to do this, but I felt it was my duty for the band.

After the concert during the load out, the sponsor wanted to talk to me. I came out of the bus to meet him. He told me that the volunteers were kids with learning disabilities, and they were excited to get to help me. They had asked him, "Why is the guy who looks like Jesus so mean to us?" Well, I was embarrassed and heartbroken. Was I completely wrong? No. The band members wanted me to step in, and the sponsor really shouldn't have allowed it. But what was easier—to hold my "just" position, or to just ask forgiveness? So I apologized to the sponsor and went to apologize to the kids. I pray they understood.

But that's not the end of the story. Afterward on the bus, one of the band members came up to me rather dumbfounded. I thought I had offended someone else! But he completely surprised me when he said that he had been involved in leading youth ministry for decades and had never heard their primary leader apologize for *anything* in all that time. He was deeply moved that I would do so. I was stunned. A leader who felt he or she could never apologize? I am usually confident of my position in leadership and ministry, but I'm not afraid to apologize when I am wrong. Plus, it is so easy to take responsibility for our part in a wrong and just ask forgiveness. Otherwise, hurt feelings become resentments and anger, and we make enemies instead of friends in Christ.

Dorotheos of Gaza

I'd like to share the classic teaching of a later father, Dorotheos of Gaza. This teaching is considered primary in living the monastic life successfully in the Christian East. It works for the West as well. But it can work only if we begin with at least a fundamentally good self-image. That is why monastic communities tend not to take folks who haven't matured to that stage. Otherwise they carry so much baggage that a new monastic life in Christ becomes nearly impossible. I will summarize in my own words.

Suppose you are walking in the monastery, minding your own business, and another monk comes up and begins to angrily read you the proverbial riot act. Our first instinct is to defend ourselves, get angry in return, and to tell the other person to back off and mind his own business. But Dorotheos says that you cannot live in peace in a monastery and follow that worldly pattern.

He says we must consider a few things. 1) The other person might be having a bad day, and we should try to bring healing with calmness. 2) Maybe we did something to offend him, and we need to repent and be reconciled. 3) Maybe we did something a very long time ago that we don't even remember, and we need reconciliation. 4) Maybe we did something to someone else a long time ago, and God is trying to get our attention through this situation so we can be healed. 5) Maybe it's just our countenance or the way we carry ourselves that the other person finds offensive.

In all these considerations, we must take responsibility for our part in the angry encounter and not blame the other person. That's a mouthful! It can be done only when we really let go of our old selves through the cross of Jesus and rise up a newborn child of God every day.

Dorotheos would say that then, after we have taken responsibility for our part in the rift, we can enter into a dialogue with the other monk and offer a correction of his anger that isn't mere self-justification, but really brings the peace and justice of God. This is a script for Conflict Resolution 101.

This attitude of self-responsibility, or what they call "self-blame," is firmly rooted in the teaching and example of the desert fathers. These teachings really make sense only in that context. As Dorotheos said, understanding and practicing this is essential to living successfully in a monastery in peace. Poemen says it's an essential rule for being a monk, period! There is no way around it if we want to live peacefully in community with others.[2]

Desert Fathers

Before Dorotheos, other desert fathers said this without the development he gave. Abba Poemen simply said that the rule of the monk is always to bear his own blame.[3] Simple. Stark. Challenging.

Like many things when viewed through the cross of Jesus, this turns on its head many things the world would consider uncomfortable or bad. Poverty becomes an opportunity for greater spiritual wealth. Chastity becomes a doorway to greater intimacy with God. Dishonor becomes a greater honor. Indeed, death becomes a doorway to greater life, both on earth and eternal life in heaven. Abba Macarius used to say that if we hold contempt as honor, blame as praise, and poverty as wealth, we will not die.[4]

Self-accusation isn't just a game of reversing blame for the bad things of life. It's also just the truth! The truth is that I do many things imperfectly, and I do some quite badly! It is

---

2. Dorotheos of Gaza, *Discourses and Sayings*, trans. Eric P. Wheeler (Collegeville, MN: Cistercian Publications, 1977), 141.

3. E. A. W. Budge, ed. and trans., *The Paradise or Garden of the Holy Fathers*, 2 vols. (London: Chatto & Windus, 1907), 2:13.

4. Budge, 2:51.

truth that opens our eyes to these things, and it is humility to
acknowledge them. As St. Francis once said, humility is just
the truth.

On a visit to Mount Nitria, Abba Theophilus asked one of
the priests there, "What excellent thing have you found on this
monastic road?" The priest answered that he always made ac-
cusations against himself and blamed himself at all times. Abba
Theophilus told him, "There is no way but this."[5]

Sin is the great equalizer. So is forgiveness. Scripture says,
"There is no distinction; all have sinned and are deprived of
the glory of God. They are justified freely by his grace through
the redemption in Christ Jesus" (Rom 3:22-24).

An old man used to say, "In all your trials blame no one other
than yourself; blame only yourself. Say, 'These things have happened to me because of my sins.'"[6]

But this doesn't mean that we blame others in order to
"bless" them! Some monastics love to "test" others with ac-
cusations and blame to see if they are adequately "spiritual."
A superior only rarely does this, but when it becomes ordinary,
it is perverse. We are always to offer honor to others. As Scripture says, "Pay to all their dues . . . respect to whom respect is
due, honor to whom honor is due" (Rom 13:7). It also tells us
to anticipate one another in showing respect (see Rom 12:10).
So self-accusation works only for yourself. We should never try
to impose it on others.

Abba Abraham asked Abba Theodore whether it is better to
blame or to praise others. Theodore responded that it is always
better to praise others and not blame them.[7] So we should look
for things in others to praise before we try to blame them. In
finding the good, we minimize the bad and pacify our need to
blame others.

5. Budge, 2:109.
6. Budge, 2:116.
7. Budge, 2:158.

Questions

1) Do you have a desire always to be right?

2) Are you aware of your own low self-image that manifests in the desire to be right?

3) How do you handle being accused, especially if you don't understand the justice of it?

4) Can you see the greater justice of God when you seem to suffer human injustice?

5) Can you rightly correct others before you take responsibility for correction of yourself?

6) Do you anticipate others in showing respect to them?

7) Is it better to blame or to praise?

30

Remembrance of Death

There's a country song that tells us to live every day "like you were dying."[1] Oddly, this modern country song is most consistent with ancient monastic tradition!

Recently as I write this, I was very ill and ended up in the hospital. During that hospital stay, I saw a glimpse the glory of heaven. I "passed over," but then was ushered back to this earthly realm. This is not an uncommon experience for those in hospital. I was so sick that it hurt to think objective thoughts and all I could do was mumble in tongues. In that state, two angels held me under each arm and ushered me to a place where I could glimpse the glory of heaven from a distance. I wanted to stay, but I was returned to my hospital room. It was most comforting. But it was also most revealing.

In that single experience I realized that in most of my monastic life I had accomplished very little. Most of my accomplishments and preoccupations, while not unimportant, are next to nothing compared to the glory of our eternal home. I put a

---

1. Tim McGraw, "Live Like You Were Dying," lyrics by Craig Wiseman and Tim Nichols (Warner/Chappell Music, Round Hill Music Big Loud Songs, BMG Rights Management US, 2004).

lot of energy into things that really didn't matter in the long run. Much of it is "much ado about nothing." Some if it is just sinful; it "missed the mark." As St. Francis said, "Brothers, let us now begin, for up until now, we have done nothing."

I was also reminded that I am now among the older generation. My time has come, and much of it has also gone! Most of my major "accomplishments" have already been done. It is now up to the next generation to pick up what was worthwhile and to forget what wasn't. Again, as St. Francis said, "I have done my part. May Christ teach you yours."

In many ways I nowadays feel like a shadow of my former self. I am only an echo of a younger and stronger voice. This is simply part of getting older. It is part of looking forward to an eternity with Jesus that makes all I have ever accomplished on earth look very, very pale. Any of my "great" achievements really seem like next to nothing when compared with what still lies ahead. But what lies ahead is no longer something on earth. It is heavenly. It is eternal. It is my true home. I long for it more and more nowadays.

Death, sin, and forgiveness are the great equalizers. No one can escape the first two. It is up to each of us to accept or reject, give or withhold grace.

Some monasteries sometimes keep an open grave in their cemetery so that monks can sit beside it and meditate on their own death and the fact that it could happen to them at any moment of any day. We never know when we are going to die. This is true for everyone, of course, but such reflection is a special part of monastic tradition.

This is not some morbid preoccupation with death. It is meant to be a positive motivation to live every day like it's our last. When I think that this might be my last day on earth, I make use of every moment to live fully for God and for others. I cannot let myself get sluggish or lazy. I cannot be self-centered. I reconcile relationships and make use of every moment to live one hundred percent as a disciple of Jesus!

St. Paul says, "Think of what is above, not of what is on earth. For you have died, and your life is hidden with Christ in God" (Col 3:2). We must consider ourselves dead to sin, but alive to God (see Rom 6:10-11).

The tradition of the monastic saints says it's only when we consider ourselves as dead that we are really free to live completely for Christ. St. Francis used the illustration of a dead body to describe the nonresistance of the truly obedient brother and the pale humility of one to whom honor is bestowed. As Paul also said, "I have been crucified with Christ; yet I live, no longer I, but Christ lives in me." (Eph 3:19-20).

Sin, forgiveness, and death are the great equalizers. We all sin, we all need forgiveness, and we all die. No one is better than another when we face these things. Popes, bishops, presidents, emperors, and kings all face these things in the same way as average and quite ordinary church members or citizens. St. James says, "My brothers, show no partiality as you adhere to the faith in our glorious Lord Jesus Christ. For if a man with gold rings on his fingers and in fine clothes comes into your assembly, and a poor person in shabby clothes also comes in, and you pay attention to the one wearing the fine clothes and say, 'Sit here, please,' while you say to the poor one, 'Stand there,' or 'Sit at my feet,' have you not made distinctions among yourselves and become judges with evil designs?" (Jas 2:1-4).

When we meditate on death, we are all equal before God, and what is important and what is not become abundantly clear. It sets our priorities straight very quickly! Love is pretty much all that survives. All good Christian theology—on the Trinity, the incarnation, the church, or anything else—is based on love. In the end, it's all that matters. Death brings us face to face with that ultimate reality.

The Desert
The desert fathers and mothers said the same thing.

Abba Silvanus told Abba Moses that if a monk is a true "laborer," he could live every day, even every hour, as though it were the first day or hour of his religious life.[2]

Evagrius gets very specific on this. He writes, "While you sit in your cell, draw in your mind, and remember the day of your death. And then you will see your body mortifying. Think on the loss, feel the pain. Shrink from the vanity of the world outside. Be retiring, and careful to keep your vow of quiet, and you will not weaken. Remember the souls in hell. Meditate within on their condition, the bitter silence and the moaning, the fear and the strife, the waiting and the pain without relief, the tears that cannot cease to flow."[3]

Abba Evagrius said that reflecting frequently on our death and eternal judgment will help us avoid temptations to sin.[4]

Buddhist monks follow a similar practice. They visualize the body at every major point of decay after death to minimize the desire for sense gratification or the attraction to carnal beauty. It is sobering.

But for the Christian, this meditation on death is only part of a larger way of life that includes other positive meditations and the practice of a rich life of virtue. It is never an end unto itself, nor morbid in character.

Describing the ideal monk, Abba John the Short offered a long list of virtues, habits, and characteristics. Then he concluded the entire litany by saying, "[Bury] yourself in a tomb as though you were already dead, and every day feeling that death is upon you."[5]

When you live every day like you were dying today, you live every day to the fullest in Christ.

---

2. Owen Chadwick, ed. and trans., *Western Asceticism* (Philadelphia: Westminster Press, 1958), 136.

3. Chadwick, 44.

4. Chadwick, 132.

5. Chadwick, 38.

Questions

1) Do you live every day at least generally aware that you could die at any moment?

2) Does this motivate you to live more positively for God and others?

3) Does meditation on death help you to consider yourself as equal to others?

4) Do you allow this meditation to be daily and appropriately specific?

5) Do you see this meditation as only one tool in your spiritual battle, or do you obsess about it in a morbid way?

Contemplation

When St. Antony told God that he wanted to go deeper into the desert because "the people will not permit me a little silent contemplation," the Lord responded to him, "If you wish to rest in greater silent contemplation, go to the innermost desert."[1]

St. John Climacus treats *hesychia* and what we call contemplative prayer at the end of his *The Ladder of Divine Ascent*. This makes sense, for contemplative life is the goal of all the meditations and disciplines of the active life.

We already treated *hesychia*, or sacred stillness, in an earlier chapter. But the whole point of going into greater solitude is to experience greater contemplative union with God. It is to simply *be* with the One Who *IS*.

We enter into solitude and silence, then, to deal with the imperfections and sins that rise to the surface through appropriate disciplines and ascetical practices. Once the vessels of our lives are substantially cleansed by God's love and truth, he can pour the greater graces of contemplative union into our souls. This is the goal of monastic life. And from this we can

---

1. E. A. W. Budge, ed. and trans., *The Paradise or Garden of the Holy Fathers*, 2 vols. (London: Chatto & Windus, 1907), 1:41.

overflow back out into the world with those same graces through various ministries of evangelization.

I've always loved solitude and silence, and I started my monastic life in a hermitage in the woods. But a community soon grew around me. I built that community based on the semieremitic pattern of the *skete*, but I was often very busy with leadership and ministry. So I personally experienced more prolonged and profound contemplation only after I retired to my personal hermitage after many years of service. I started this first for three days a week, then for five days a week. Since then, I've experienced it for even greater periods at times. I am immensely grateful to my community for allowing this and for creating a protective barrier and space where I could do so in a more uninterrupted manner. It was there that I began to experience something of the deeper contemplative life I had read about in monastic books but only experienced in part. I am still descending deeper into this eternal well and will do so for the rest of my life.

As a musician I've always intuited things more than intellectualized them. Somehow, I've always intuited the eternal things in and through the things of space and time. Be it a Scripture passage or a tree in the forest, I've always been able to intuit the eternal in such things. Perhaps that's what people sensed in my music and why it was so popular?

But it was only after I sensed the deeper calm of the hermitage in purer reclusion that I somehow dropped deeper. There, without the thought of another music or book project, a community meeting, or an outside ministry, I could discover the deeper *me*, my *being* in God who is beyond the "me" who is identified with what I do for God. It is almost impossible to conceptualize such things, let alone write about them. But once experienced, my being and my ministry cannot be separated into nice and neat categories. Everything simply *is* in God, the One Who *IS*.

The Desert

The contemplative life isn't treated explicitly in the early sources of the desert fathers and mothers. You simply won't find any developed methods of sacred reading, meditation, prayer, and contemplation, or the divisions of active and contemplative life there. These all come a bit later in the monastic traditions. Later still come full-blown systems that are elegant and beautiful. But they are all rooted in the primitive sources of the desert.

Typically, Christian contemplation means that which is beyond all human understanding or description. Most of our lives are "active," focused on the things we can know about God and our lives of following him. Jesus is indeed the Word made flesh. But the contemplative life is a union with God so pure that it is a communion of our beings with his Being. It cannot be described or grasped with images, forms, or ideas. It can only be intuited.

While not developed, this contemplation isn't absent from the desert fathers and mothers either. It is almost present on every page, but as an intuition and understood point. It is rarely mentioned explicitly. It must be mined like gold from the sources. Once we do that, we discover a veritable gold mine of contemplative sources.

Abba Isadore experienced contemplation: "My mind departed and was carried away by contemplation, and I was snatched away by the similitude of a thought, and I was fed with the food of glory, which, however, it is impossible for me to describe."[2]

Of Brother John the Recluse, Prophet of the Thebaid, it was written: "He had been a strenuous man and had loved the life of quiet contemplation all his days, and he excelled greatly in prayers, and in singing praises, and in multitudes of visions, and spiritual manifestations were revealed unto him with such scrupulous exactness, some in revelations and some in dreams,

2. Budge, 1:90.

that finally he was able to walk in the footsteps of incorporeal beings."[3]

Abba Abban "passed his whole life in silent contemplation and in humility, and in his manner of life he was as one of the angels, and he clothed himself in the deepest humility."[4]

Macarius the Alexandrian used to say,

> I have kept every kind of rule of the life of self-denial and fasting which I have desired to observe with all my heart. But I desired for my mind to be with God in heaven only for five days, and that I might be exalted above the anxious cares and thoughts of material things. And having meditated upon this, I shut the door of the courtyard and of the cell, and I disciplined myself that I might not give a word to anyone at all. And I continued in that way. I began to fulfill this thought on the second day of the week, and I commanded my mind, 'You shall not descend from heaven, for behold, there you have angels, and the princes of angels, and all the hosts which are in heaven, and especially the Good and Gracious God, the Lord of all. You shall not come down from heaven.' And continuing like this I was fine for two days and two nights. I constrained the Evil One to such a degree that he became a flame of fire and burnt up everything that I had in my cell, even the mat I stood on blazed with fire, and I thought that I should be wholly consumed. Finally fear of the fire took hold of me, and my mind came down from heaven on the third day, because I was unable to keep my mind collected in the state in which it had been. So, I came down to the contemplation of the world and the things in it. And this happened so that I might not boast.[5]

3. Budge, 1:329.
4. Budge, 1:337.
5. Budge, 1:121–122.

Syncletica said, "We have lost a means to excellence, yet we can contemplate the glory of God with the inward eyes of the soul."[6]

One of the desert fathers said: "The Lord Christ abides in us and with us, and watches our life. And because we bear him with us and contemplate him, we ought not to be negligent but ought to make ourselves holy as he is holy."[7]

Another said: "No one can see his face reflected in muddy water: and the soul cannot pray to God with contemplation unless first cleansed of harmful thoughts."[8]

Of Abba John the Short we read, "His mind was occupied in the contemplation of God."[9]

Later writers and teachers developed the stages and methods of contemplation based on these early sources. The stages of active and contemplative life—that is, the cataphatic, or knowable things about God and life in God, and the apophatic, or things beyond human knowledge—were first developed by Evagrius based on his experience in the desert. Most of the later monastic descriptions are highly influenced by him.

John Climacus

St. John Climacus says simply in his *The Ladder of Divine Ascent*: "Prayer is by nature a dialogue and a union of man with God. Its effect is to hold the world together. It achieves a reconciliation with God. . . . The beginning of prayer is the expulsion of distractions from the very start by a single plot; the middle stage is the concentration on what is being said or thought; it's conclusion is rapture in the Lord. . . . When a man has found

6. Owen Chadwick, ed. and trans., *Western Asceticism* (Philadelphia: Westminster Press, 1958), 86.

7. Chadwick, 64.

8. Chadwick, 143.

9. Chadwick, 133.

the Lord, he no longer has to use words when he is praying, for the Spirit Himself will intercede for him with groans that cannot be uttered (Romans 8:26). . . . Do not form sensory images during prayer, for distraction will certainly follow."[10]

Evagrius

It was Evagrius, who lived in the desert and visited the fathers, who developed a more complete treatise on contemplative prayer, or what he called "pure prayer." He describes moving through and beyond any ideas, images, or forms, even of God. This is radical, and many have objected to it. But through the centuries great monastic and mystical writers and teachers have found the wisdom of his description, embraced it, and taught it to countless others who have benefitted from it.

This kind of prayer can be very difficult for monks, much less for the average Christian! I have found the incorporation of the Jesus Prayer very helpful in this process. I have written about the Jesus Prayer in other books rather extensively. Suffice it to say that you sit comfortably and quietly, breathe in and out slowly, and incorporate the phrases of the prayer with your breathing. Slowly, you move beyond words, images, and forms, and enter into a pure contemplative union of God's divine Being with your being.

Spiritual Father or Mother

Again, it's very important to get an experienced teacher to help you with this prayer and contemplative way. A spiritual father, mother, or elder is vital in learning this way correctly. Trying to do it simply from what you read in books or by your own

---

10. John Climacus, *The Ladder of Divine Ascent*, trans. Colm Luibheid (Mahwah, NJ: Paulist Press, 1982), 43.

experimentation can be dangerous, because you can easily delude yourself into thinking that you have found something, when in fact you haven't found anything at all.

We already treated this in the chapter on the spiritual father and mother. Suffice it to say here that I recommend finding a good monastic who is experienced in this way as a spiritual director or teacher.

Questions

1) Have you tasted the graces of contemplative prayer in your own prayer life?

2) Have you gone through the preceding stages of the active life properly before entering into the contemplative life?

3) Have you been able to move beyond ideas, images, and forms even of God in order to be in union with God?

4) Do you find it difficult to pray without ideas, images, and forms of God?

5) Do you find incorporation of the breath in disciplines such as the Jesus Prayer helpful?

6) Do you have a good, experienced spiritual director to teach you the proper way to contemplation?

Conclusion

The delights and dangers of the desert are abundant. But they can be stark. They are primitive but foundational, simple but not simplistic. In this book we have investigated some of the rich heritage as it applies to our lives today. Other authors have presented even more. Hopefully the questions at the end of the chapters are penetrating and helpful regarding your own personal life in the modern world today. I'm sure you might have more.

As we have seen, the teachings and lifestyle of the desert fathers and mothers are rugged and challenging. But they aren't a fully developed mystical or monastic theology by any stretch. That was left to later generations to compile. We hear very little about moving from the active to the contemplative life, from the knowable things of God in cataphatic theology to the way of divine darkness and unknowing in the apophatic way. Most of what they taught was what we would consider active life, things that we can do or know about God and our lives in him.

The delights and dangers of the desert provide a pattern for the so-called "nones" and "dones" of today's cultural and religious experience. They teach us an alternative that is complimentary to the typical diocesan or local church expressions of modern Christianity. The desert was a place where folks who simply wanted more could go to dive deeper into their spiritual life in Christ. They also show us an environment that provides an alternative to the divisive and angrily polarized climate of our own modern culture, secular or religious. But they aren't opposed to these cultures either! They teach us how to leave the secular and religious world without hating either one. And in a way that can help both.

The desert fathers and mothers address the problems of the "big, bad" outside world by beginning with the world within the attitudes and actions of our own lives in Christ. They accept no excuses for self-indulgence. In the desert, it was complete self-sacrifice or nothing. But they were also very realistic about the human condition. They knew that men and women needed to grow into perfection. It wasn't automatic. Monastics weren't perfect people. They understood the psychology of the spiritual life long before our formal spiritual directors or professional counselors. And good spiritual directors and counselors today are usually quick to recognize their wisdom. The mediocre ones know them only by reference. The bad ones don't have a clue.

The desert fathers and mothers show us some helpful, tangible steps of letting go of the old self through the cross and resurrection of Jesus Christ. The eight thoughts that come from Evagrius and Cassian are classic and timeless; they still reach across the ages to speak to serious seekers today. The principles we learn in the desert teach us how to be alone yet in communion with all. They teach us how to be poor yet rich, and really free in obedience to God and a good spiritual father or mother. They show us how to be full in fasting, intimate with God in celibate chastity, and rich by relinquishing possessions and the need to control. They teach us how to be released from the prison of anger and bitterness, to beat boredom in healthy labor, and to find ourselves by losing ourselves through the cross and resurrection of Jesus Christ.

The desert shows us how to proverbially "drop out" by "dropping in." It teaches us not to just drop out, but to drop deeper. In other words, the problems of the world are really problems of the human condition. They are solved when we dare to adventure within ourselves and discover the deeper things of God there. Then we have something to give to others. The way of the desert shows us how to be separated from all and united with all. It offers an alternative to the modern church and world in a way that can heal both.

I ask you to go back to these chapters and sources repeatedly. One read is simply not enough. It has taken me decades to even scratch the surface of the wisdom of the desert fathers and mothers. The desert without their guidance is alluring in its delights but dangerous to the uninitiated. This is the message of the delights and dangers from the desert.